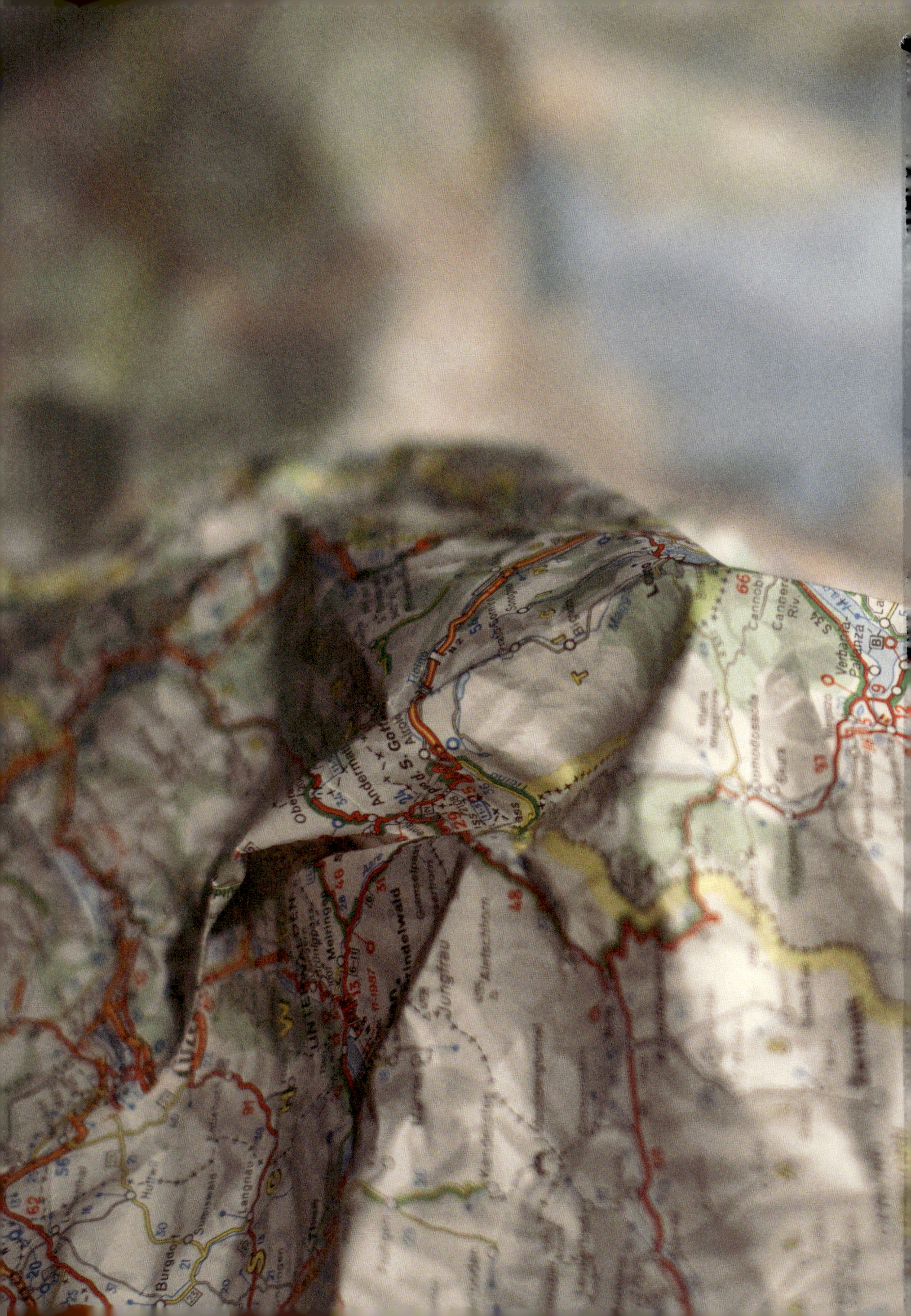

Ticino
Gottharo
S. Gotth
Airolo
Andermatt
Oberalp
Maggia
Cannobio
Cannero Riv.
Verbania
Pallanza
Cannobbio
Fusio
Meiringen
Grindelwald
Jungfrau
Lauterbrunnen
UNTERWALDEN
Langnau
Burgdorf
Huttw
Sumiswald

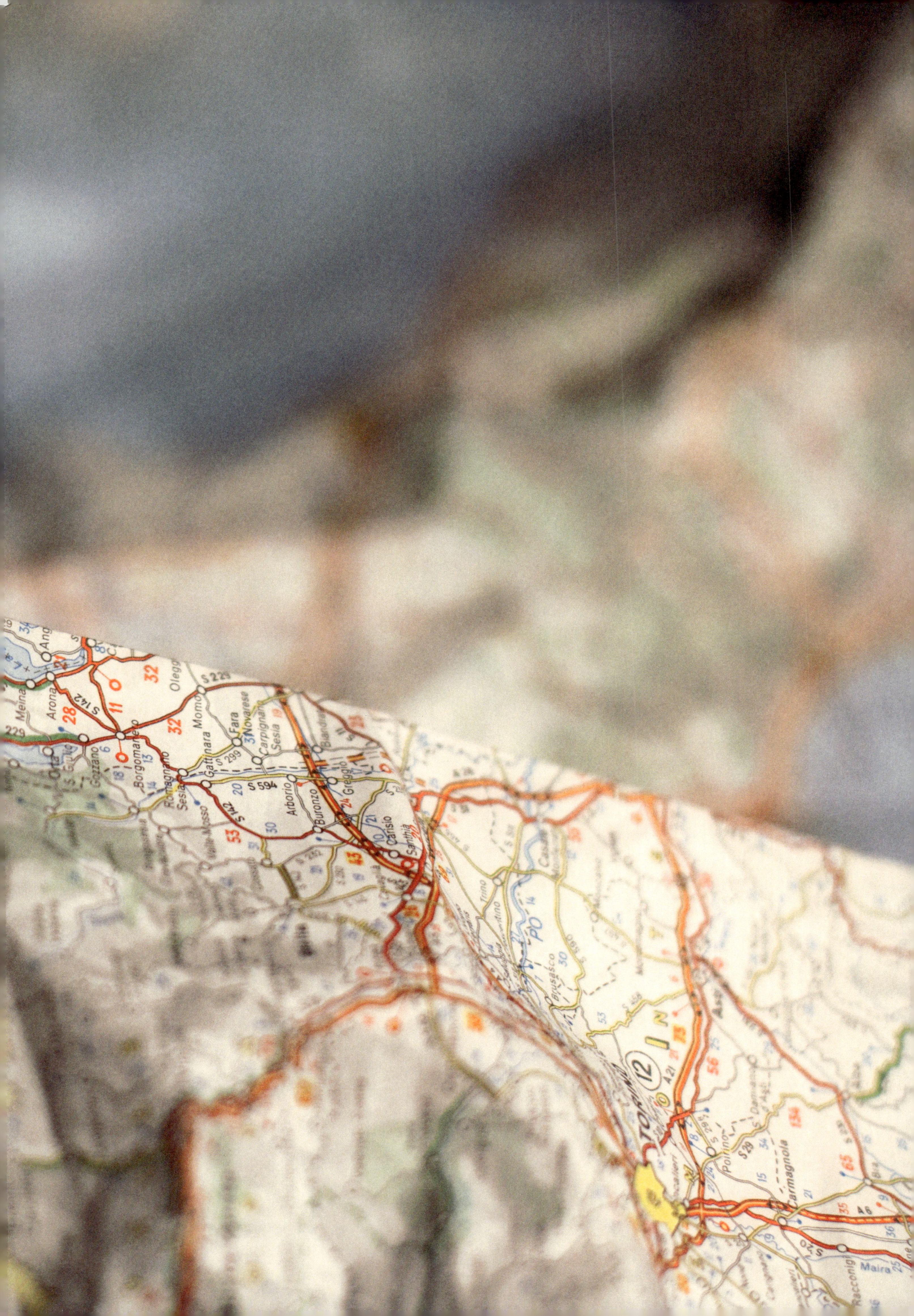

Landmarks *was the title of my first show almost thirty years ago
and it seemed fitting to bookend this epoch by naming this book and
survey with the same title. The word "landmark" can refer to an
event, a place, or an object. I like that this word can simultaneously
represent these very different types of things.* —JB

This book is dedicated to Cannon Hudson.

JENNIFER BOLANDE

LANDMARKS

with essays by

DENNIS BALK

JACK BANKOWSKY

ROSETTA BROOKS & CHRISTINA VALENTINE

NICHOLAS FRANK

INGRID SCHAFFNER

edited by NICHOLAS FRANK

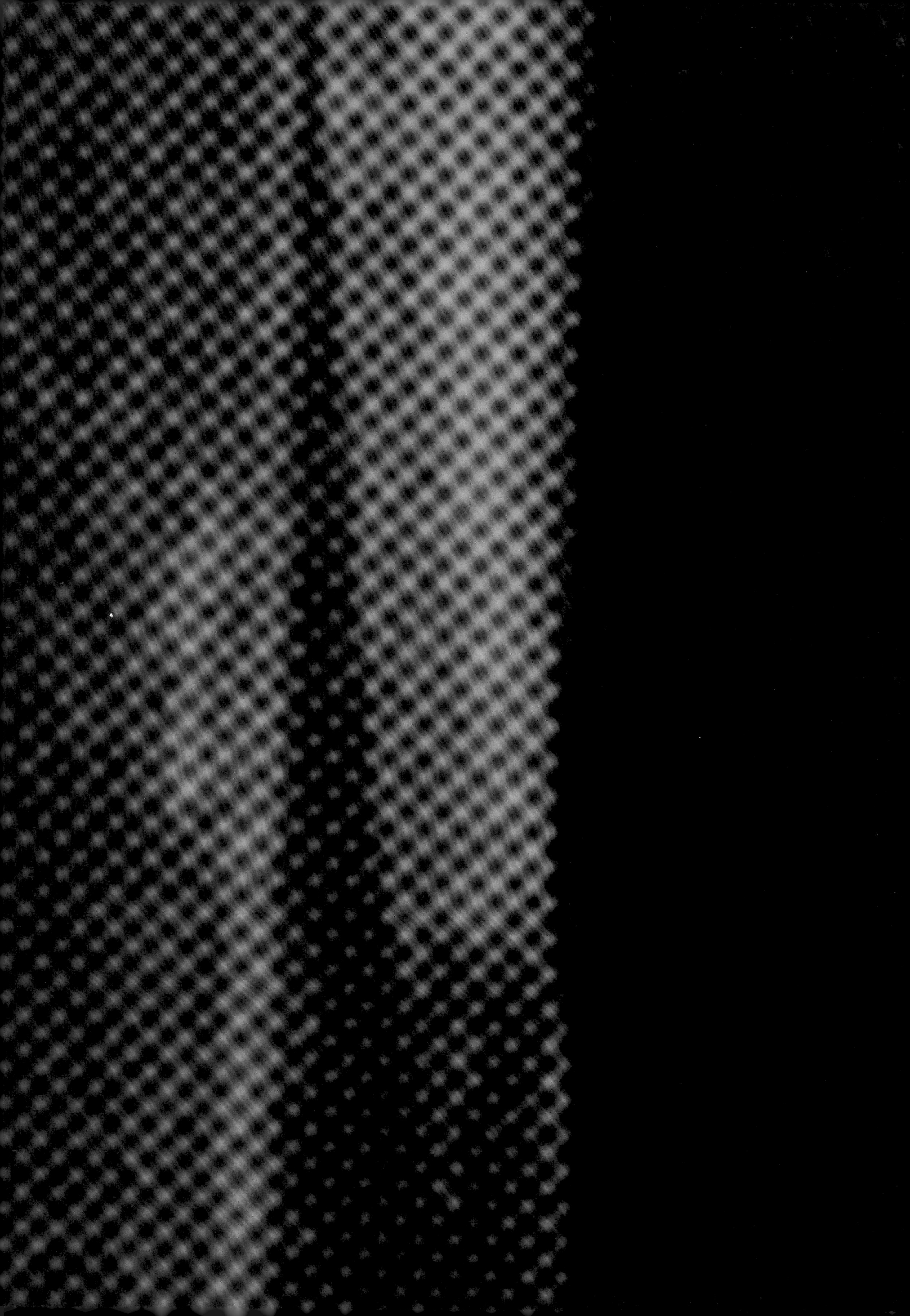

JENNIFER BOLANDE, AN INVITATION…

First, there are these Bolande objects. Put-together components really, mostly familiar, not in the sense of gallery-familiar, but from the street or a friend's apartment or garage, maybe the storage of a retail store. Looking at these things the tendency is to glance over most of them as things already understood; they're handsome, but what are they doing here, stacked up like this? All the references and associations, the glut of distractions begin to flood in. Then another veneer, an unfamiliarity, a skewing of these very same objects; this is not quickly understood; the sure becomes unsure; they don't have the familiarity of the artist's hand. There's also a picture, a photograph, and oddly, it's a picture of what I'm looking at. This changes the situation and pulls in a particular frame of focus. An invitation, maybe a suggestion, the viewing shifts away from just seeing and calculating these objects, and it's now clearly about this process I myself am engaged in, this process of considering.

The white-ghetto-chic glamour of the late 1980s East Village for me was rough and depressing. I lived on 6th and B. It was a tough time, having just moved in from Venice Beach, I didn't know yet how to get my bearings and get myself set up. Building after building burned out or half torn down. I saw a kid walking down the street, not too far ahead of me, get the back of his head caved in by another kid with a two-by-four. Open fires, etc. A few storefront galleries dug in and put up shows, and to call these galleries outposts is really accurate. The good ones weren't mimicking the recent conceptual aesthetics, they had moved past pictures. These artists and artist/dealers favored strategies over expression, intellect over the damaged genius persona, and emerge they did, from the burned-out ruins of SoHo. I remember the night of the Koons "Rabbit" debut, and the moment when a distraught art-lover ripped the toilet seat off Meyer Vaisman's *The Whole Public Thing*, 1986. These were the headiest of days, when a renewed earnestness and ambition ran deep into the status of the object. This work didn't look like art, it wasn't art. It was something else, something we hadn't yet seen or considered.

Jennifer came up through this New York. Alongside the commodity work, her objects and pictures had a different quality of purpose, a bit tighter focus, a new opportunity. The piece *Conjunction Assemblage*, 1988 [38], understands the construction and randomness of our attention. Here is where we get the invitation. The objects and the surfaces become something to do with culture, something we know, but not really. The picture shifts the attention to the process of looking. That's culture too, something we're trained to know, but not really, as the work takes you gently by the hand, walks you out into the open landscape past the elaborate grey busy buzz of activity, and once there, you're prompted to turn around. And there it is, the point-to-point process you just assembled, the culmination of all the agreements, concessions and predeterminations that were your comprehension.

Those are the steps you just went through to get to where you are right now, looking at those steps. Stay there for a little while and look at that aspect of the object.

In Jennifer's work, the fundamental operative is that the object is the thing it says it is, without the dependent references of elsewhere. It's not discursive retaliation. Her compositions are necessarily straight-on, in a way that diverts the process of looking from becoming a disconnected dive into the habitual aesthetic or the prosey mental space of ambiguity and embellishment. That level of glee isn't part of this. The objects and printed pieces are clearly calculated but not with a cold conceptualist's formula. There is a soft generosity to the work; this connects back to the artist, and this is also part of the invitation. Across her work, this invitation takes different forms of presence and announcement.

Over many years of exhibition and studio work she has constructed an inventory of approaches and a vocabulary she can draw upon to elicit further associations and connections; some point out to the world, and some point back in to the body of her work, expanding the potential trajectories of her language. It's not a private language, but rather the cultural landscape of pictures and objects, the primary sets of head-on significance that communicate and inform our shared knowledge and identities. Her work reveals passages into a broader subterrain, where the emotional physics and transient adhesives that connect objects to a fluidity of meaning are at play. Here, we discover a connection, share a sympathy with what we had previously not thought or seen. Everyday objects, the taken-for-granted variety, suddenly are creating a different language we can read and follow, the trip is the revelation, a world we didn't know to look for. The truth of the process, without the messy involvement of truth.

Bolande's work establishes a Romanticists' alignment with the unseen forces of everyday objects and images. An artist firmly in the domain of the contemporary, she redefines the language of the "Natural Landscape." Her work facilitates the mysteries and subtlety of phenomena called up and presented, allowing us to experience the world in an unexpected and astounding "it was right there all the time" kind of way. Providing the viewer, in the field of her ongoing projects of objects and pictures, a glimpse into the perfect worlds within the world.

Bolande chronicles the barely noticed objects and image potentials scattered around us. Her images function as indices to an historical dreamtime that floats in and around our collective concordance, the unspoken agreements that allow us to speak and sometimes communicate. In the swapped-out bass drum band logo, the draped and crumpled photo, and the pedestrian signboard, all indicators of cultural process and production, we begin to realize how the invitation part of the program ends and the process of the work has begun. At other times she frames the out-of-frame moments preceding some exotic, theatrical event. On the other side of the curtain, in the main event, are the forces and unacknowledged deep rifts within the base vocabulary of object-presence and cultural identity. Here, we participate in this drift that sluggishly attaches and reattaches whole areas of cultural meaning onto objects and representations.

As a frequent visitor to Jennifer's studios over the years in Manhattan and Joshua Tree, the conversations were on the order of a magician's technician, constructing the sleight of hand and discovering the process at the same time. She was never interested in calculating the Pop mute object of personal reflection, or configuring a debatable statement of condition. Her objectives were perfecting the playwright's formula, beginning with the object that announces itself as a chunk of the world, to then facilitate the travel within the work, the channels and possibilities, the tender calculation that allows the viewer to discover on their own what is necessary. The activity of her work is the opportunities in the work. A Bolande piece in a sense begins outside the gallery with the obvious objects we barely see.

Inside, the work deflates studied expectations, and in the process we pass through a Chandleresque world of language-spies and material witnesses, cerebral allies and adversaries always concerned to implicate the viewer as part of the action. Where a Bolande work finally resides is open business. The invitation in the work continues back out into the open air and sunlight where the relations between things have a suspicious altered quality, inseparable from our consideration. As Rachael says to Deckard in *Blade Runner*, "I'm not part of the business, I am the business."

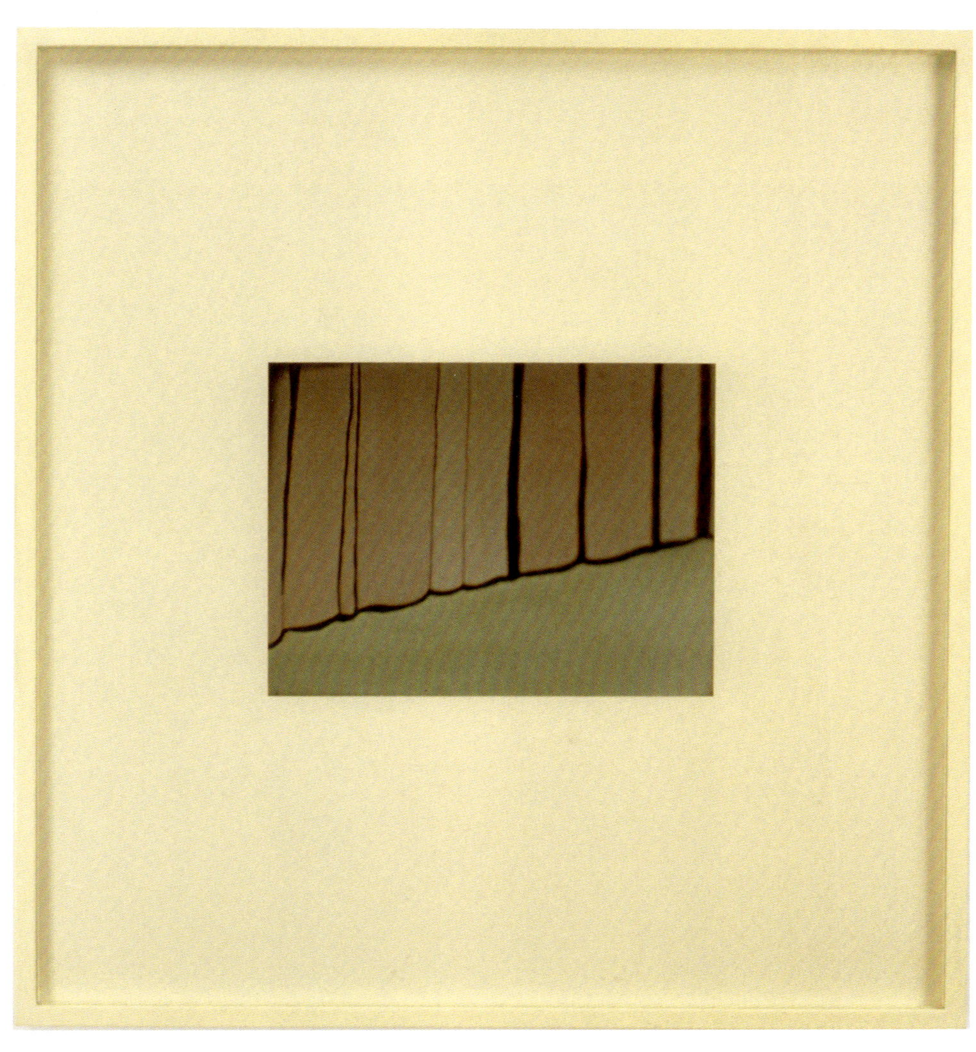

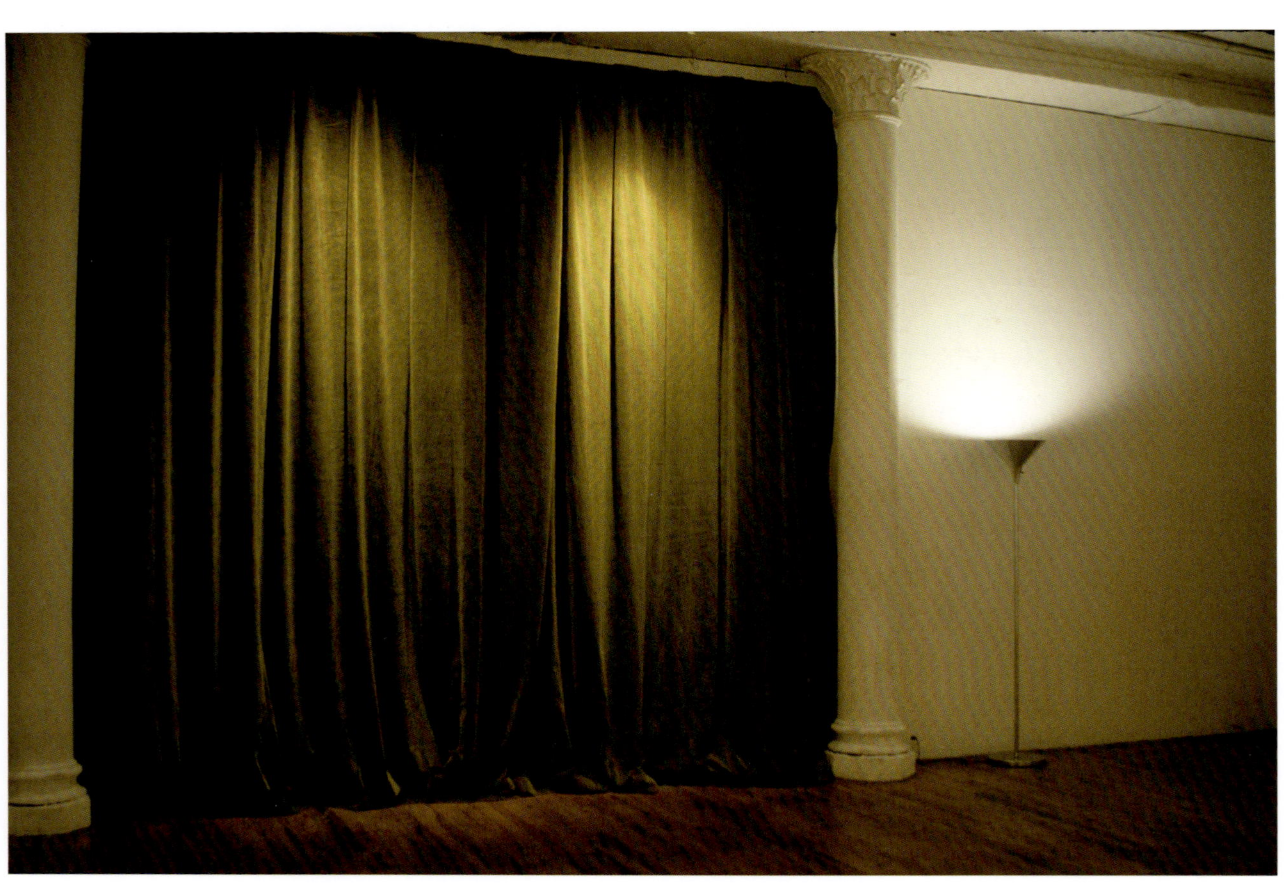

[3] Installation view: *Landmarks*, The Kitchen, NY, 1982   [4] *The Formal Gardens Series, #16*, 1982

[5] *Central and Mountain*, 1985

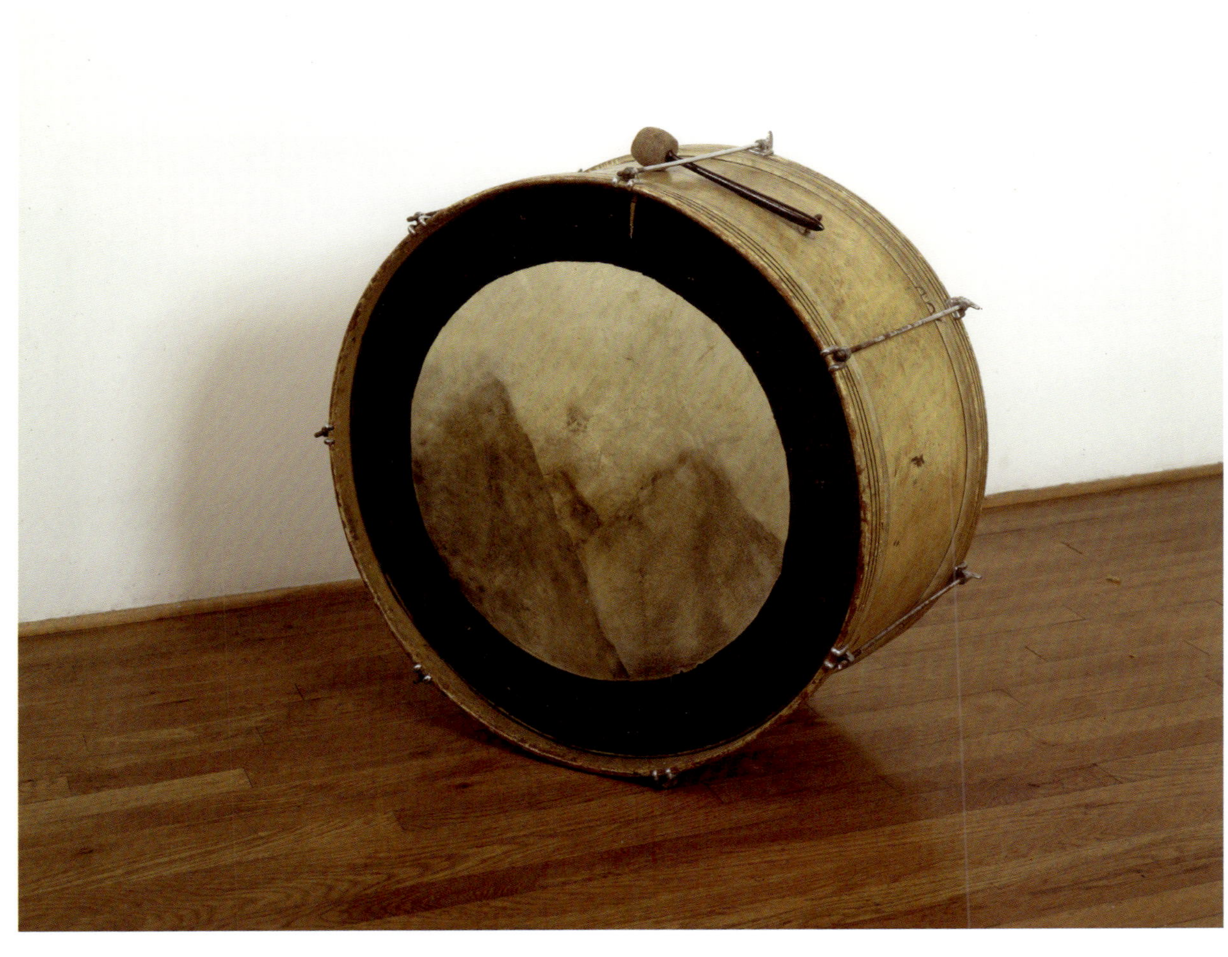

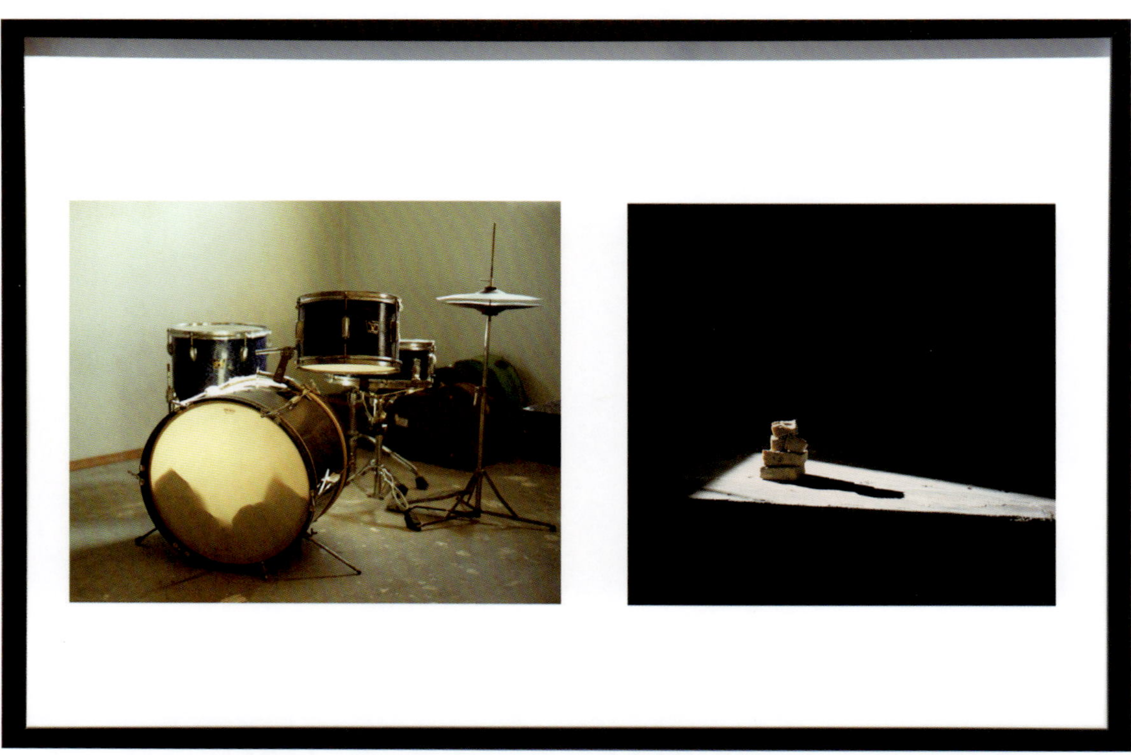

[6] *Diptych #38*, from the series *Space Photography*, 2009

[7] *Green Towel Sequence #1*, 2004

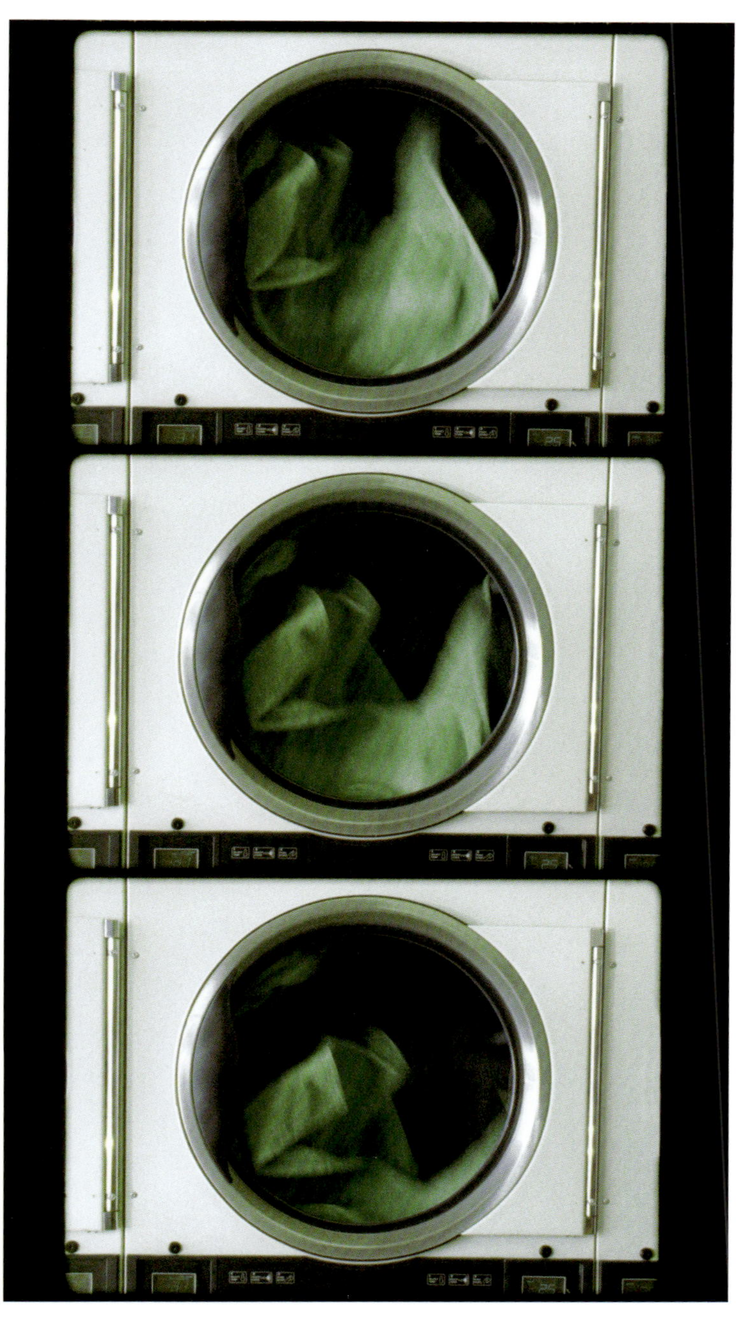

[8] *Cascade*, 1987

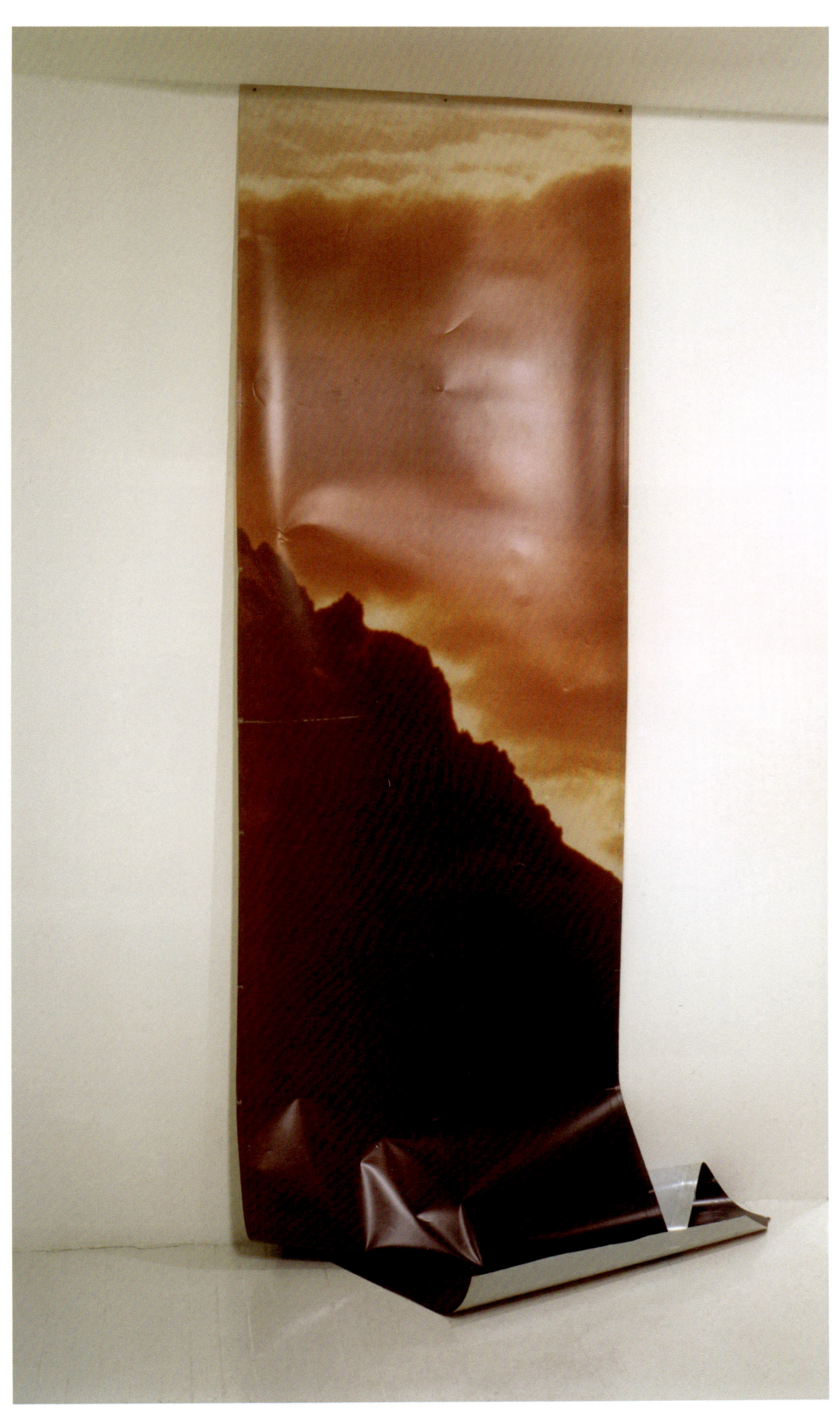

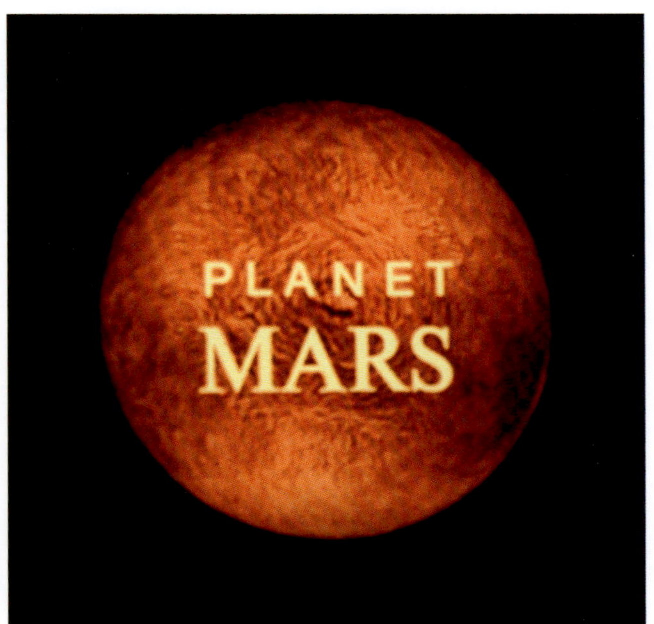

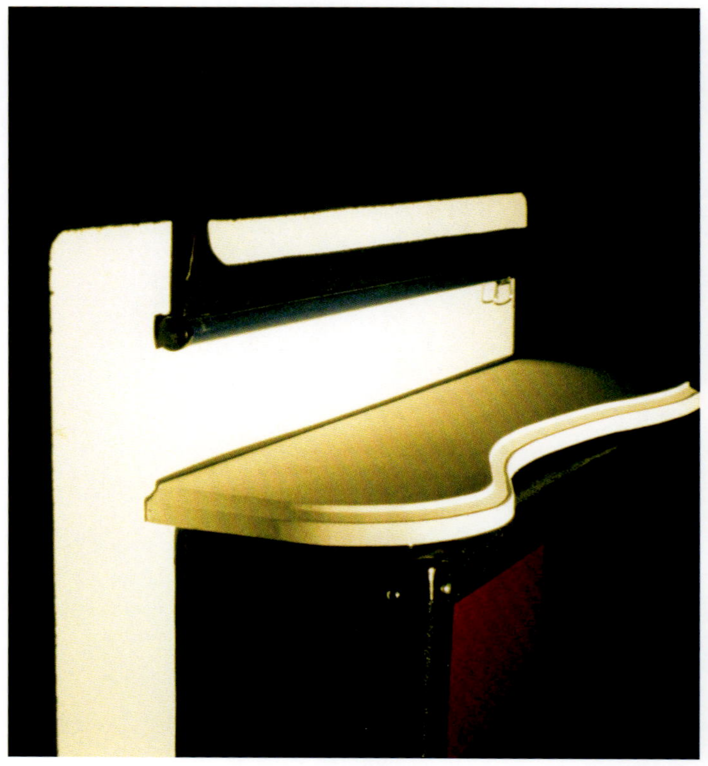

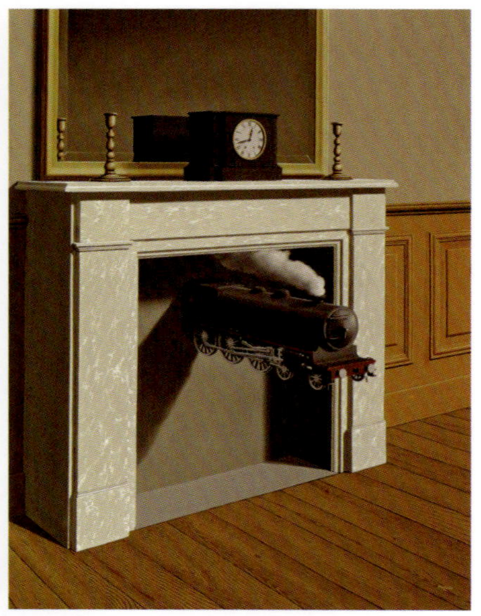

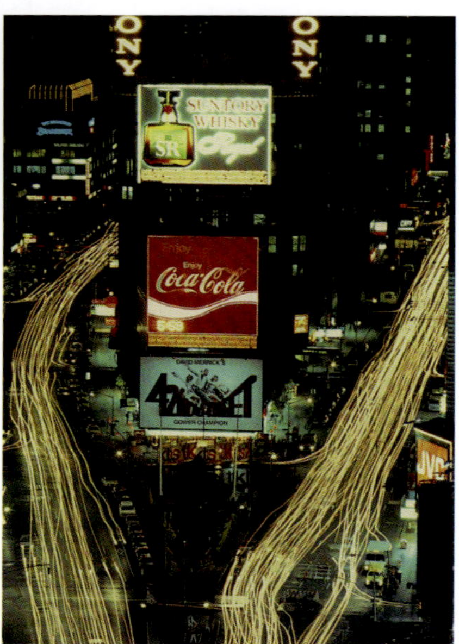

[9] reference: NASA film still   [10] reference: René Magritte, *Time Transfixed*, 1938   [11] reference: postcard Times Square   [12] *Untitled*, 1992

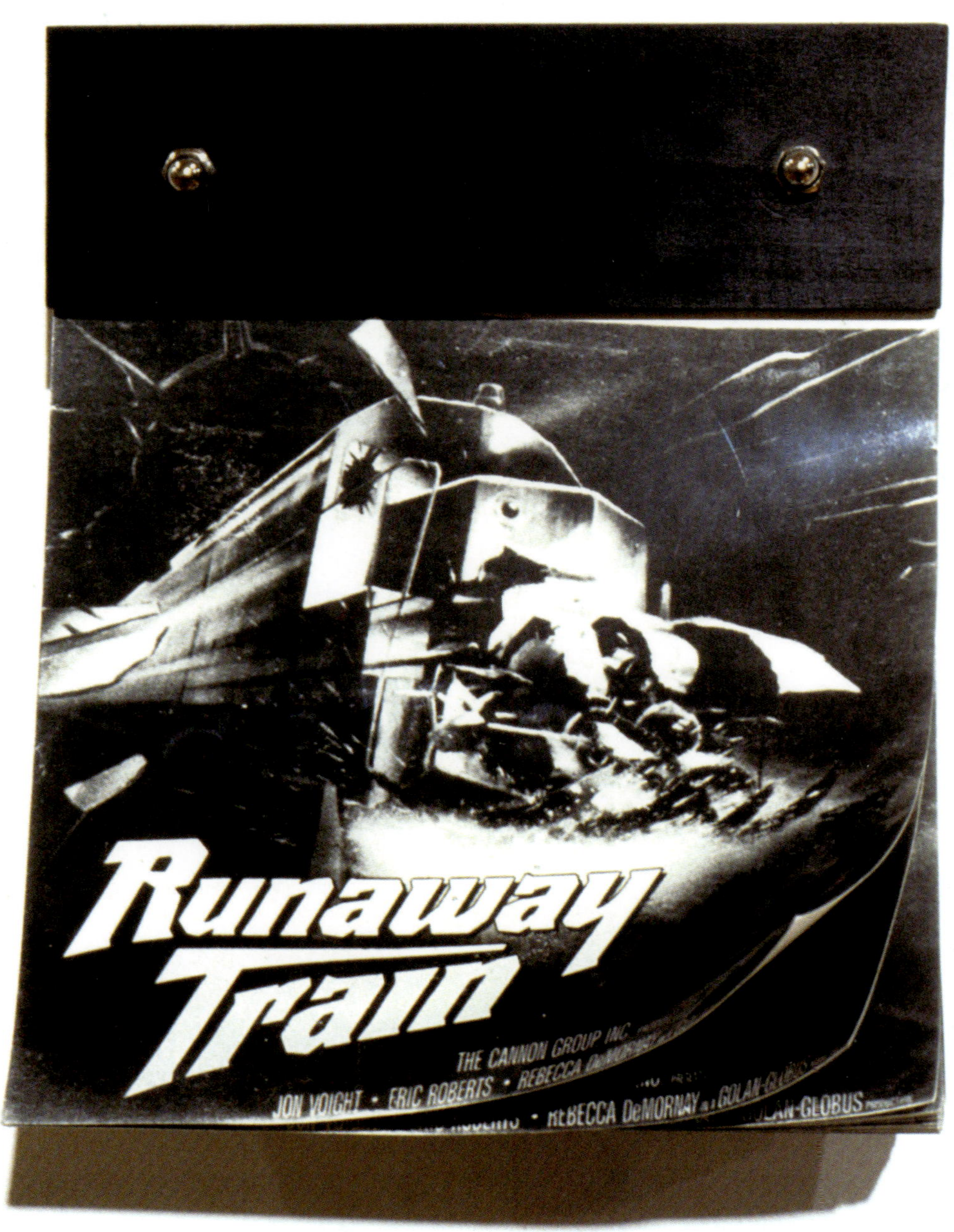

RUNAWAY
Train
THE CANNON GROUP INC.
JON VOIGHT · ERIC ROBERTS · REBECCA DeMORNAY
REBECCA DeMORNAY · GOLAN-GLOBUS

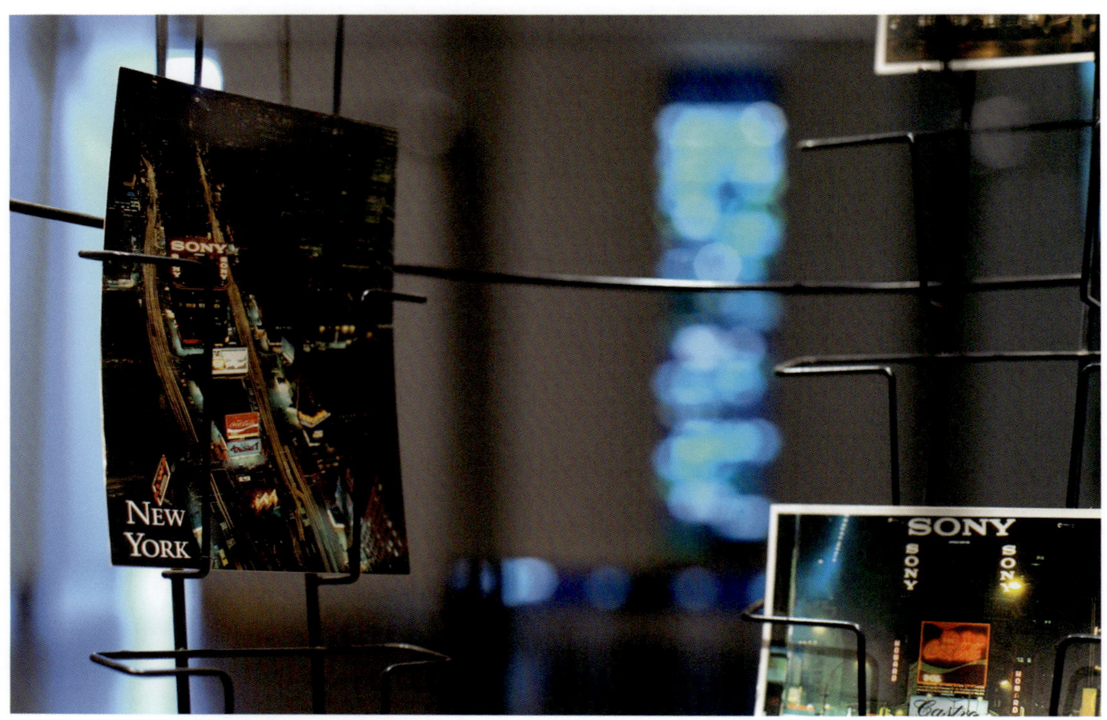

[14] *Times Square Cone* (and detail), 1989

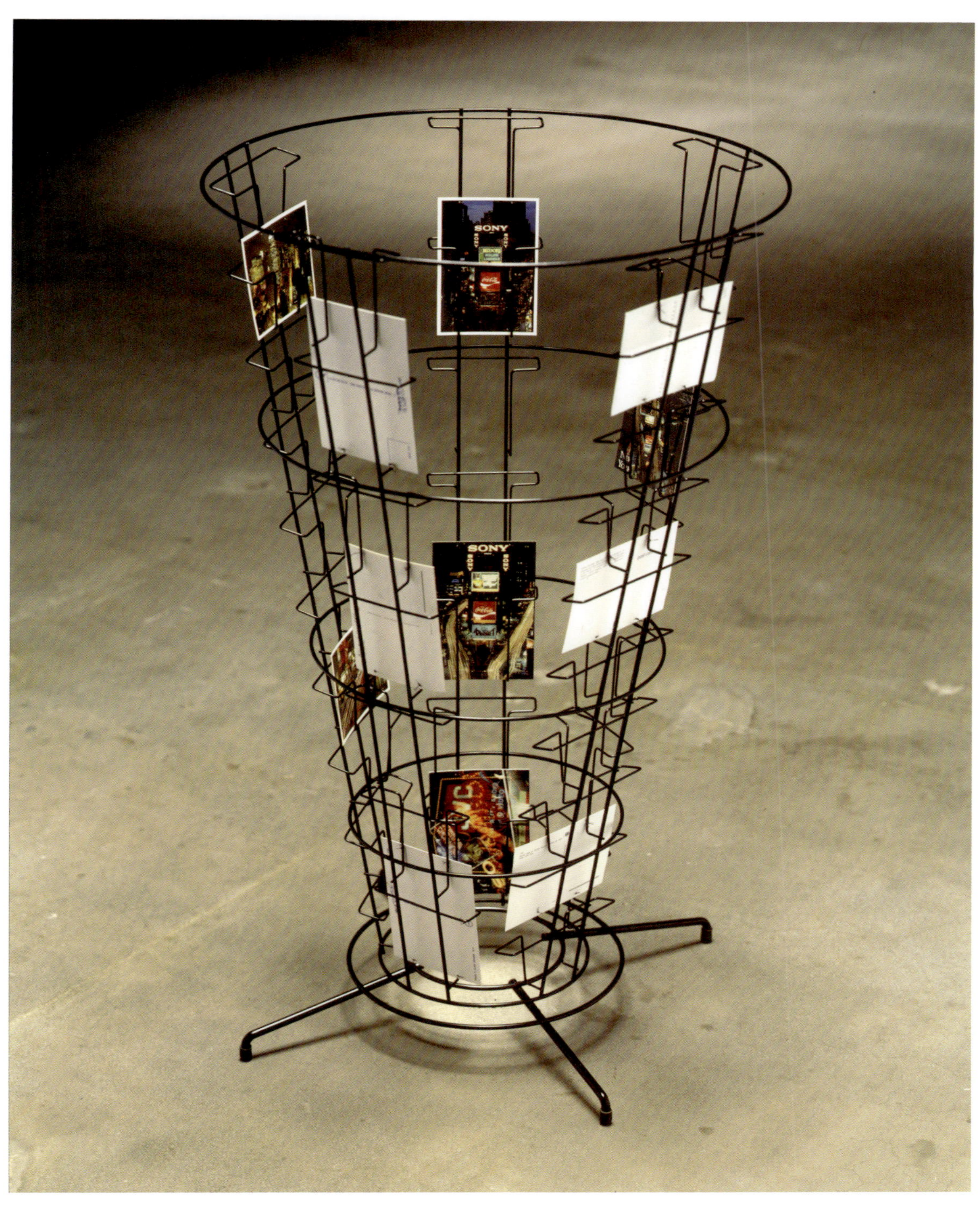

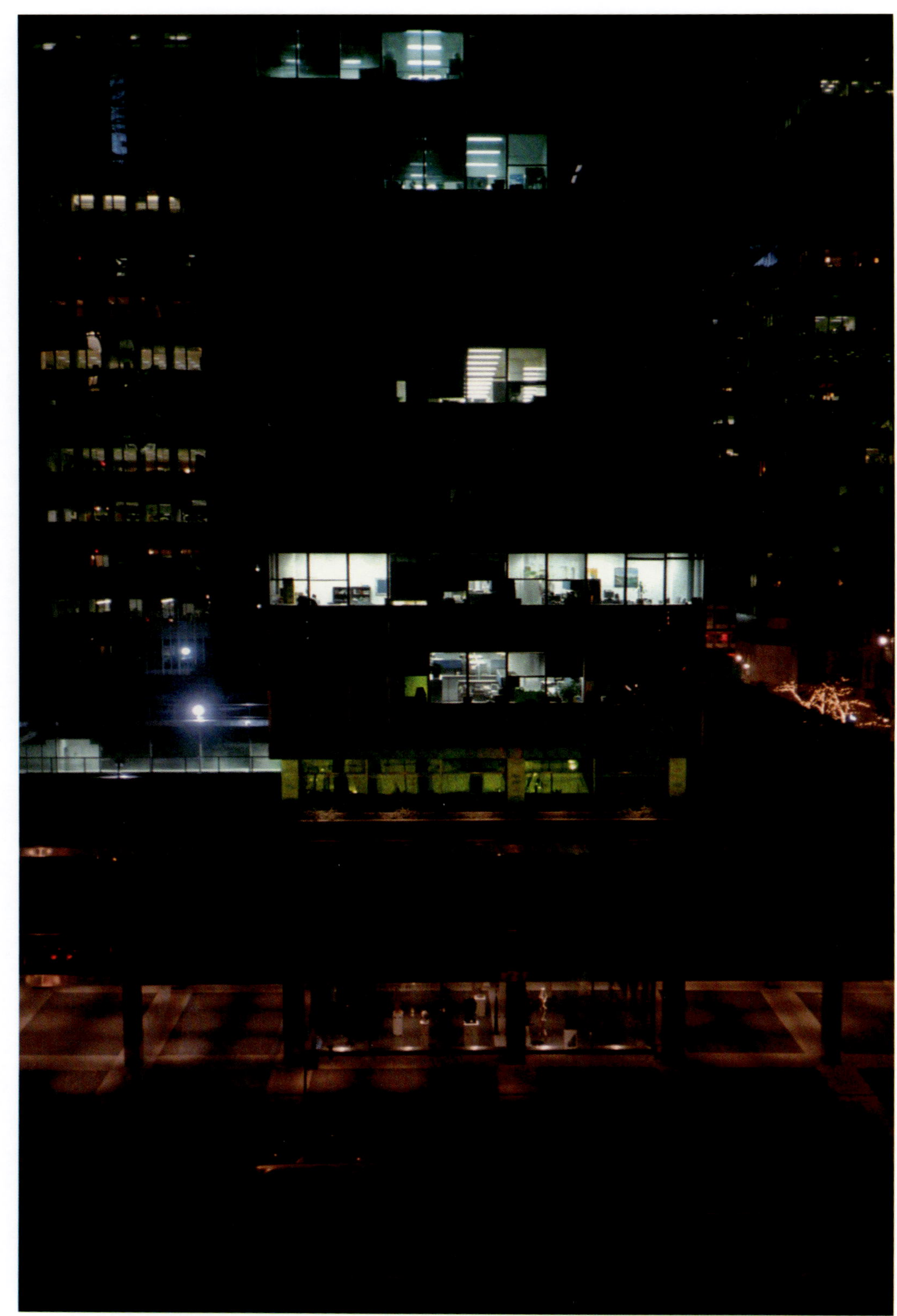

[15] *Lever House*, from the series *The City at Night*, 1998

[16] *Alley*, from the series *The City at Night*, 1998

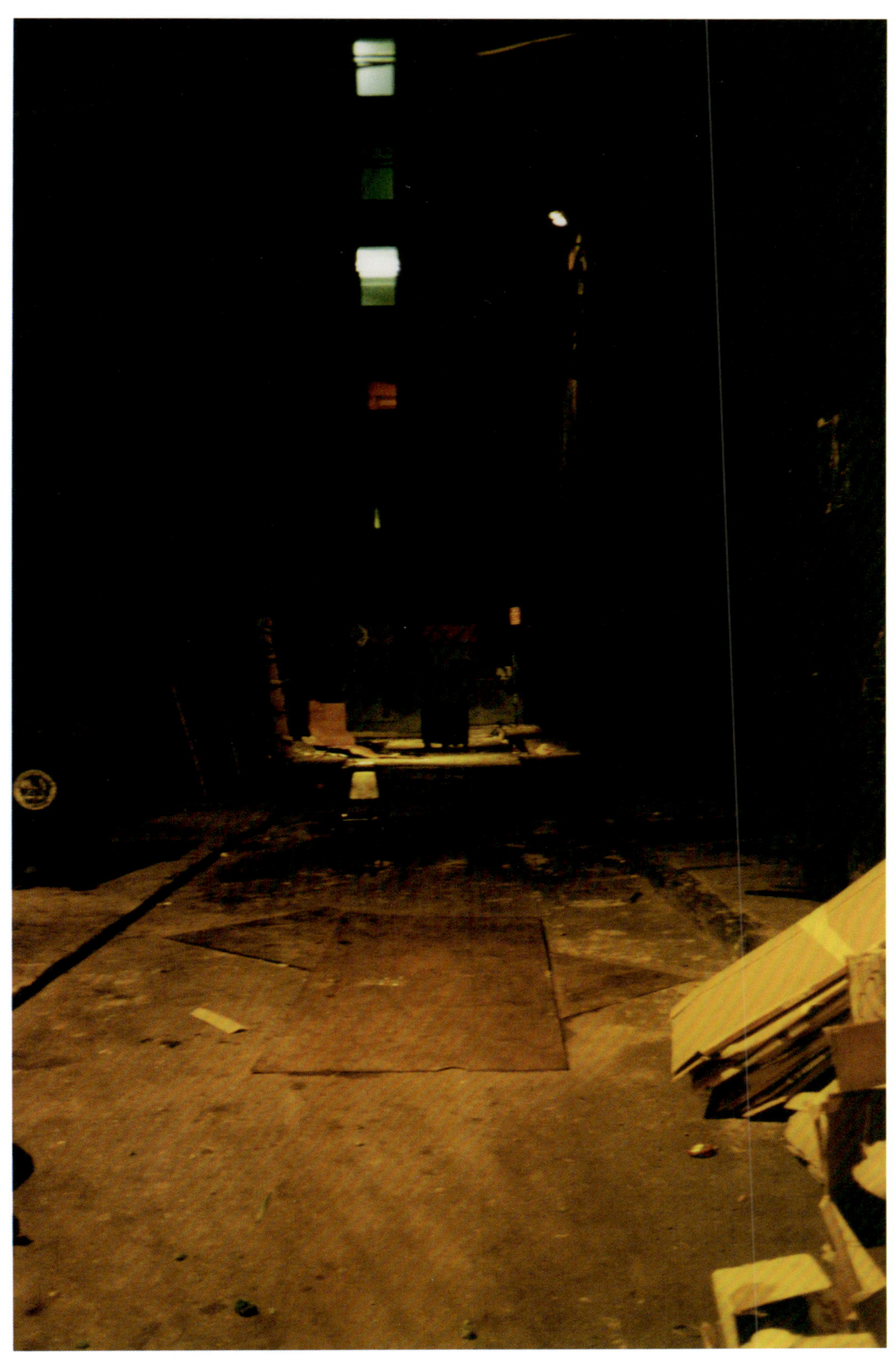

[17] *Appliance Store,* from the series *The City at Night,* 1998

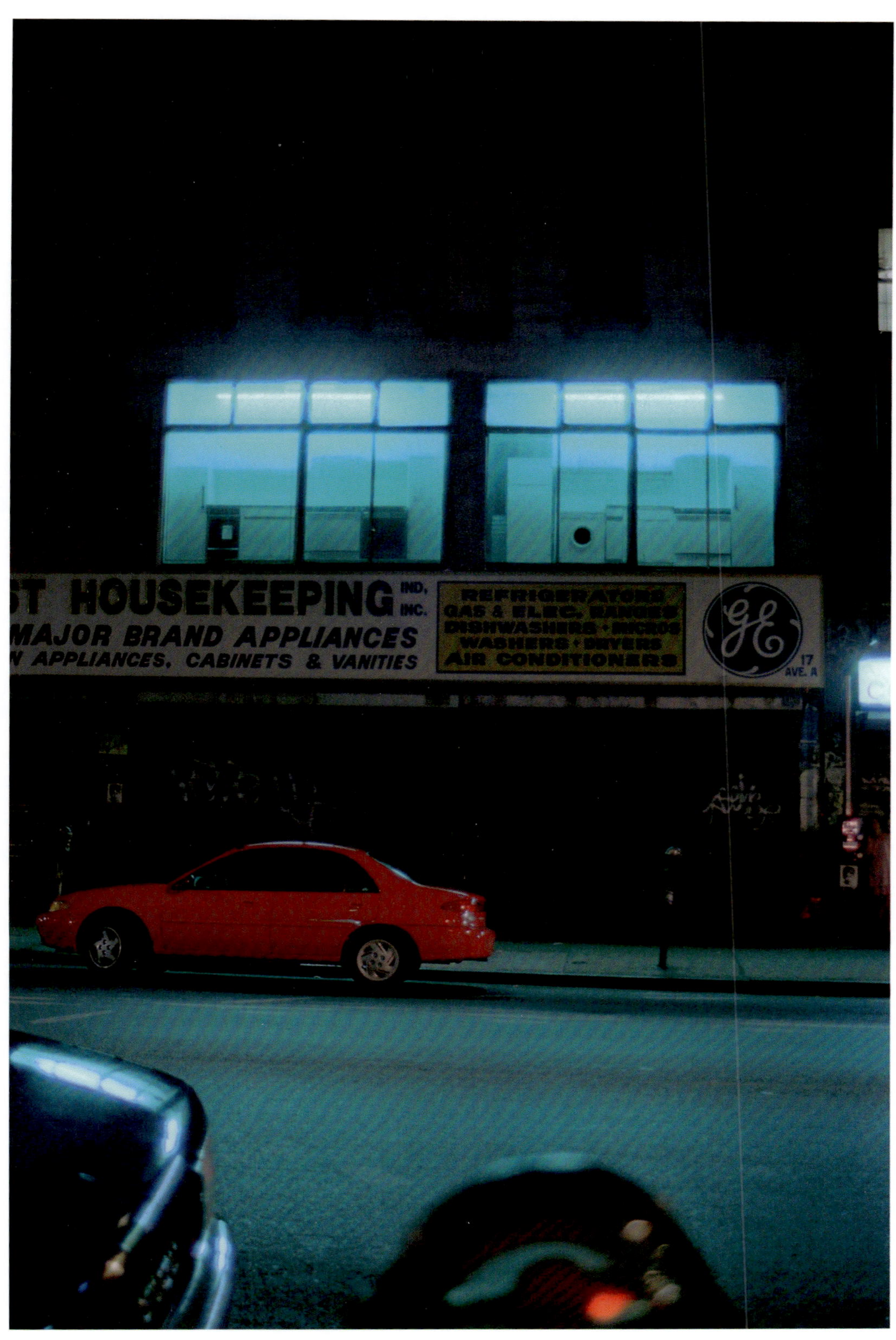
ST HOUSEKEEPING IND, INC.
MAJOR BRAND APPLIANCES
N APPLIANCES, CABINETS & VANITIES
REFRIGERATORS
GAS & ELEC. RANGES
DISHWASHERS • MICROS
WASHERS • DRYERS
AIR CONDITIONERS
GE
17
AVE. A

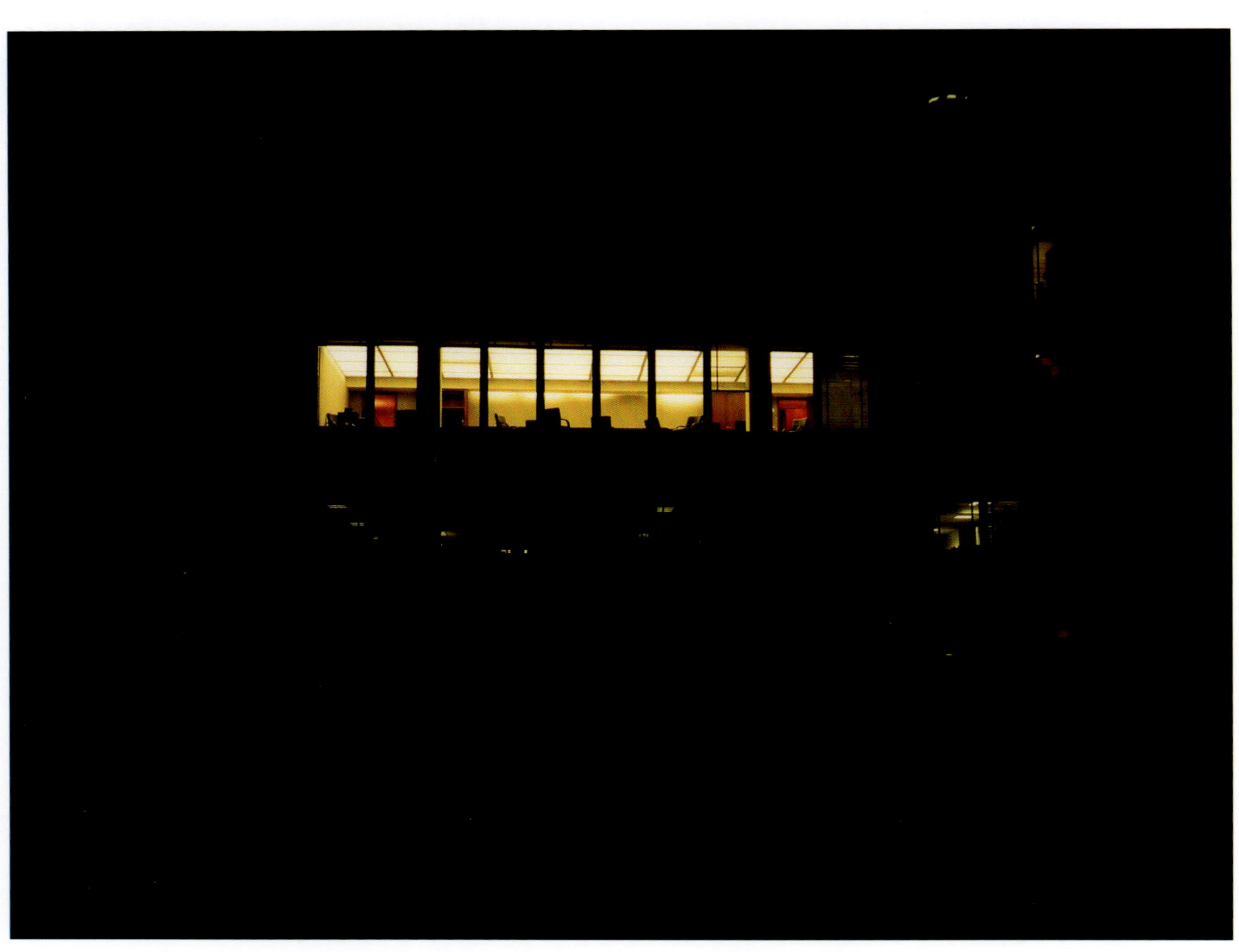

[18] *Conference Room*, from the series *The City at Night*, 1999   [19] *Appliance Contact #1*, 1999

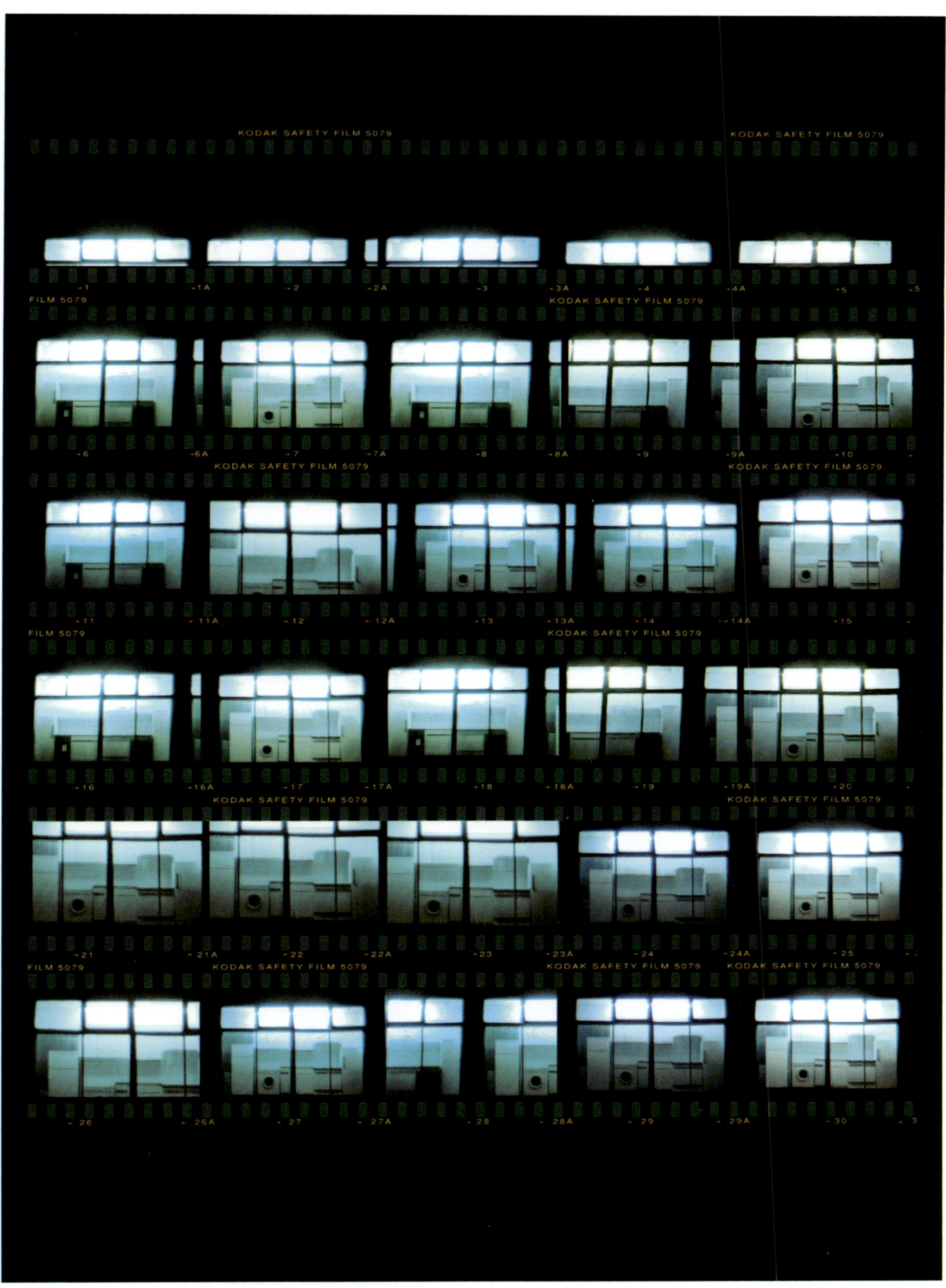

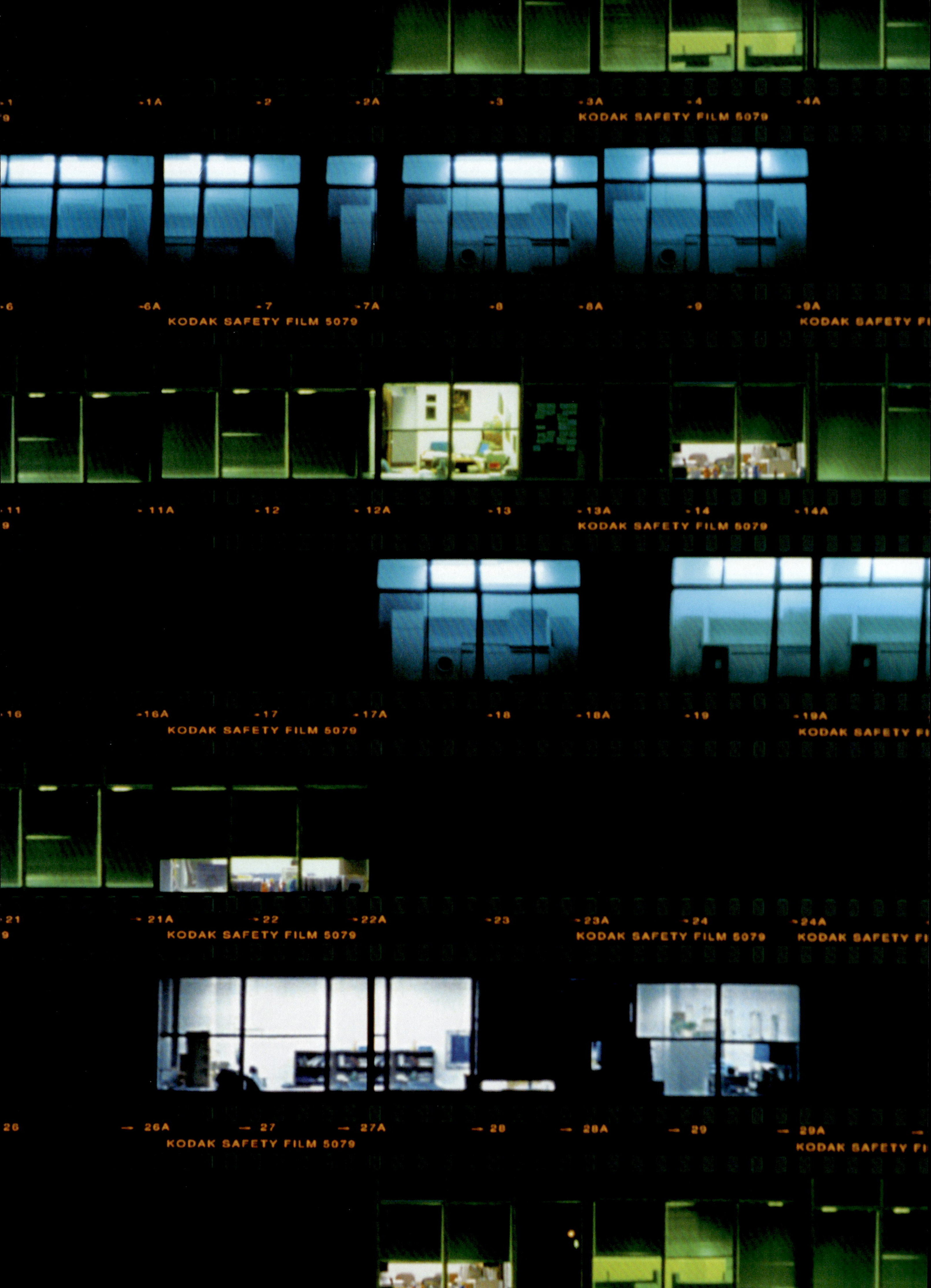

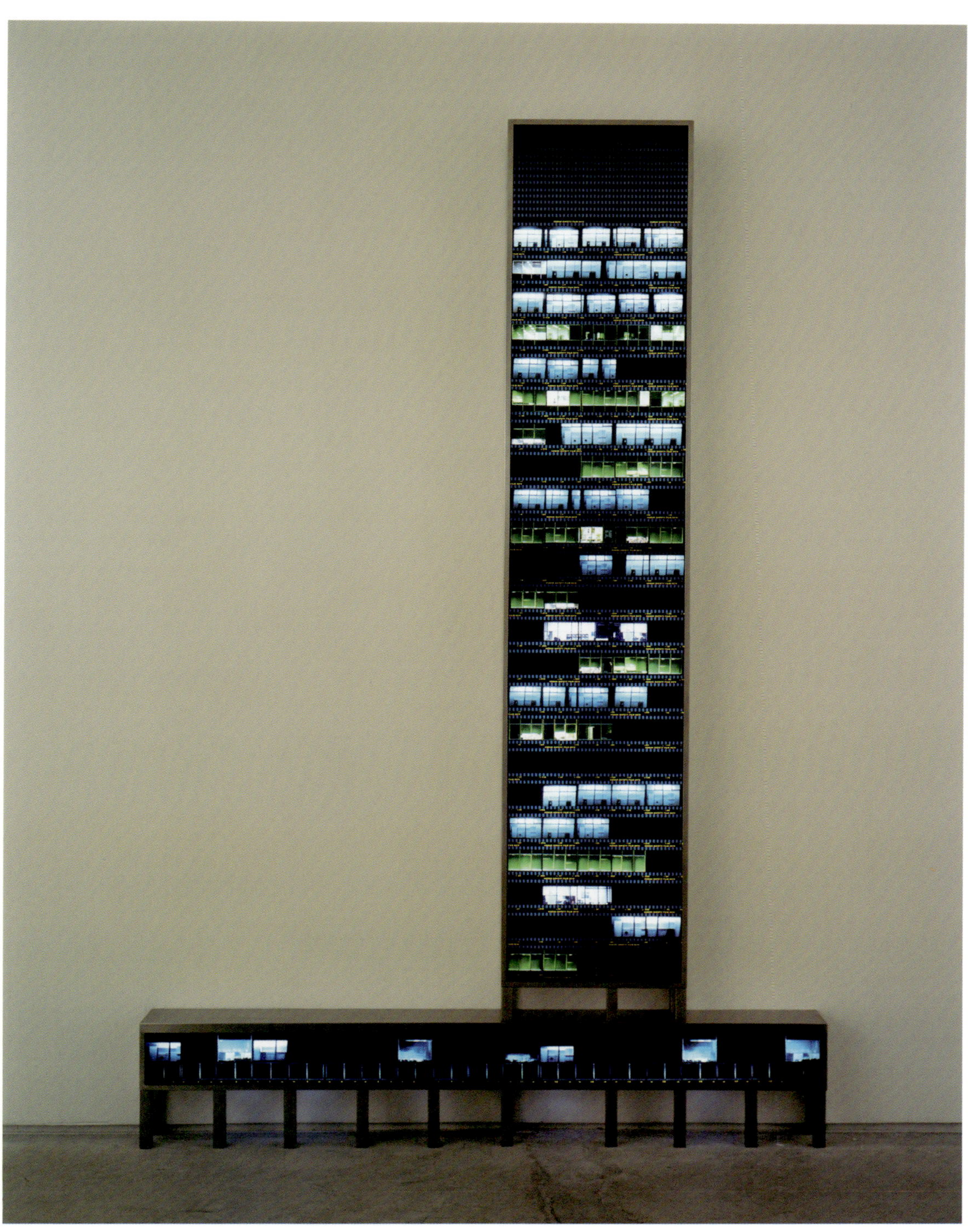

[20] *Appliance House* (and detail), 1999

[21] detail: *Appliance House*, 1998

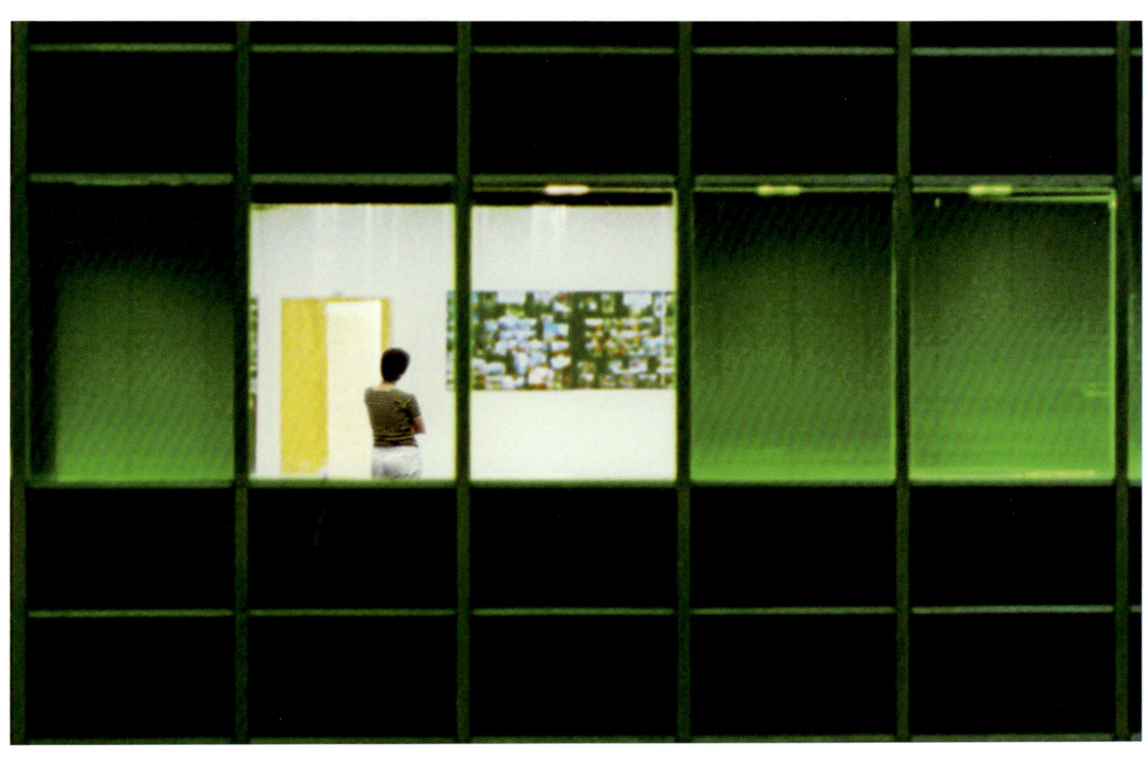

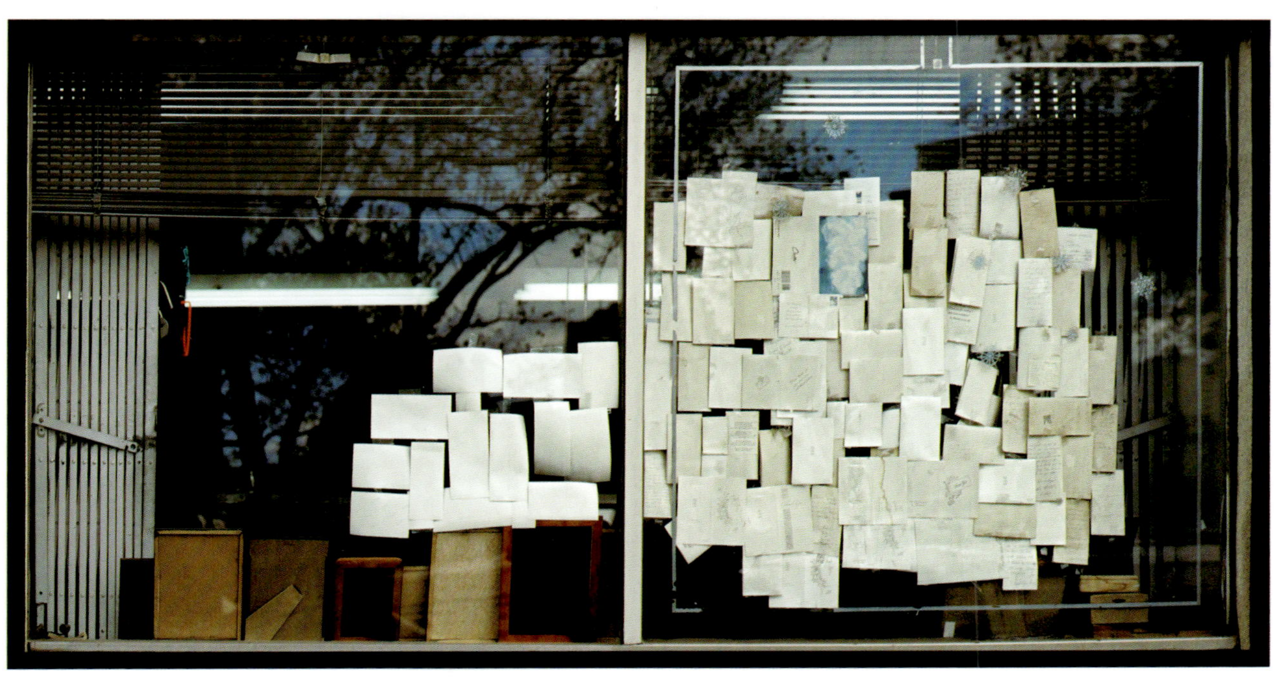

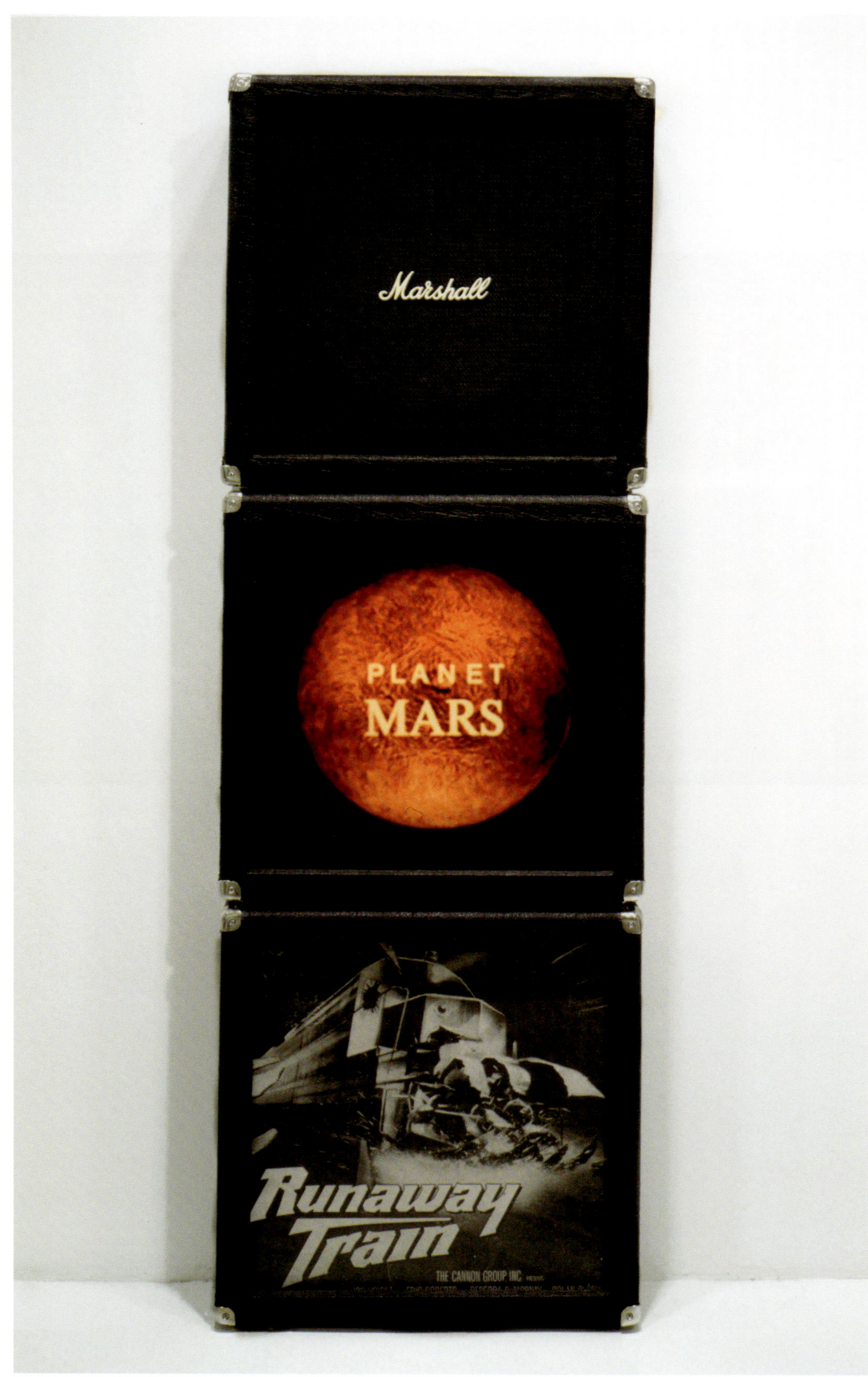

[23] *Marshall Stack*, 1987

UNPLUGGED: JENNIFER BOLANDE'S SPECIAL THEORY OF RELATIVITY

Hail, hail, rock and roll, deliver me from the days of old.
—Chuck Berry

I love my Marshall Amps, and I am nothing without them.
—Jimi Hendrix

Rock was already old when I first stumbled on the art of Jennifer Bolande, in the form of a couple of amplifiers, modestly assisted versions of the black-box archetype that, in my estimation, stand as the bicycle wheel of her period [25], a latter-day readymade whose disarming power to make the everyday uncanny is rivaled only by Jeff Koons's Hoovers encased in Plexiglas. [26]

Bolande is roughly (pop-scholarly hair-splitting aside) the same age as Rock 'n' Roll, and her inspired election of the untrumpeted workhorse behind the electric spectacle of rock made Chuck Berry's tribute of her birth year feel suddenly olden—poignant even. How many youthful generations had staked their salvation on this futurist prayer? And where, Bolande's silent totems make us ask ourselves, did this epoch-making phenomenon come from? What made that simplest of formulas—a guitar, a drum kit, a gyrating vocalist, and the inevitable pyramid of amplifiers—so durable, so much the mortar of our modern myth-space that it should require Bolande's estranging poetry to enliven us to the mystery of it all?

Rock is huge—and strange. But what isn't, when you come to think of it, which is what Bolande's art reliably inspires us to do. This is not to suggest that the sweep of her endeavor is in any sense encyclopedic; on the contrary, her artistic obsessions are decidedly particular. Indeed, Bolande tends to work a few fascinations repetitively (think of an artist like Vija Celmins), to worry a single figure through a slowly modulating series of variations, so that her subject, finally, is less, for instance, amplifiers—or washing machines or Modernist office towers (to name a few of her favorite things)—than the quicksilver nature of meaning and the improbable ways we manufacture it.

The date of my first encounter with Bolande's work was 1986; and the venue, the East Village storefront Nature Morte, just a few short blocks, as it happens, from the establishment where Koons would launch his juggernaut of a career.[1] The show, Bolande's third or fourth, depending on how you do the math, included a range of more or less related works, but it was *Speaker I*, 1986 [33], and *Speaker II*, 1986 [32], the first official "sculptures" in a series that would come to include some thirty amp-related pieces made over nearly as many years, that stopped me in my tracks.[2] *Speaker I* comprised a pair of stacked amps, stripped of their fabric-facing and perforated with a pair of crisp circles roughly where the four internal speaker cones would normally sit. One cone is visible, floating loose inside its cabinet, but the remaining three seem to have gone missing, leaving two mostly hollow shells.

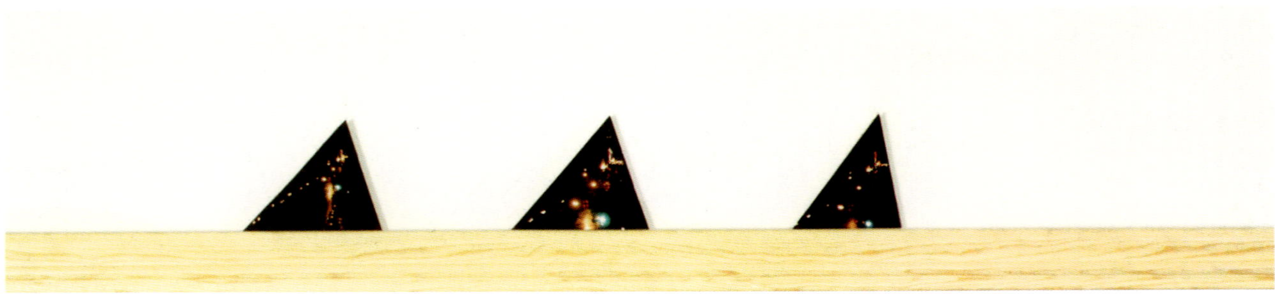

The control panel is absent too, replaced by a couple of shims of raw wood sandwiched together with black enamel paint that visibly oozes out at the edges. The longer we stare, the more alien these familiar appliances look—an experience that is amplified by the row of diminutive, barely legible photographs, laminated onto triangular chips of wood and lined up along an unvarnished scrap of chair railing. Displayed in the same sequence in which the photos were shot, these dark shards (Bolande calls them "Times Square triangles") [24] capture car lights moving up 46th Street as viewed through the windows of the artist's studio at the time, and yet their tiny scale and shiny, chiplike format undermine our sense that we are looking at a recognizable scene, challenging us to square this improbable part of the work with the larger whole. I am tempted to call this photographic flourish typical Bolande, if by "typical" we mean that it is utterly unexpected.

If *Speaker I* is king ("The photo triangles," the artist offers, "remind me of the points on a crown"),[3] then *Speaker II* must be his queen. Made in the same year, *Speaker II* consists of the sliced-off top end of a single speaker cabinet, a black veil affixed to its upper edge and trailing loose in front of it, as if the facing had been blown out by a sonic blast. This time the "cones," fashioned of common aluminum screen and sewn together in an overlapping manner ("like a Venn diagram"), sit before the veiled speaker directly on the gallery floor. Biomorphic, and faintly Arte Povera in feel, the shapes must, we gather, represent speaker cones, but they register no less as mini-mountains and dunce caps as funnels or sieves.

Bolande's X-looks-like-Y-feels-like-Z–stream-of-consciousness improvisations have a way of moving viewers from the local (a mute appliance) to the big imponderables: time (that of an aging idiom, rock) and art (her own attempts to mark and make knowable the world she passes through). Indeed staring at those unplugged gangs of speakers made strange by Bolande's selection was a lot like staring at a star-strewn summer sky. In the face of the incommensurability of it all, our efforts to connect the dots seem puny and a bit beside the point.

All of this may sound light-years from the Koons of the Hoovers, and yet I summoned him at the start not merely to exploit the juxtaposition of the *povera* and the slick, but rather to highlight a fundamental period affinity underlying the differing places their art has taken them. Measured against the broader range of 1980s artistic options (think Neo-Expressionist painting), Bolande and Koons are siblings before they are antagonists: Both are children of television, the American suburb, and Madison Avenue—that is to say, of the then incipient image culture of which the photograph was fundament. And though one would no more call Bolande a photographer than one would Koons, the photograph is the fulcrum of her art, just as it was for her *Pictures Generation* precursors.

In *Mouthpiece*, 1987 [31], a favorite work of mine, the photograph plays a role at least as disarming as it does in *Speaker I*. Here, the speaker that anchors the ensemble consists of a face without the cabinet, really just a board wrapped in fabric and cut through, once again, with four holes where the absent amplifying cones would go. A tiny, brass placard nailed in the bottom corner features not, as one might expect, the speaker's brand name, but instead a simple patch of etched crosshatching visually echoing the fret cloth weave. And yet the decisive element, the detail that makes the piece, is a photograph, an innocuous snapshot tucked casually next to the speaker front like a Kodak moment slipped into the frame of a dressing table mirror. The print is beginning to curl at the edges (the way loose snapshots are wont to), and what it pictures is, well, next to nothing. A barely differentiated outtake—a throwaway from all appearances—the image registers only a few stray

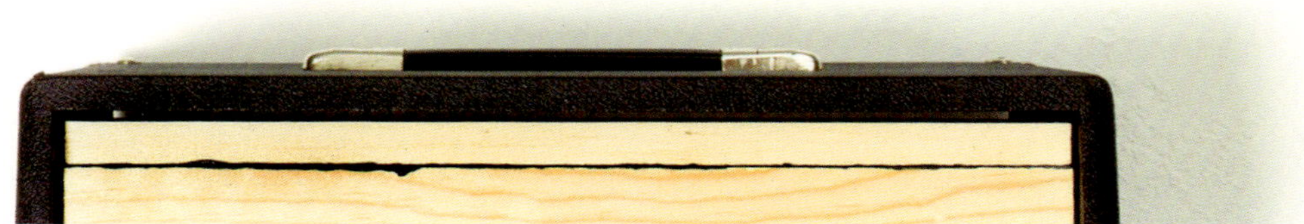

twinkles of light. Are they glints off a frontman's microphone stand as it tilts in the glare of the stage lights? In point of fact, the subject of the photo was again Times Square, a night shot enlarged to the point where the lights of that celebrated crossroads register as disembodied flashes, and yet in typical Bolandean fashion, the rhyme between the grainy texture of the enlarged image and the weave of the speaker facing, between the "star dust" captured in the photograph and the glisten off the metallic threads that run through the fret cloth, is the associative breadcrumb that sets us down the forking trail of improbable meaning. Because the image is so slippery, so intractably objectlike in its curled paperiness—so hard, that is, to step through as a window on a represented world—it seems to mock photography as a way of capturing anything at all. In a final twist, a sheet of Plexiglas glazing that separates the viewer from the art (a seemingly traditional touch!) is punctured with a circular configuration of holes that resemble the vent in a ticket vendor's window. Exemplifying the sort of "figuring of mediation," the representation of those moments of transit and interface that constitute the lodestone of her endeavor, the detail is as curious—and as much the main event—as the fugitive, and suddenly magical snapshot.

Bolande puts the photograph through its paces—teases at it, tortures it, turns it inside out. *Milk Crown*, 1987 [56], perhaps her best-known work, turned Harold Edgerton's famous photograph [58] of a splashing droplet of milk into a three-dimensional object cast in porcelain. If *Milk Crown* one-ups Edgerton's claim to show us more than we can see with our own eyes, exposes the real as surreal and, in so doing, wreaks gentle havoc with the photographic plain truth, *Cascade*, 1987 [8], takes a more bare-knuckled approach to the medium. Tumbling down the gallery wall is a 12-foot-long slice from the middle of what appears to be a billboard image picturing an atmospheric sunset scene, the excess length crumpling in a pile on the floor. The drama of the object, of the massive duratrans—more a big piece of paper than a Madison Avenue fantasy glimpsed from the highway—makes for the work's effecting friction.

If the *Pictures* artists made the power of the photograph—its uses and abuses in the social sphere—the subject of their appropriations, Bolande responded to the medium's objectifying gaze by turning the tables and "objectifying" the photograph itself. Indeed, the "Photo Object" was a period catch phrase for the impulse that saw not only Bolande but a number of her peers (most notably, Alan Belcher) beat up on the print. With Belcher's blocks of wood wrapped in ad-art-slick color images of themselves, the photograph, in its simultaneous quality as an image and a material object, becomes a *reductic ad absurdum*. Treating the prints more like lumber than image, Belcher literally hammered the pictures to their subject, employing grids of nails altogether out of scale with the task at hand. Bolande similarly roughed up the image in *Coda Stack*, 1988, where she sanded the surface of a print, exposing the layers of pigment that make up the emulsion.

Of course Bolande's gesture was less brash than Belcher's, her rough treatment of the print but one move in a larger poetic complex.[4] Whereas, for instance, the sanded surface of the print in *Coda Stack* suggests a cosmic event, an eddy of the Milky Way, the fact that the upper corner of the image appears to be peeled back, exposing the Kodak logo (minus the final K) on the company's signature yellow ground, lands us squarely back on earth. Riffing on the company's long-running ad campaign, the *trompe l'oeil* gimmick sets the stage for a crisp Ektachrome—of, say, a beaming Every-Family vacationing at the lake—but offers instead an impossibly oblique anti-photograph.

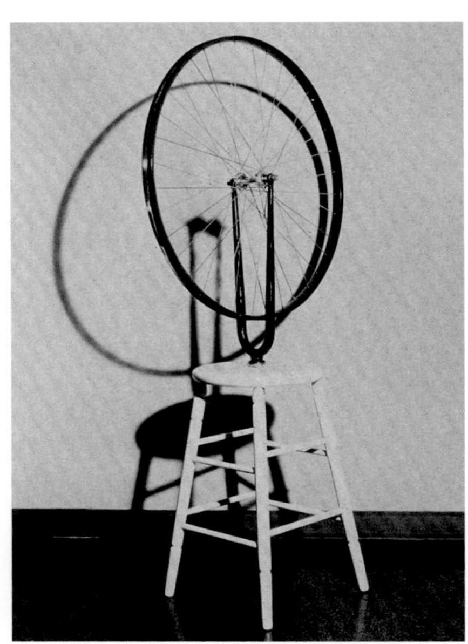

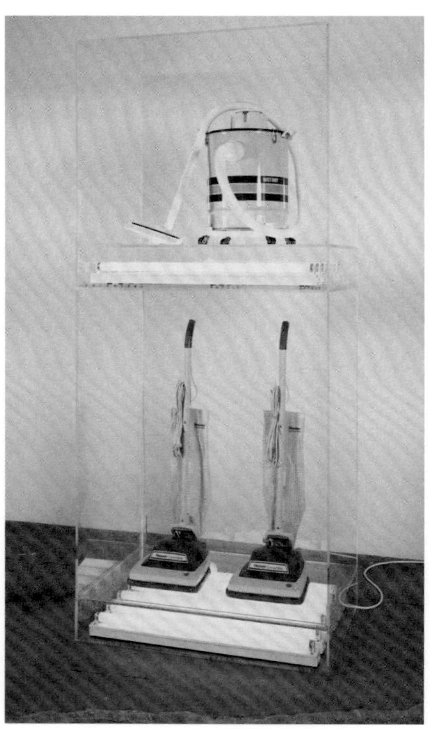

Coda Stack is not only characteristic of the devious ways Bolande uses the photograph to slip a wedge between what we think we see (and know) and what we actually do or don't; it exemplifies her more general (and deep-seated) drive to undermine any surety we may have as to where we stand in the cosmos. Instability, one might almost say, is her art's most stable value. In *Coda Stack*, the sanded image is framed in a speaker cabinet (one of three), and the tower as a whole lists gently to the left, the rough wood shims inserted between each amplifier, as if to level the proceedings, doing exactly the opposite.

Mistakes are Bolande's stock-in-trade. She savors undecided spaces: cracks, holes, but also thresholds (the leader, the 11-10-9-8 reverse countdown before the movie begins, is a filmic trope she has evoked on more than one occasion). Bolande tends to go after "meaning" on the way in—or out. She works, in fact, to capture meaning in the making—meaning at the moment it coalesces into something graspable and transferable, or just as it eludes us again. This explains her devotion to the framing games she plays, her habit of summoning the rhetoric of display, the conventions of presentation, only to expose them for their artfulness. It's no coincidence that speakers look a bit like framed canvases, the weave of the linen evoked, as she herself has pointed out, by the knit of the fabric facing. *Single Speaker*, 1987 [28], another black-box amplifier cut with a large round hole, houses a tiny drawing. Executed in pencil on gessoed board, the thumbnail sketch spotlights a drawing of nothing—a framed blank—leaning against a wall. Emerging from the dark ground like a deer in the headlights, the sketch is "just a pathetic little image […] really sort of dorky," the artist laughs, but it is also, for this reason, an easy art object to love. Bolande calls it "the pathos rectangle."

The road-not-taken forkings that are the best way around Bolande's individual artworks also provide the surest path between them. If a piece like *R.Shldr.*, 1990 [40], comprising one corner cut out of a speaker with a shoulder pad resting atop it, evokes a playful anthropomorphism that runs deep in Bolande's art, *U.N.titled Speaker*, 2002 [69] makes the humble amplifier monumental. Based on the moderne tower that houses the United Nations' midtown Manhattan headquarters and cast in concrete, the speaker/skyscraper is faced on one side with Fender speaker

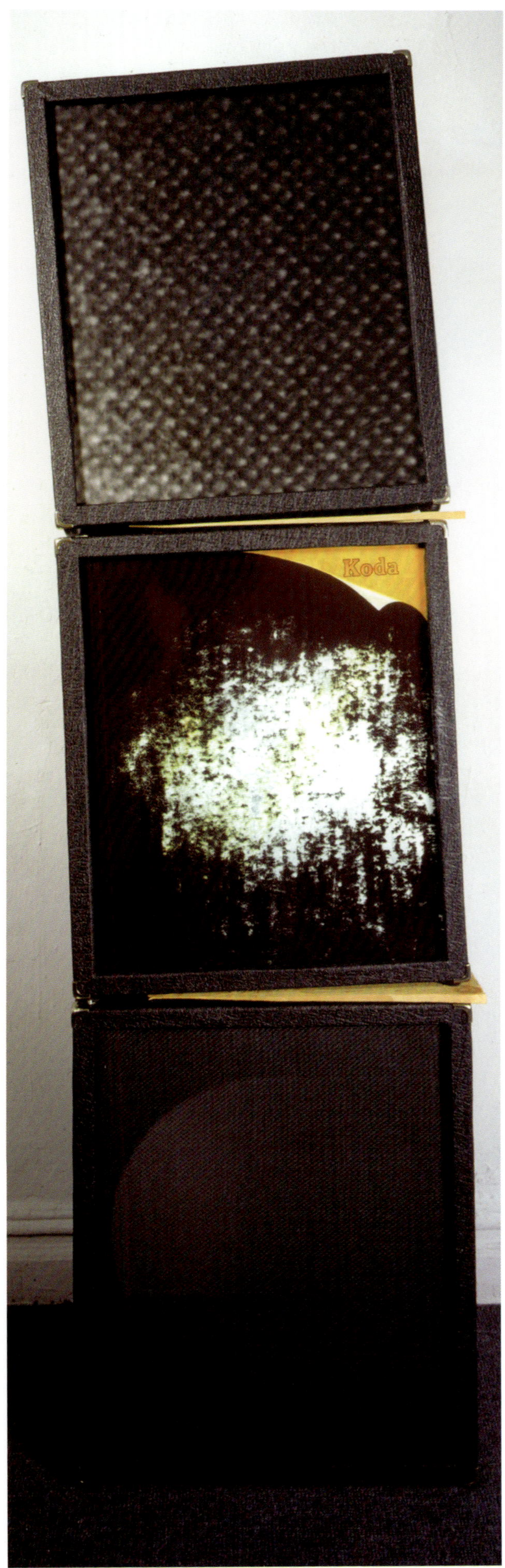

fabric, which happens to come laced with blue fibers, recalling the coloration of the building's mostly glass façade. The reverse face features a photograph Bolande shot of the building's actual façade, in which the scale and grid of the window-wrapped floors echo the weave (we have been here before) of the speaker fabric.

If in Bolande's universe a speaker can be both building and body (the sculptural body), then so can a washing machine, another favored Bolandean artifact that joins forces with the amplifier in her latest and largest work in the speaker sequence, *Earthquake*, 2004 [39]. Conceiving of the piece on the tenth anniversary of the Northridge, California, disaster, she describes the work as "almost a bodily memory" of the event— a memory in the form of a monumental cube built of two washers; two dryers; and eight oversize amps stacked tightly and bolted together, so that when the spin cycle kicks in, the entire ensemble shakes.

Washing machines may not be quite as central to Bolande's oeuvre as amps, but the impulse that drew her to both involves more than simply the improbable formal affinity of these unlike appliances. One night on Manhattan's Lower East Side an illuminated, second-floor store window stocked with household appliances caught her eye and inspired *Appliance Store*, 1998 [17], a photograph that would, in turn, beget a second work based on a modernist tower, this time the Gordon Bunshaft–designed midcentury masterpiece Lever House. *Appliance House*, 1999 [20], incorporates photographs of the Lower East Side storefront, with a series of *Rear Window*–style glimpses (also shot at night) into the midtown Manhattan headquarters of the British laundry detergent concern Lever Brothers Soap. Assembled in a contact-sheet-like configuration and inserted against a grid representing the building's celebrated curtain wall, Bolande's gesture connects the company's humble product and the quintessential International Style glass-box skyscraper, though her motive is less exposé than archeology— or even better, poetry (in Bolande's world, the three are frequently one). Both buildings exert not only the inevitable *Nighthawks* tug at the heart strings but the palpable nostalgia for the just-vanishing past— here the high-industrial *Mad Men* past in both its cut-rate and uptown incarnations.[5] Ever self-conscious of art's place (and her own) in this meditation on lost time, Bolande inserts into the *Rear Window* scenario an image of herself posed in one of the building's offices, looking at what recalled to her a Gerhard Richter color grid—though, she owns, it was likely just a bulletin board. [21]

"Hail, hail, rock and roll, deliver us from the days of old"—but hail too photography, and, for that matter, avant-garde art. Bolande revels in the melancholy of obsolescence, whether of an idiom (rock) or an object (the old tube speakers, a kind of style fetish used by rockers today to evoke the legends of the pre-solid-state era); whether it's the demise of an idea (modern art/architecture), or just the passing of a neighborhood (the Lower East Side), or of a city, a civilization from one technological phase into another. There's an image the artist keeps close, by her Brit Pop forefather Richard Hamilton, that pictures a computer of his own design next to Duchamp's famous fountain [52]. For Bolande, this picture—the shifting sands of time, of our times and our art it disarmingly summons—makes it feel a lot like home.

Marshall Stack, 1987 [23], adds another ripple to her meditation on time's passage. Inspired by René Magritte's celebrated 1938 painting *Time Transfixed* [10], in which a locomotive emerges from the solid back wall of a coal-burning fireplace, the piece consists of an uninflected speaker (save for its

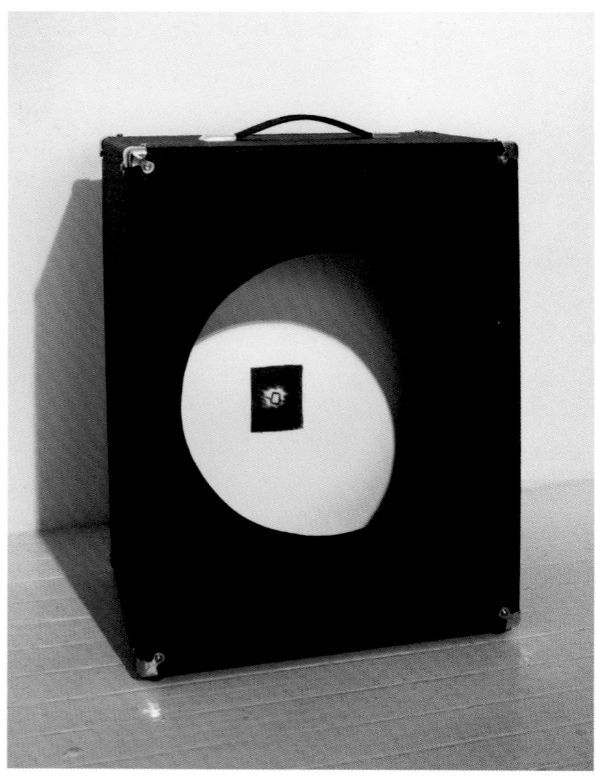

atypical shallowness) set atop a stack in which the two below it are treated as frames. In the middle amp Bolande has replaced the fabric facing with a still from a NASA-produced film titled *Planet Mars* [9], a personal landmark in her obsessional cosmos. Bolande grooved on the place the "red planet" held in the popular imagination of her childhood as a kind of dark double of earth, the locus of "life-in-space" projections ("the home of the monster," as she puts it, but also, more benignly, of a popular 1960s TV serial like *My Favorite Martian*). The opening sequence of *Planet Mars* simply features a red circle of light made to stand in for the planet and its mythos. Is it the fourth rock from the sun or a beam of light? The *trompe l'oeil* playfulness is so neatly tailored to the artist's sensibility that she surely would have come up with the image herself if the NASA creatives had not beat her to it. By contrast, the bottom speaker frames a promotional illustration from the 1987 movie *Runaway Train*, a production starring Jon Voight, Eric Roberts, and Rebecca De Mornay, remembered for, among other camp delights, a climactic battle between the male leads atop a locomotive careening toward disaster to the strains of Vivaldi's *Gloria in D*. Bolande, like most artists of her generation, is a connoisseur of such pop-cultural chestnuts (the *Runaway Train* image has made several appearances in her work), but what elevated it to an *objet fixe* was the locomotive's status as an out-of-date symbol of the Industrial Revolution (a dry-ice update of Turner's steam-hiss sublime). *Marshall Stack*, Bolande says, is about various "sites of projection coming together and ricocheting off each other": the Marshall amp implicitly projecting its sonic message outward (you can almost see cartoon sound waves), the projector projecting its beam onto the movie screen, and the train as outmoded industrial symbol, "sort of projecting from past to future." *Marshall Stack* is Bolande's special theory of relativity.

Indeed, "unplugged" is as good a word as any to capture the mood not only of Bolande's speaker works but of her performance as a whole. When Bob Dylan plugged into a Marshall stack, it was because he knew the times were a-changin', and he meant to change with them. Bolande is that other kind of witness, which may have something to do with why she remains something of a cult taste, a coffeehouse alternative to Koons's Electric Circus.

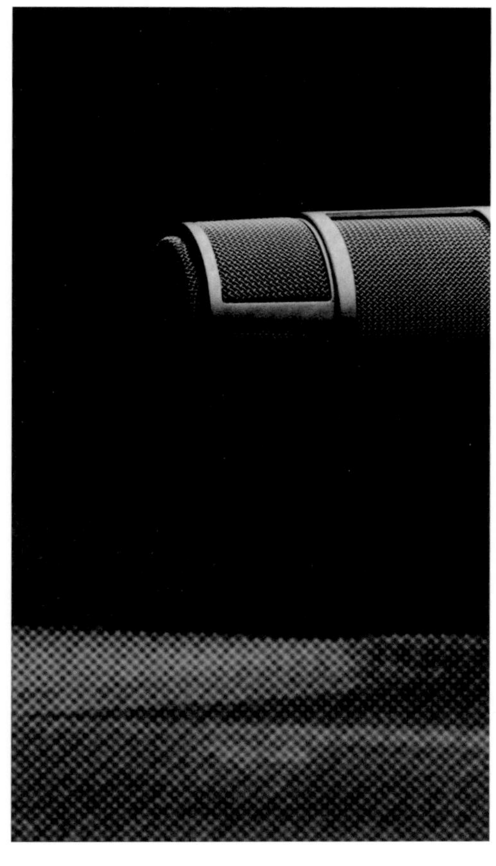

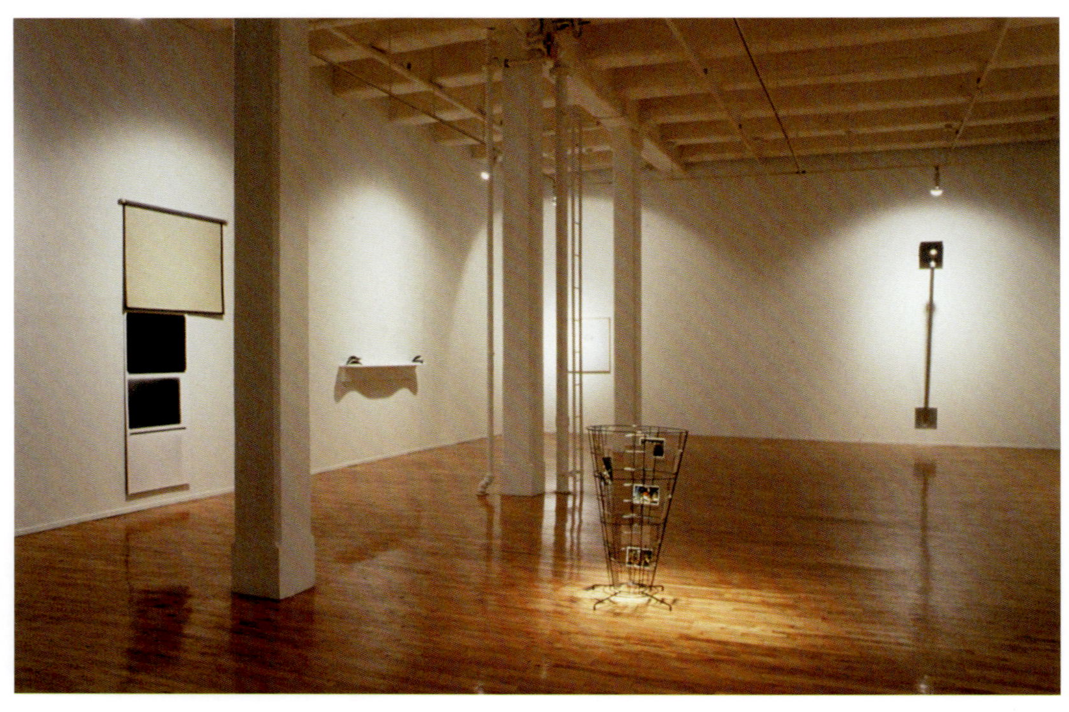

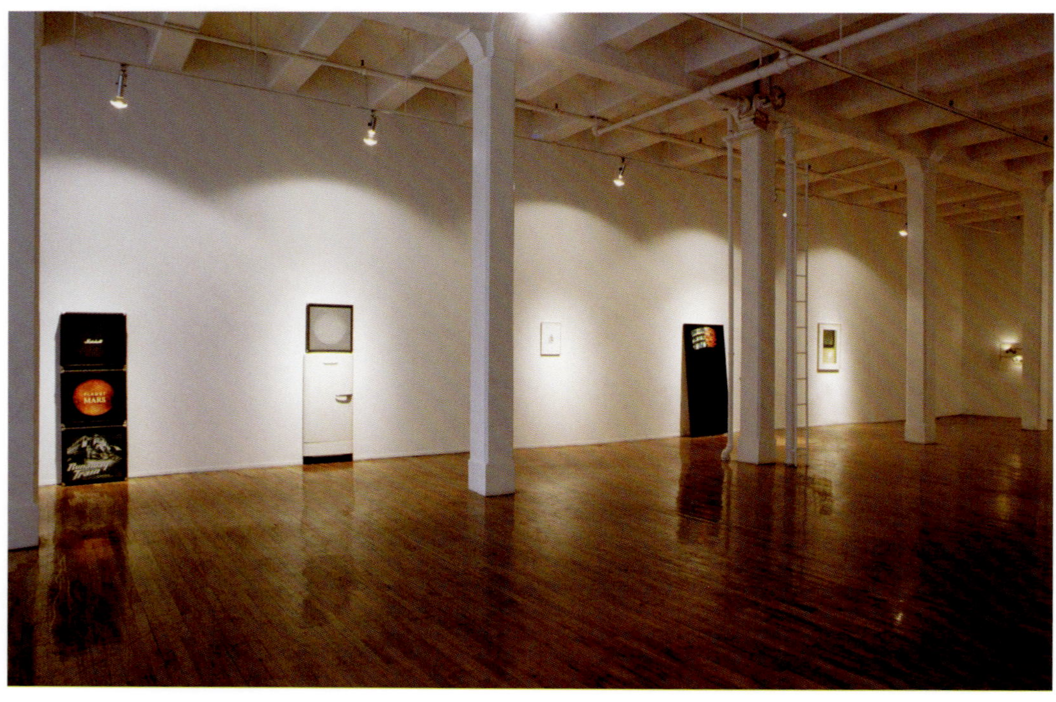

In 1988, shortly after signing up with the big-time gallery Metro Pictures (her essential diffidence would be the cause of her departure not long thereafter), Bolande imagined her own retrospective.[6] It took the form of a drawing in which her work to date was shown lined up against a long wall in reverse chronological order and receding dramatically toward a vanishing point. There's *Marshall Stack*! And also *Coda…* And there's the "pathos rectangle" (well, I can't quite make it out, but it must be tucked inside of *Single Speaker*, which I can clearly see). Rendered in a childish hand and clumsily perspectival (all the works appear to be careening backward), Bolande's modestly sized sketch makes a quizzical counterpart to, for instance, Warhol's "Retrospectives" and "Reversals," those late-life celebrations of the Pop master's transmogrification into a household brand, or Ed Ruscha's puckish mid-career refusal, *I Don't Want No Retro Spective*, 1979.

How weird, she seems to muse, that I made all this stuff—and how funny/strange the whole art thing! Landing just on the right side of the wry, no-stakes regard of a *New Yorker* cartoon, *Retroperspective*, 1988 [98], the title punning at once on the conventions of artistic depiction and the exigencies of self-packaging and career, conjures a perfectly equanimous "Good for me if I join the firmament with the immortals; but OK too if I don't." It's a posture in tune with her elusive, slow-boil contribution, one whose rescue, she seems to wink, depends on us. The broad visibility today of a younger artist like Rachel Harrison, an artist who also deploys photography with all its material specificity as a medium in sculptural assemblages, cannot but make a case for the prescience of Bolande's rule-breaking gestures of the middle-1980s.[7] Indeed, if—imitation being the sincerest form of flattery—recent appearances of her signal obsession, the speaker, in work by artists from Kaz Oshiro to Banks Violette are any indication, *Retroperspective*, like Bolande's legacy generally, should work its time-release magic on the visitors to the show it imagined some two decades ago.

1. The burgeoning East Village gallery scene at the time featured some 50-plus establishments. Among the most prominent of them, Nature Morte and International with Monument (Koons's launching pad) shared overlapping programs that defined the more conceptually oriented side of the scene, which is typically contrasted with a second celebrated camp that drew on street art and Expressionist idioms.

2. *Speaker Family Drawing*, 1986 [34], a drawing in ballpoint pen on paper based on a promotional still arraying a full line of one company's amplifiers, was perhaps the real first work in the series.

3. All quotations except where noted from an interview conducted by the author in Bolande's Los Angeles studio on March 26, 2010.

4. Together with the art of another period peer, Meyer Vaisman, Belcher's brasher, more Pop sensibility might be seen to anticipate the aggressively hands-on, resolutely low-tech photomechanical circus of the contemporary duo Guyton/Walker.

5. I owe a debt to Katy Siegel's sensitive reading of the piece *Appliance House*, 1998–1999. See "Tumble, Sigh," *Artforum*, New York, Vol. XXXVIII, No.5 (January 2000), pp. 88-89.

6. While Bolande's pointedly modest, at times almost abject-seeming sensibility and at least apparently casual facture ran counter to those of her ambitious dealers at the time, her example would soon look prescient next to such rising stars as Mary Heilmann (belatedly recognized in the very early 1990s), Jack Pierson, and Karen Kilimnik.

7. A recent Museum of Modern Art (MoMA) show devoted to the interface of photography and sculpture, *The Original Copy: Photography of Sculpture, 1839 to Today*, singled out the work of Harrison but missed the opportunity to tease out a suggestive thematic with respect to the work of Bolande and her 1980s peers. The show, curated by Roxana Marcoci, took place August 1–November 1, 2010.

[31] *Mouthpiece*, 1987

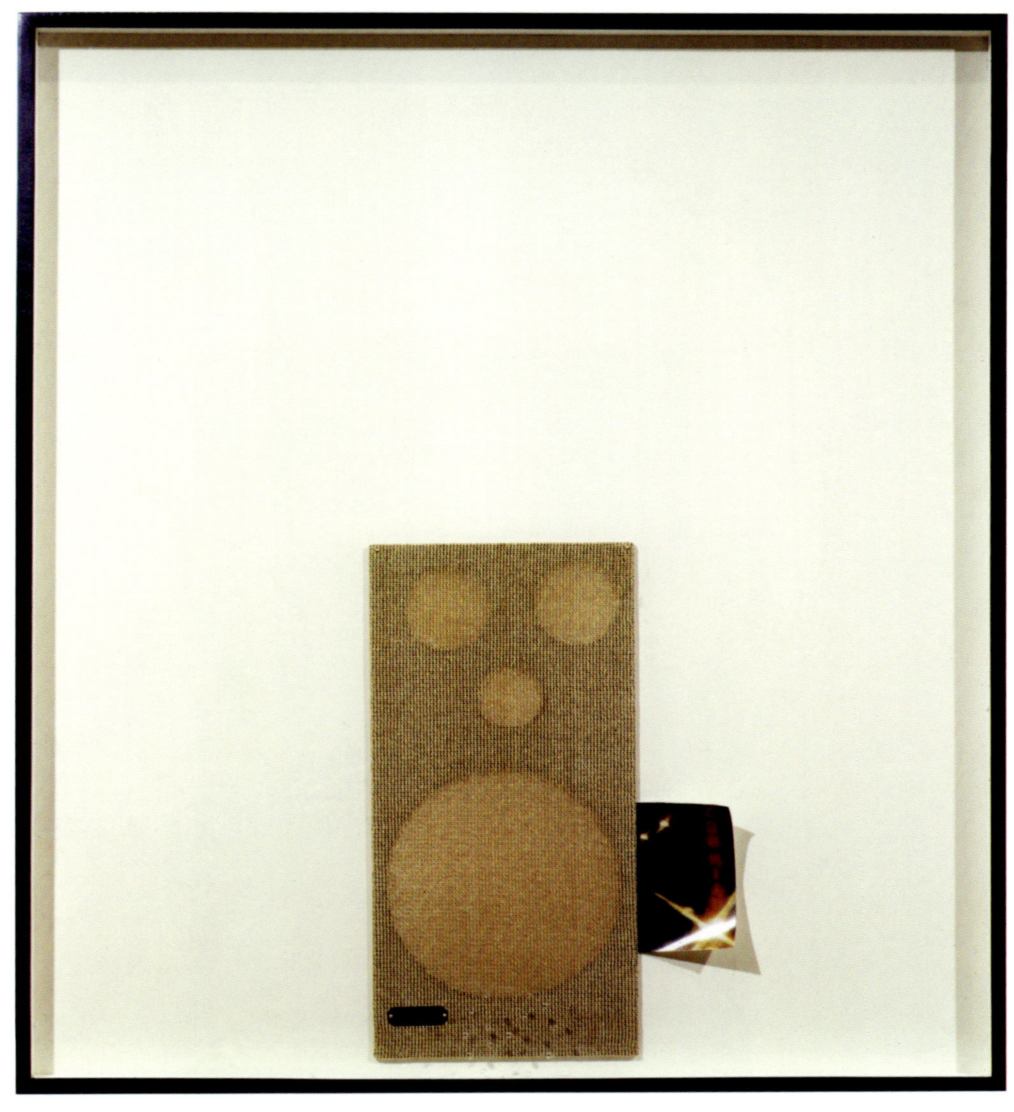

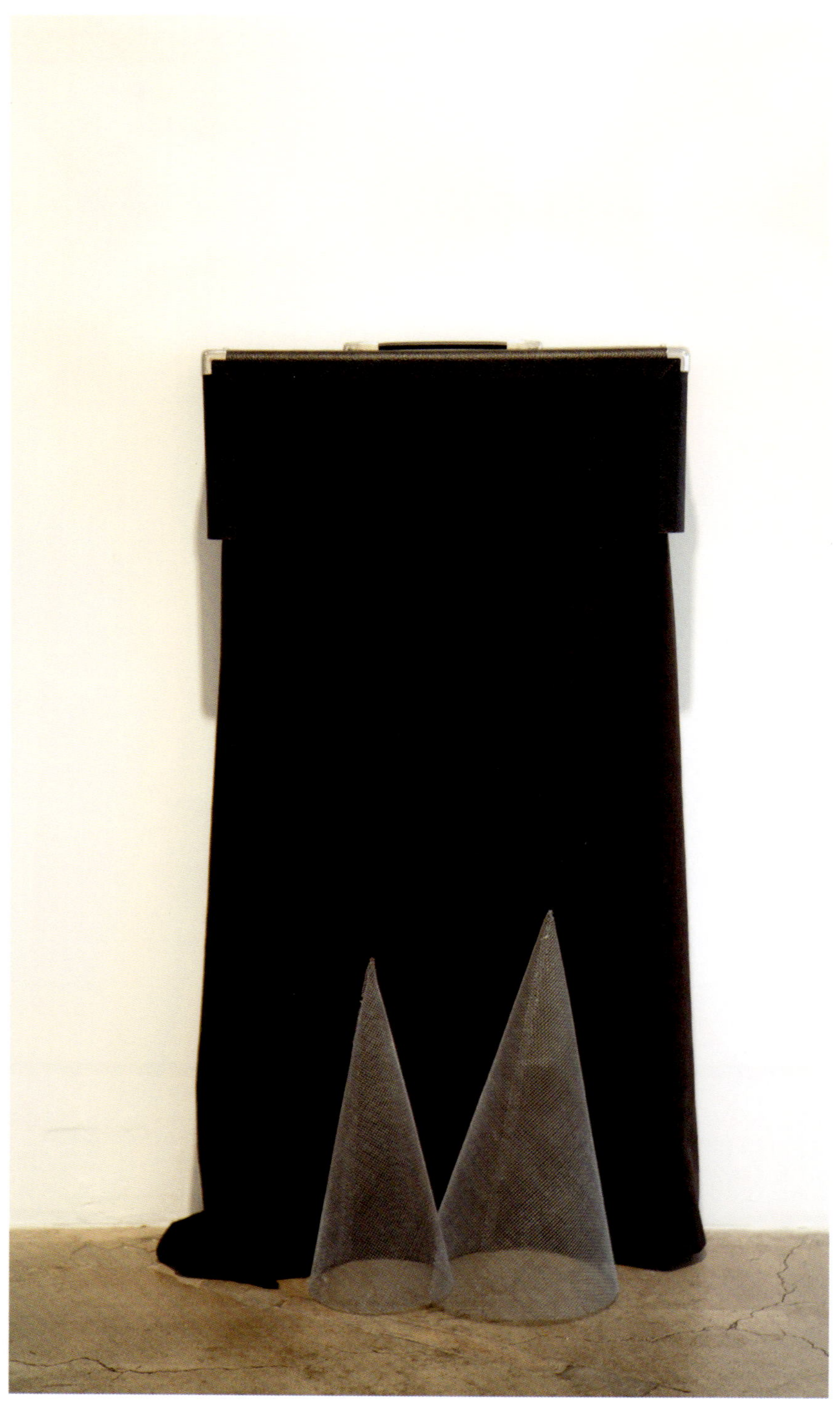

[32] *Speaker II*, 1986

[33] *Speaker I*, 1986

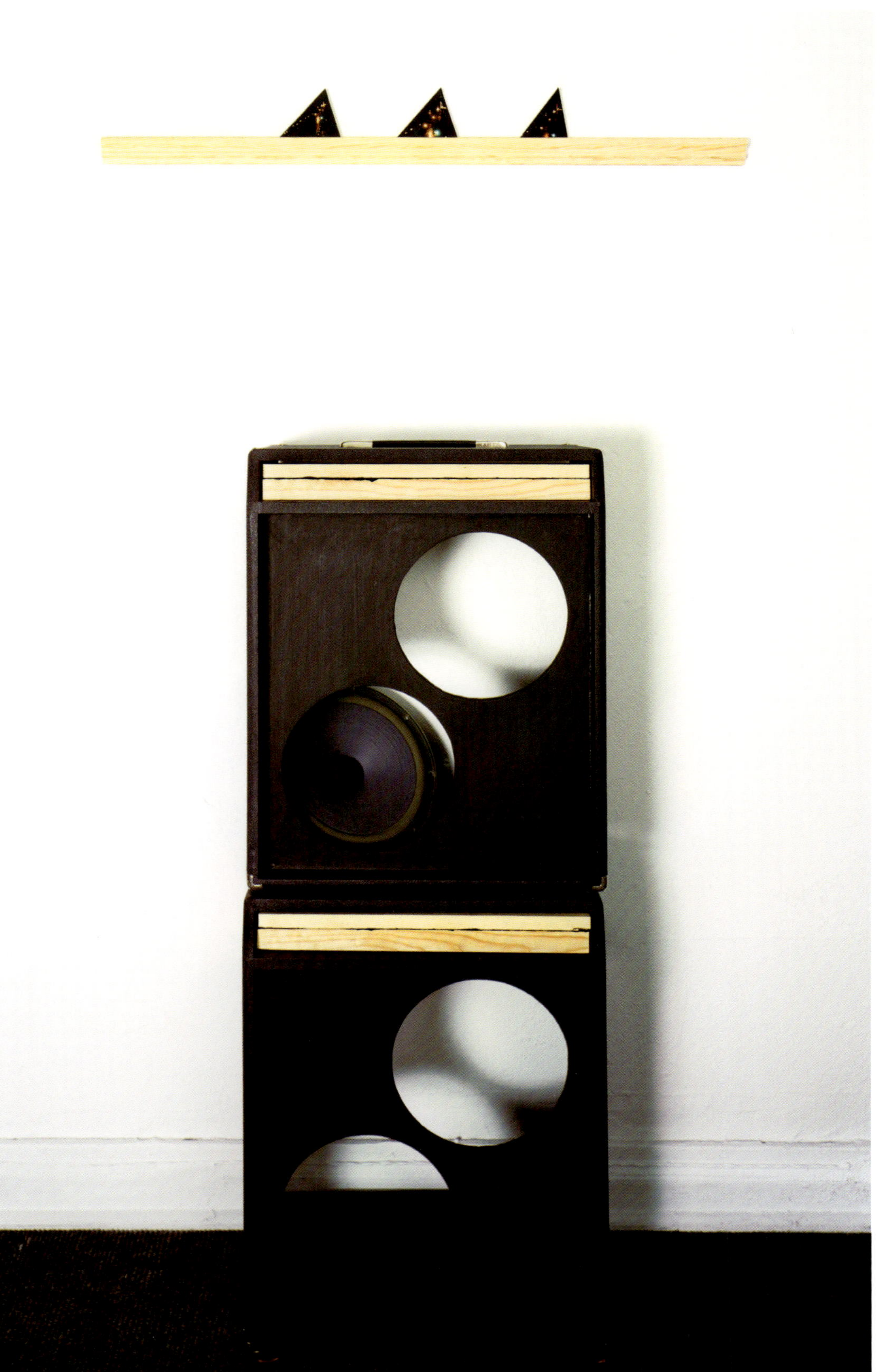

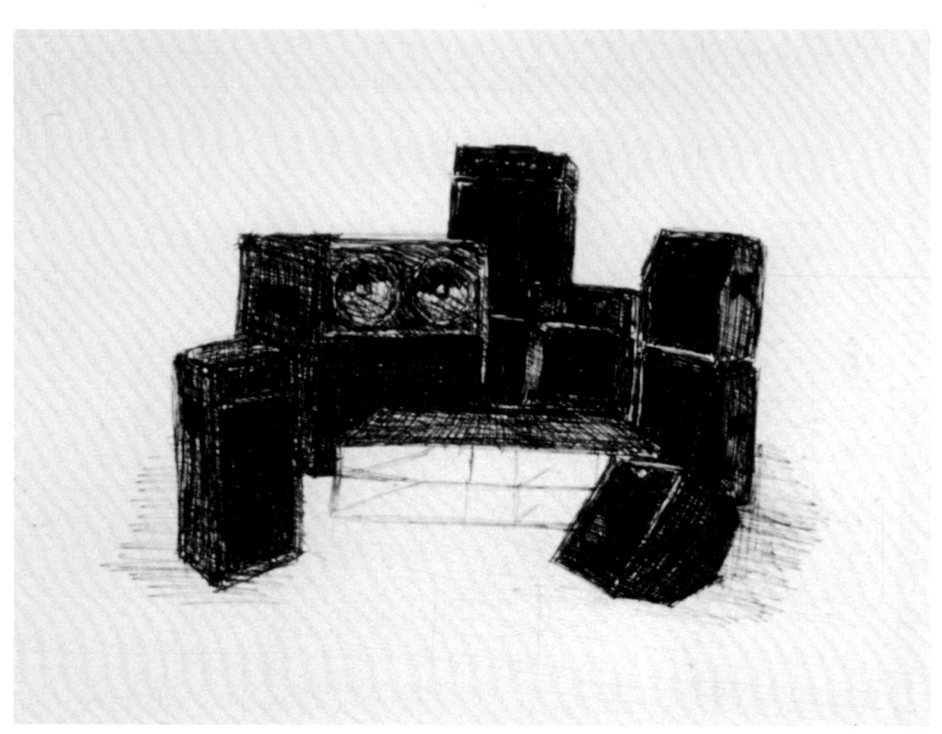

[34] *Speaker Family Drawing*, 1986

[35] *Marshall Contact Sheet*, 1995

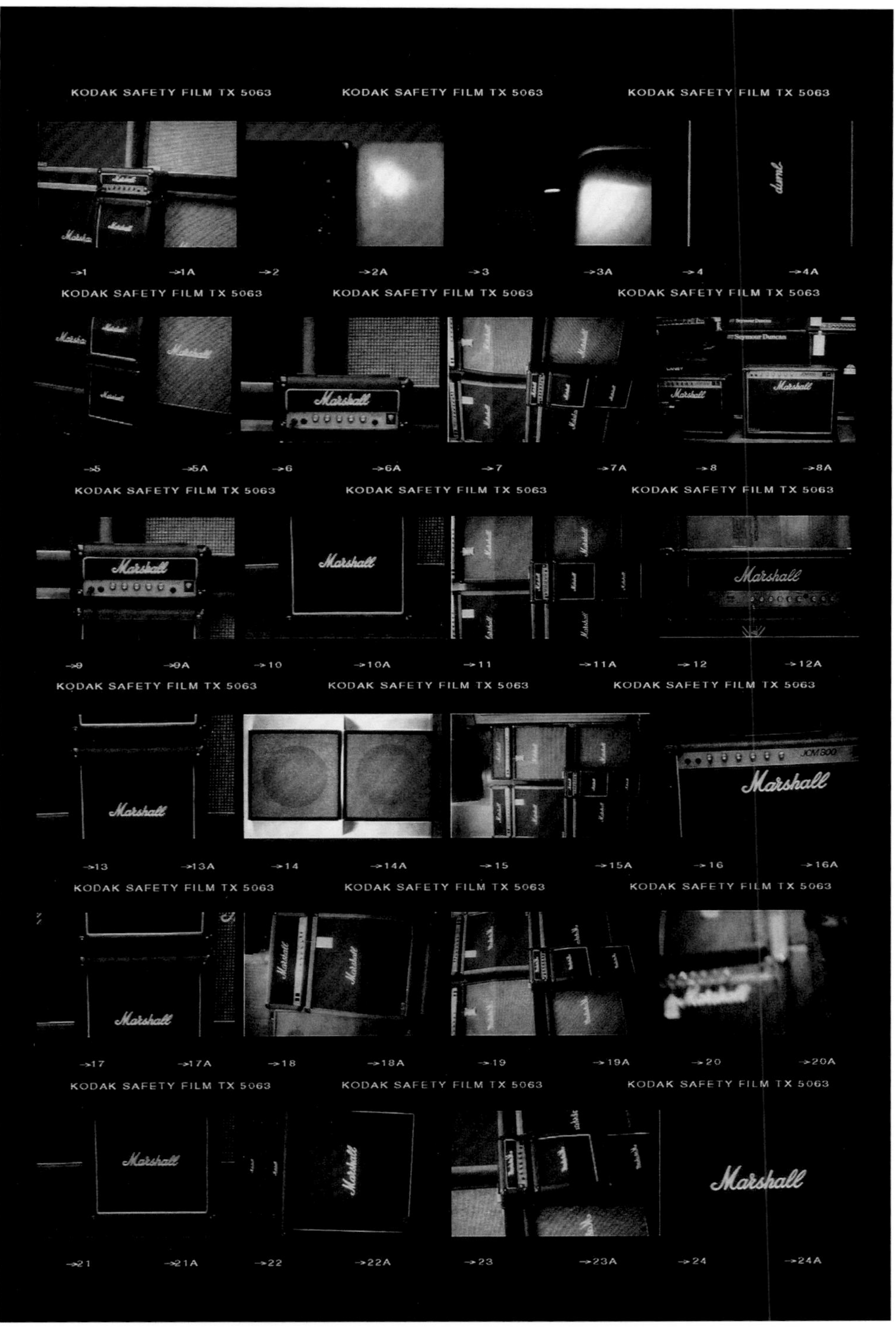
KODAK SAFETY FILM TX 5063
KODAK SAFETY FILM TX 5063
KODAK SAFETY FILM TX 5063
→1   →1A   →2   →2A   →3   →3A   →4   →4A
KODAK SAFETY FILM TX 5063
KODAK SAFETY FILM TX 5063
KODAK SAFETY FILM TX 5063
→5   →5A   →6   →6A   →7   →7A   →8   →8A
KODAK SAFETY FILM TX 5063
KODAK SAFETY FILM TX 5063
KODAK SAFETY FILM TX 5063
→9   →9A   →10   →10A   →11   →11A   →12   →12A
KODAK SAFETY FILM TX 5063
KODAK SAFETY FILM TX 5063
KODAK SAFETY FILM TX 5063
→13   →13A   →14   →14A   →15   →15A   →16   →16A
KODAK SAFETY FILM TX 5063
KODAK SAFETY FILM TX 5063
KODAK SAFETY FILM TX 5063
→17   →17A   →18   →18A   →19   →19A   →20   →20A
KODAK SAFETY FILM TX 5063
KODAK SAFETY FILM TX 5063
KODAK SAFETY FILM TX 5063
→21   →21A   →22   →22A   →23   →23A   →24   →24A

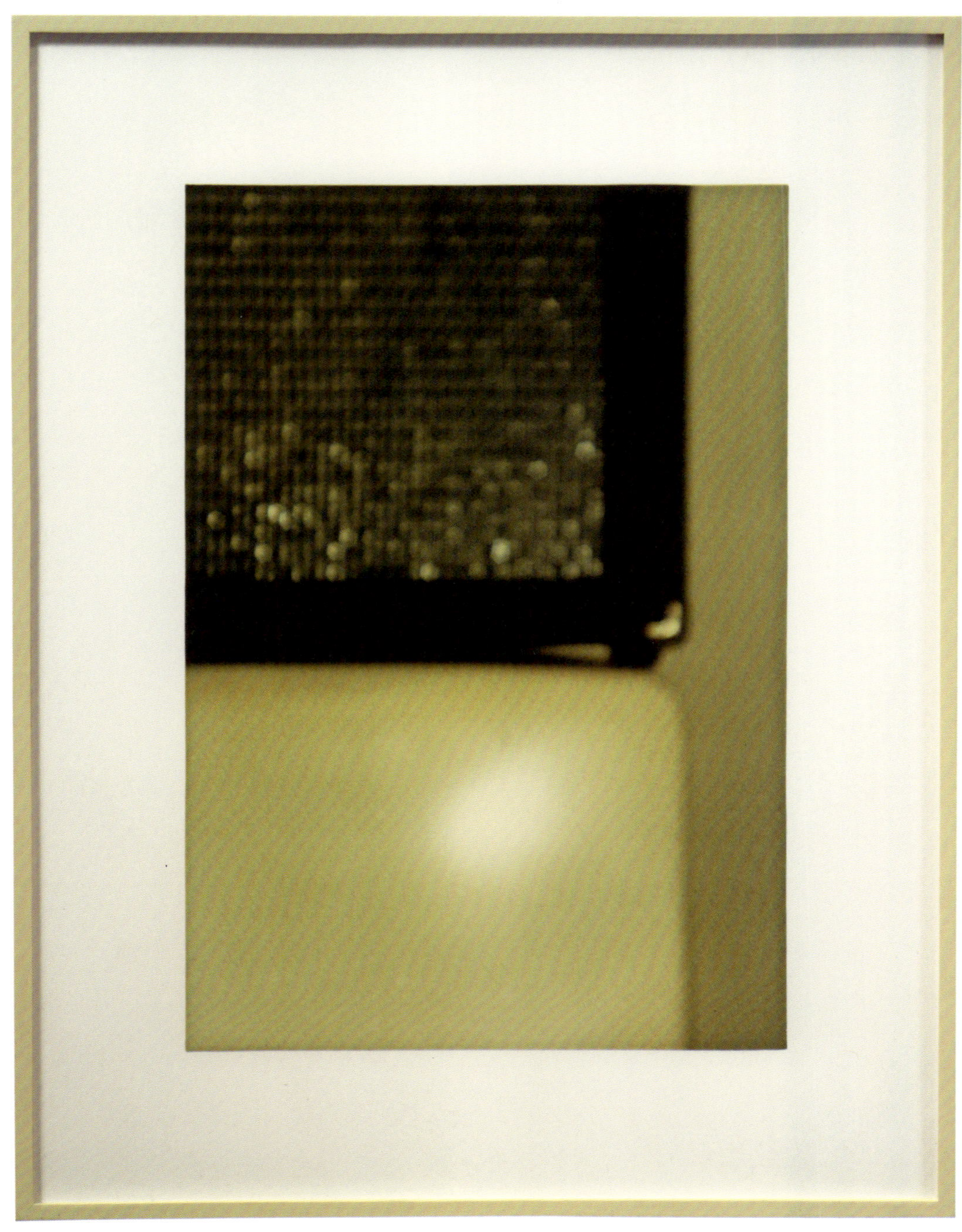

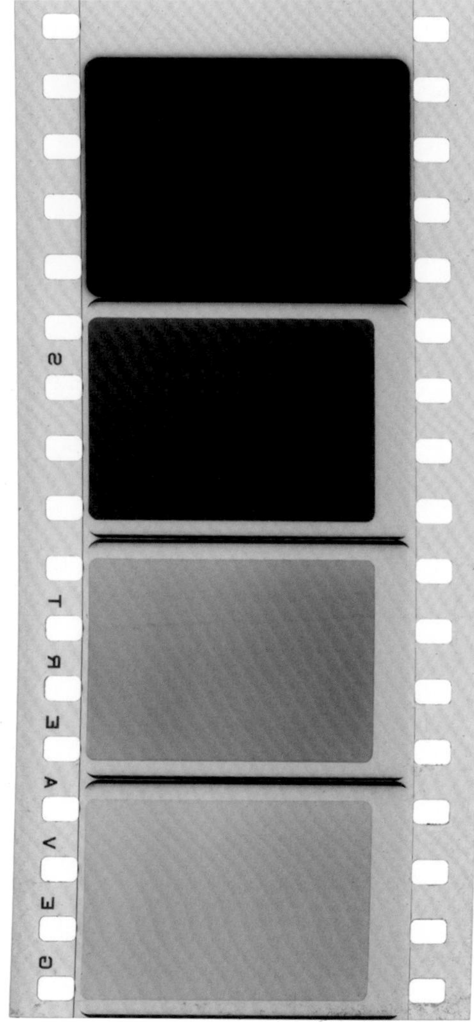

[37] reference: segment of 35mm film leader, "Rothko element"

[38] *Conjunction Assemblage*, 1988

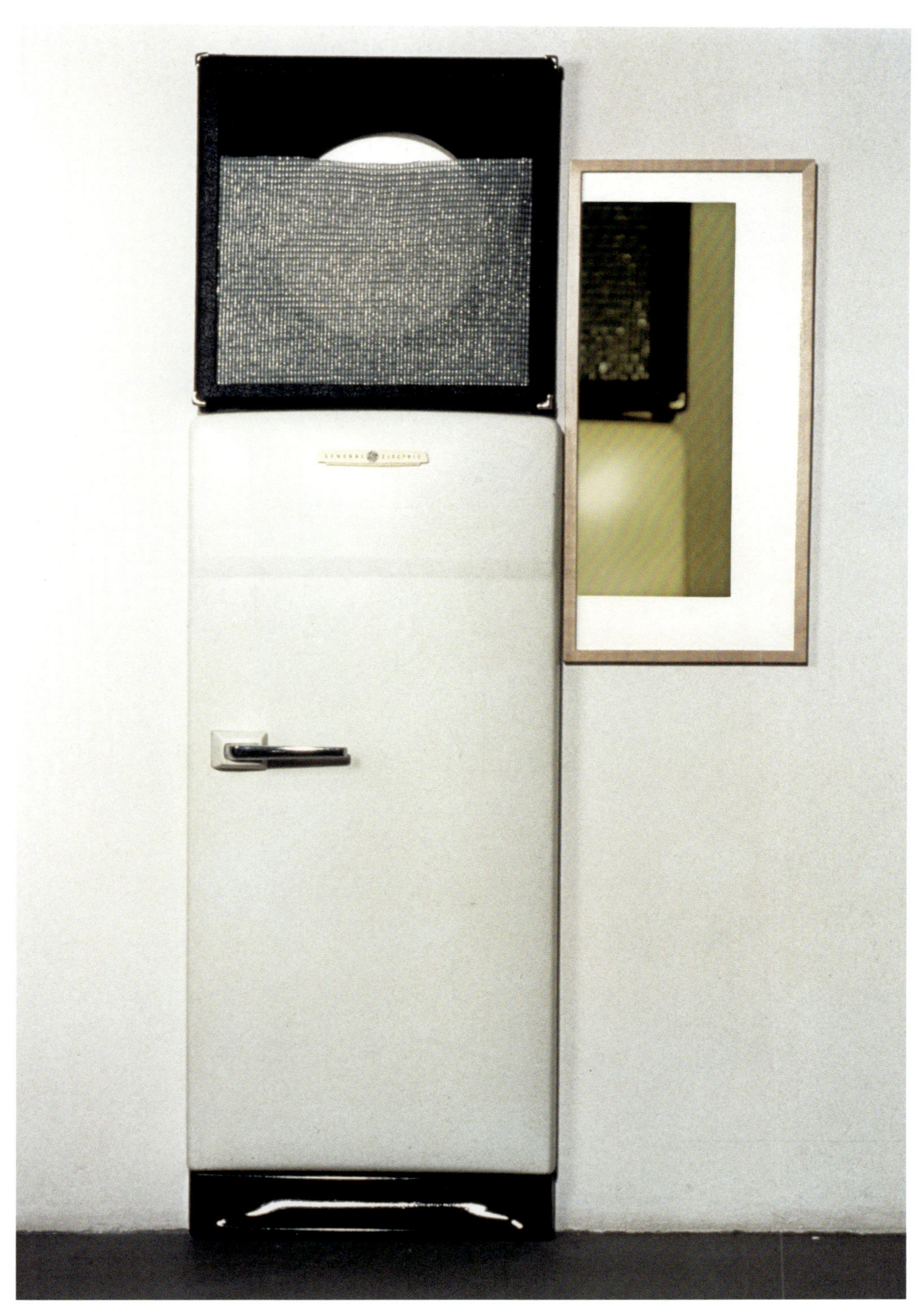

GENERAL ELECTRIC

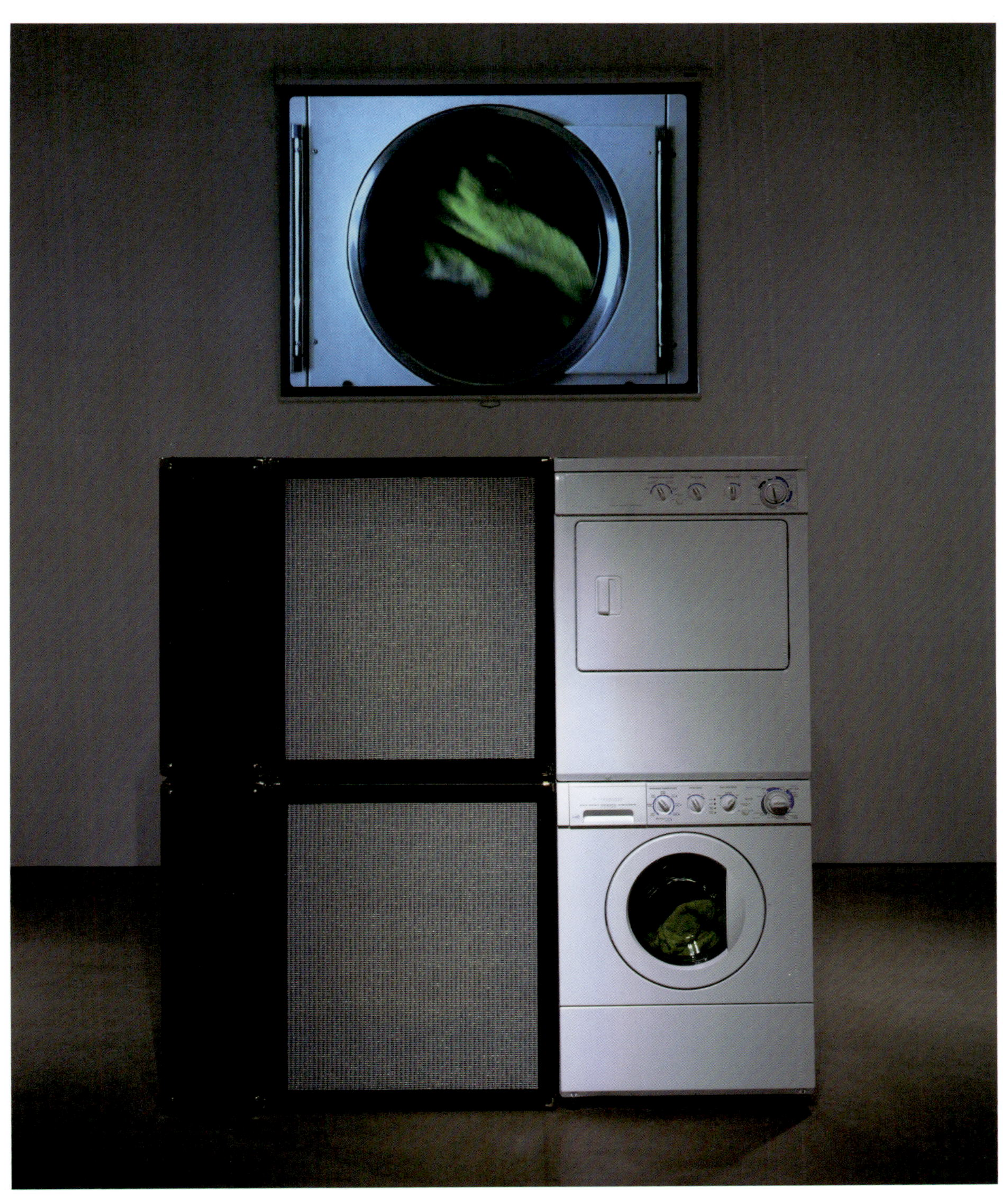

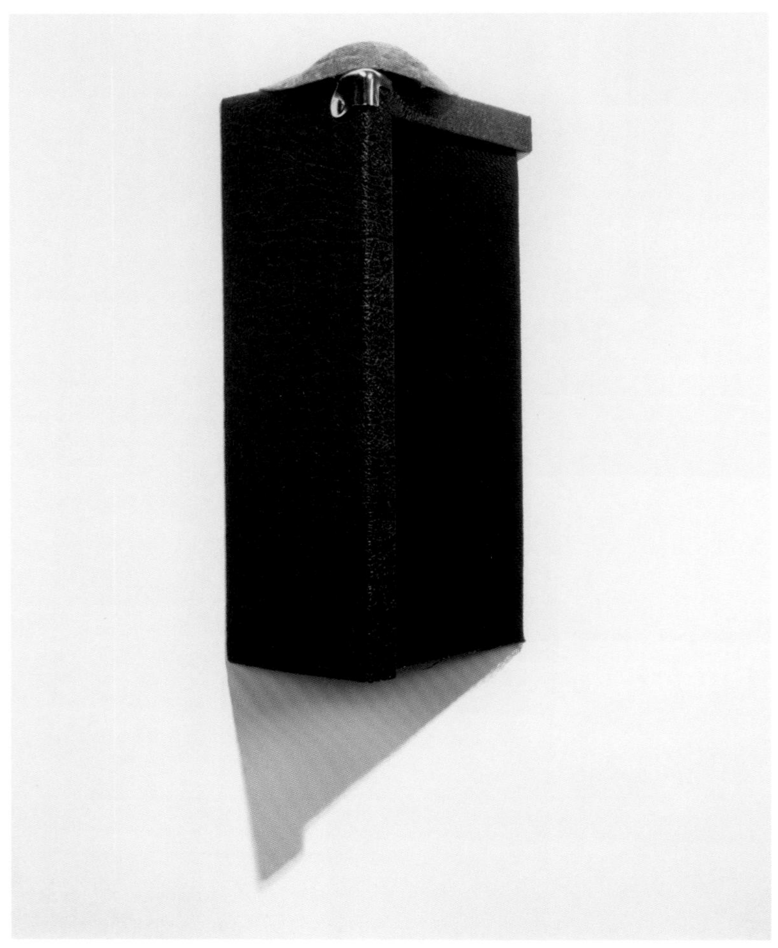

[40] *R. Shldr.,* 1990

[41] *The Rounding of Corners,* 1991

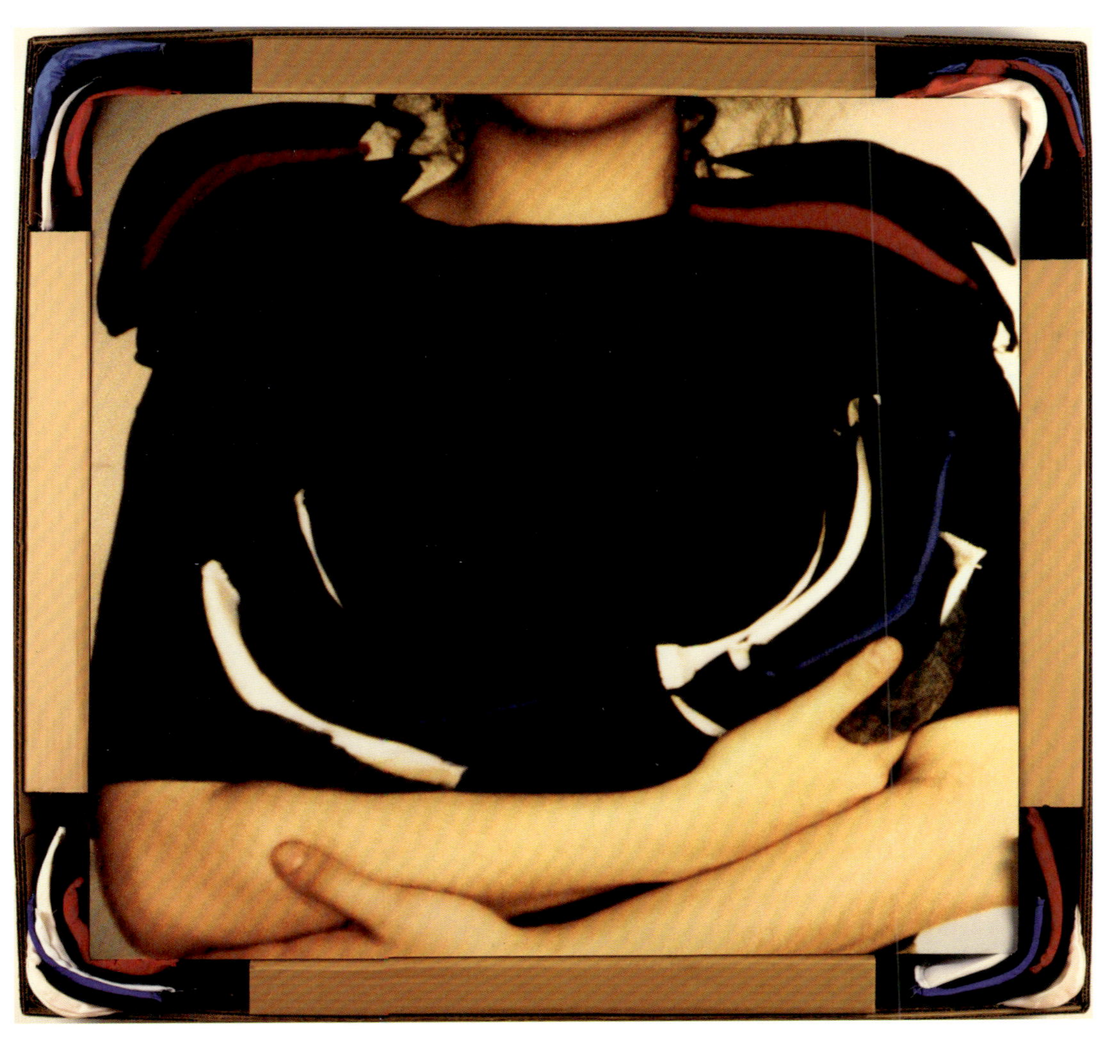

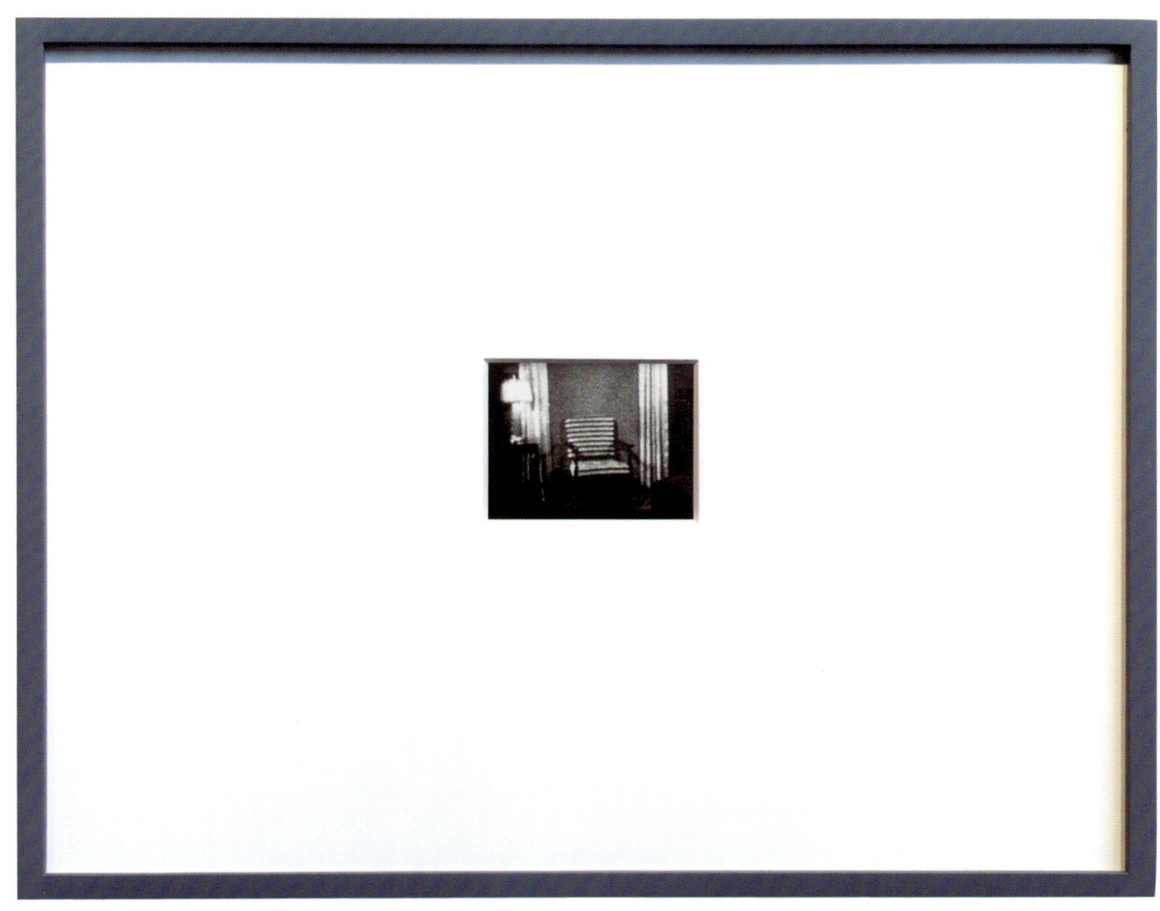

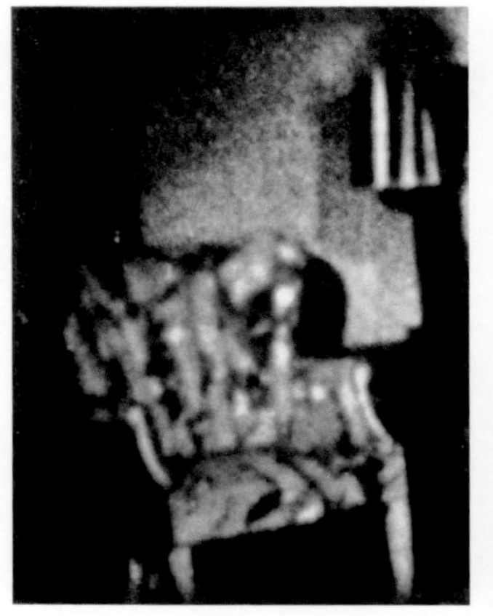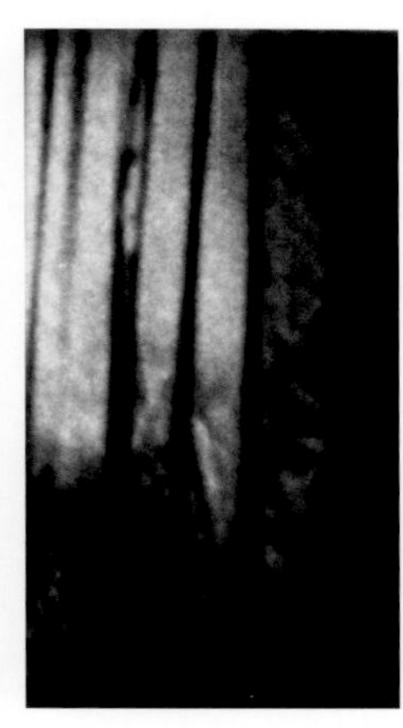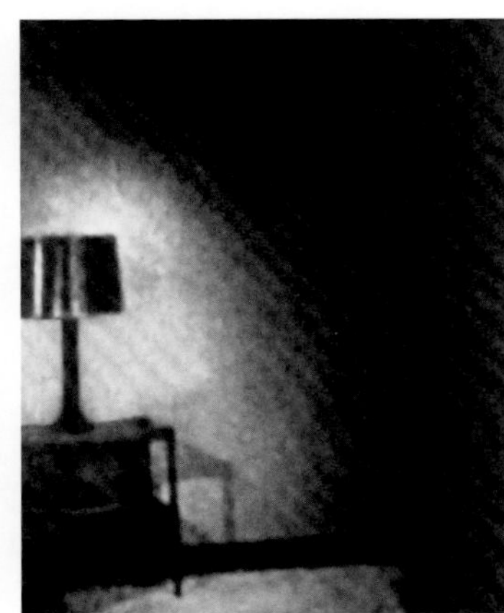

[43] details: *The Porn Series, #2-7,* 1982

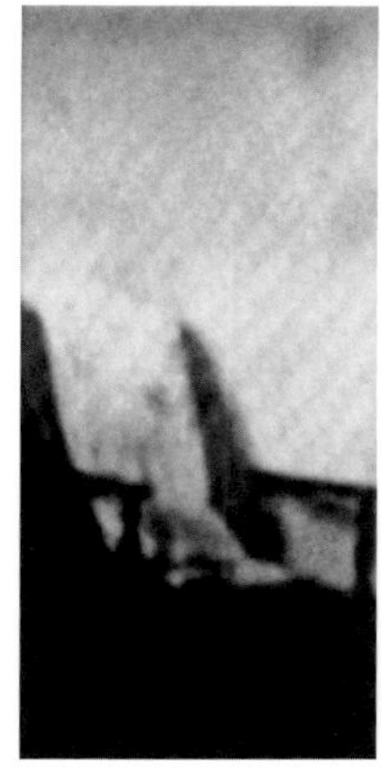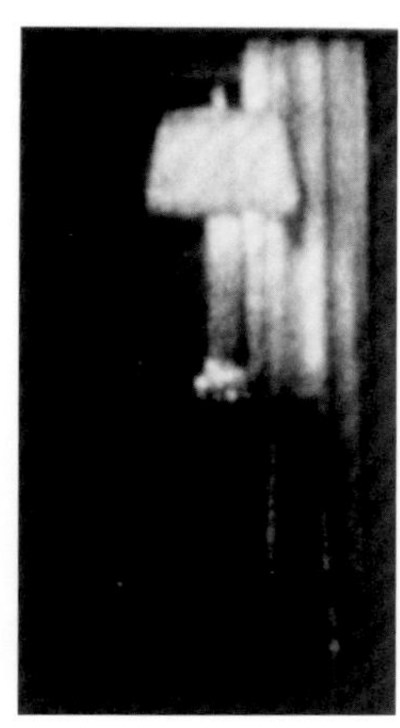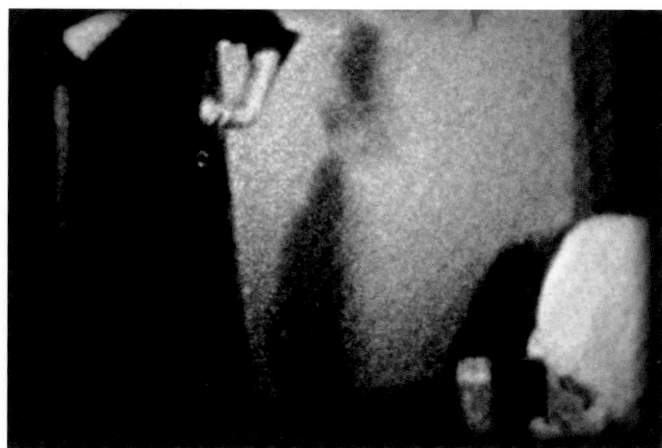

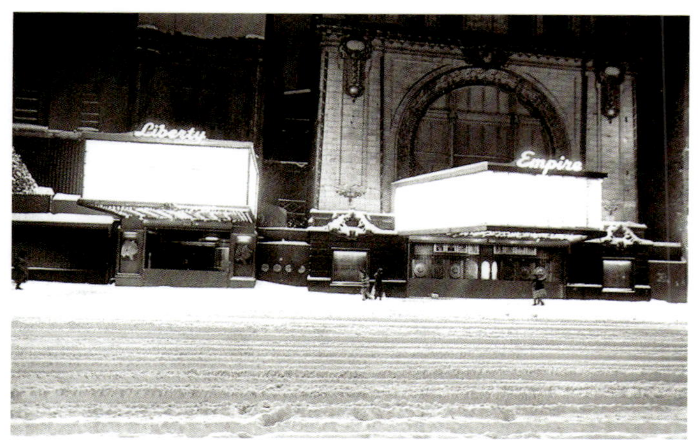

Liberty
Empire

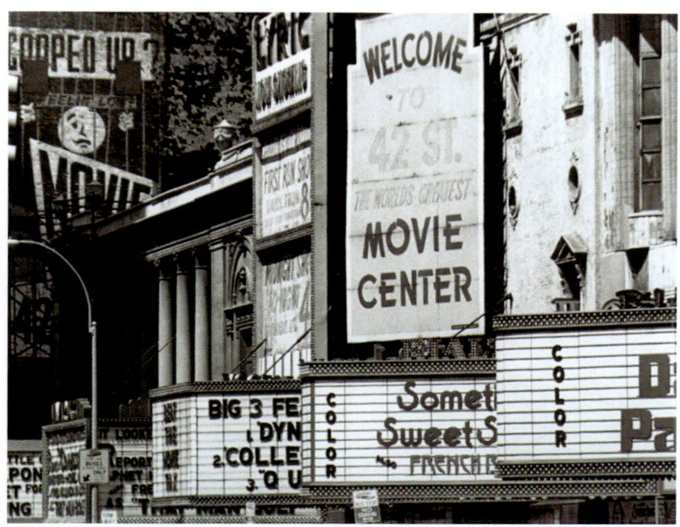

COOPED UP?
MOVIE
WELCOME
TO
42 ST.
THE WORLDS GREATEST
MOVIE
CENTER
COLOR
COLOR
BIG 3 FE
DYN
COLLE
QU
Somet
Sweet S
FRENCH
Pa

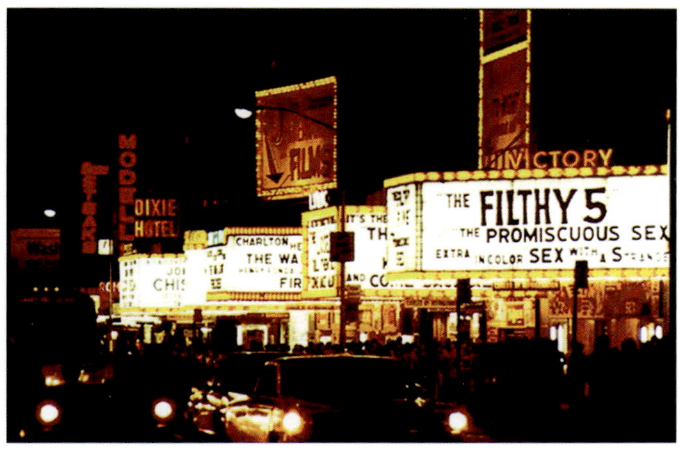

MODELL
DIXIE
HOTEL
FILMS
VICTORY
THE FILTHY 5
THE PROMISCUOUS SEX
EXTRA IN COLOR SEX WITH A STRANGE
CHARLTON
THE WA
FIR
CHIS

[45] *Study for Untitled Tower*, 1999

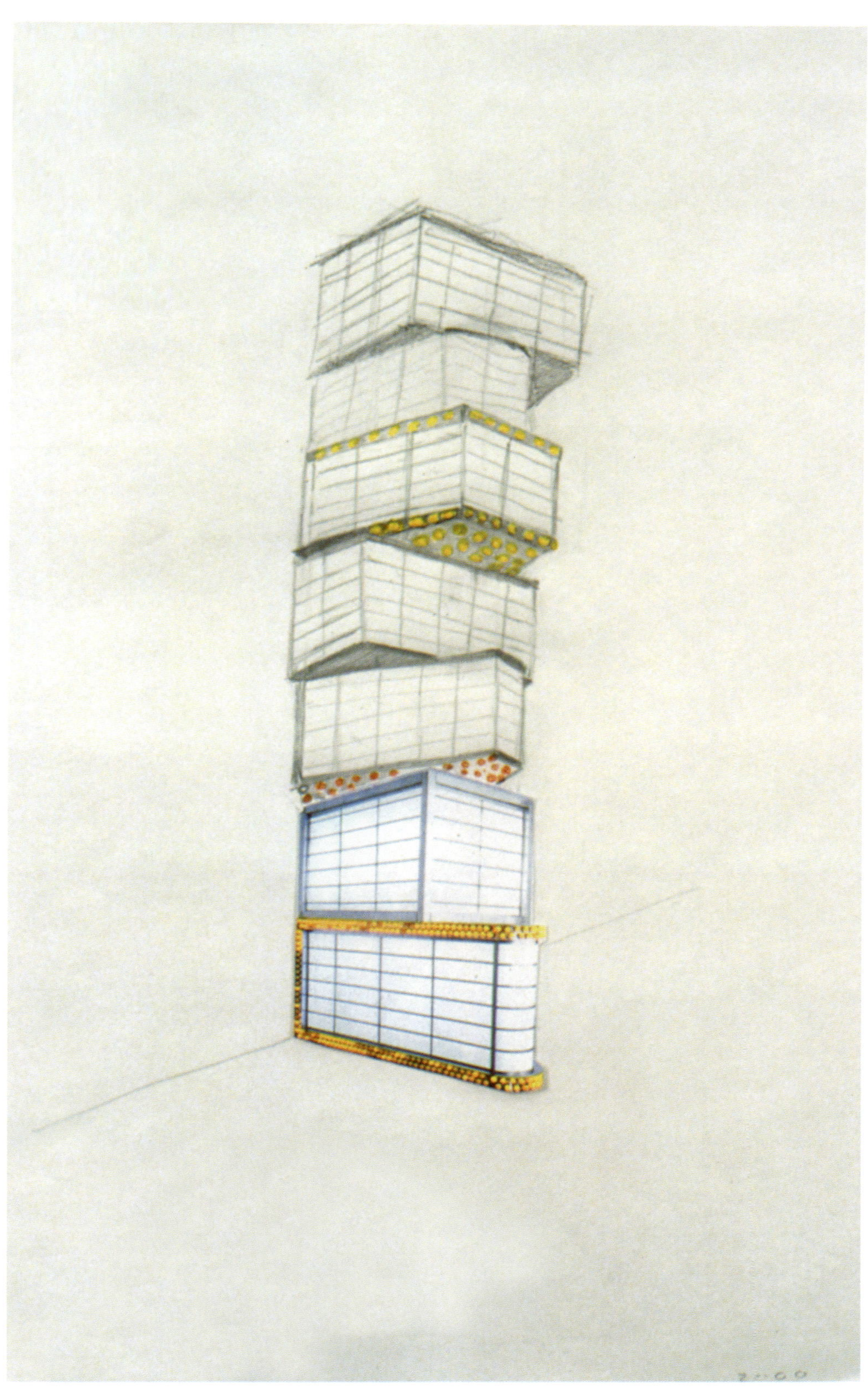

[46] *Tower of Movie Marquees*, 2010

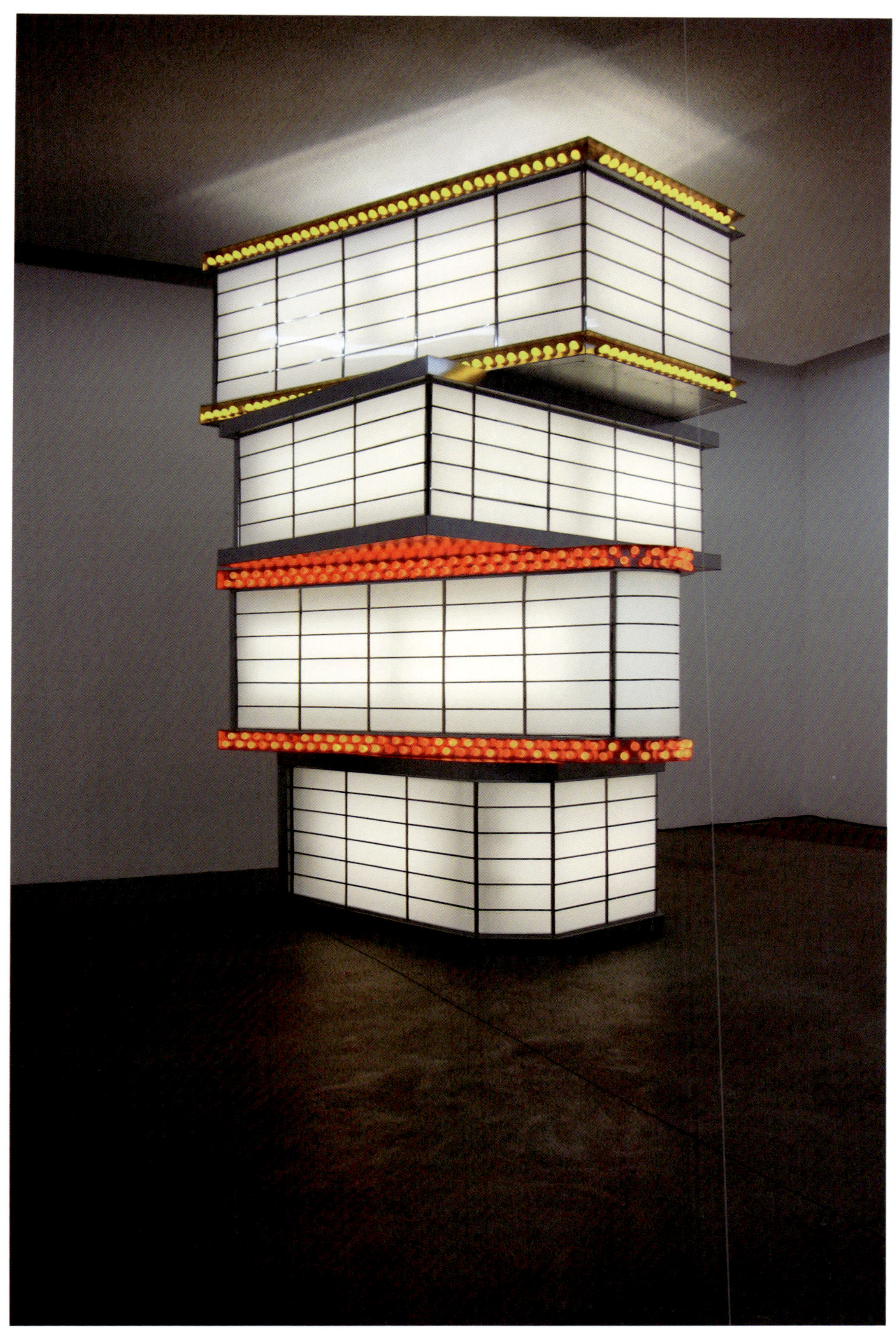

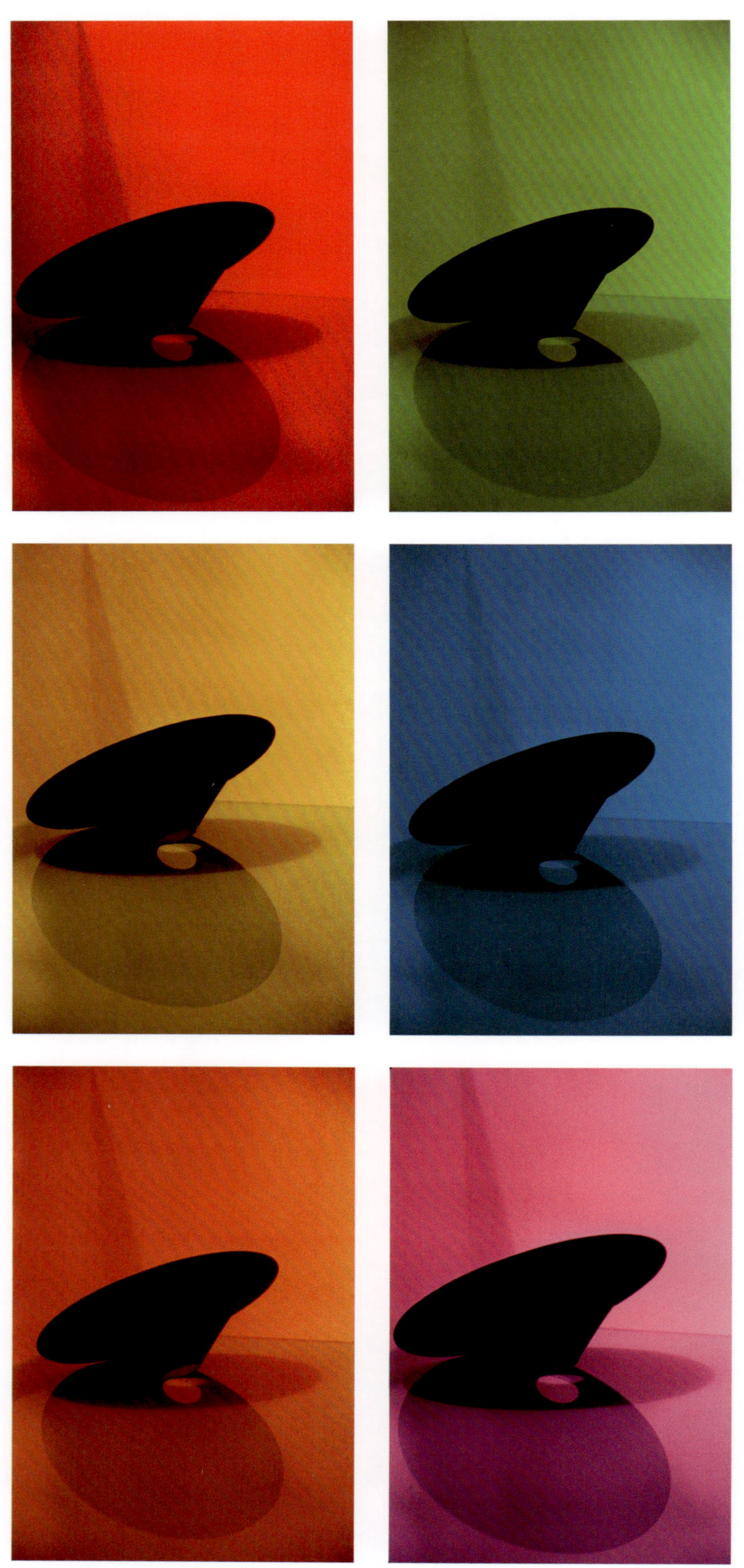

[47] *Composition with Speaker Cone* (various colors), 1990   [48] *Broken Bulbs*, 2010

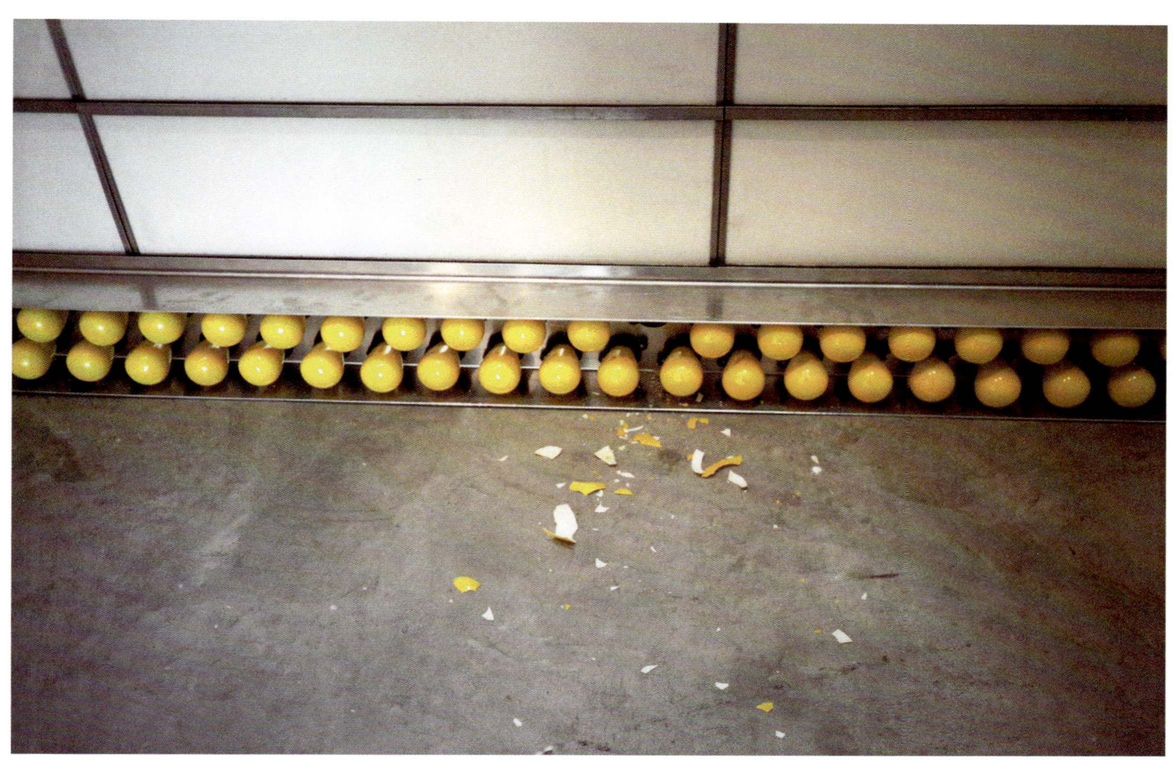

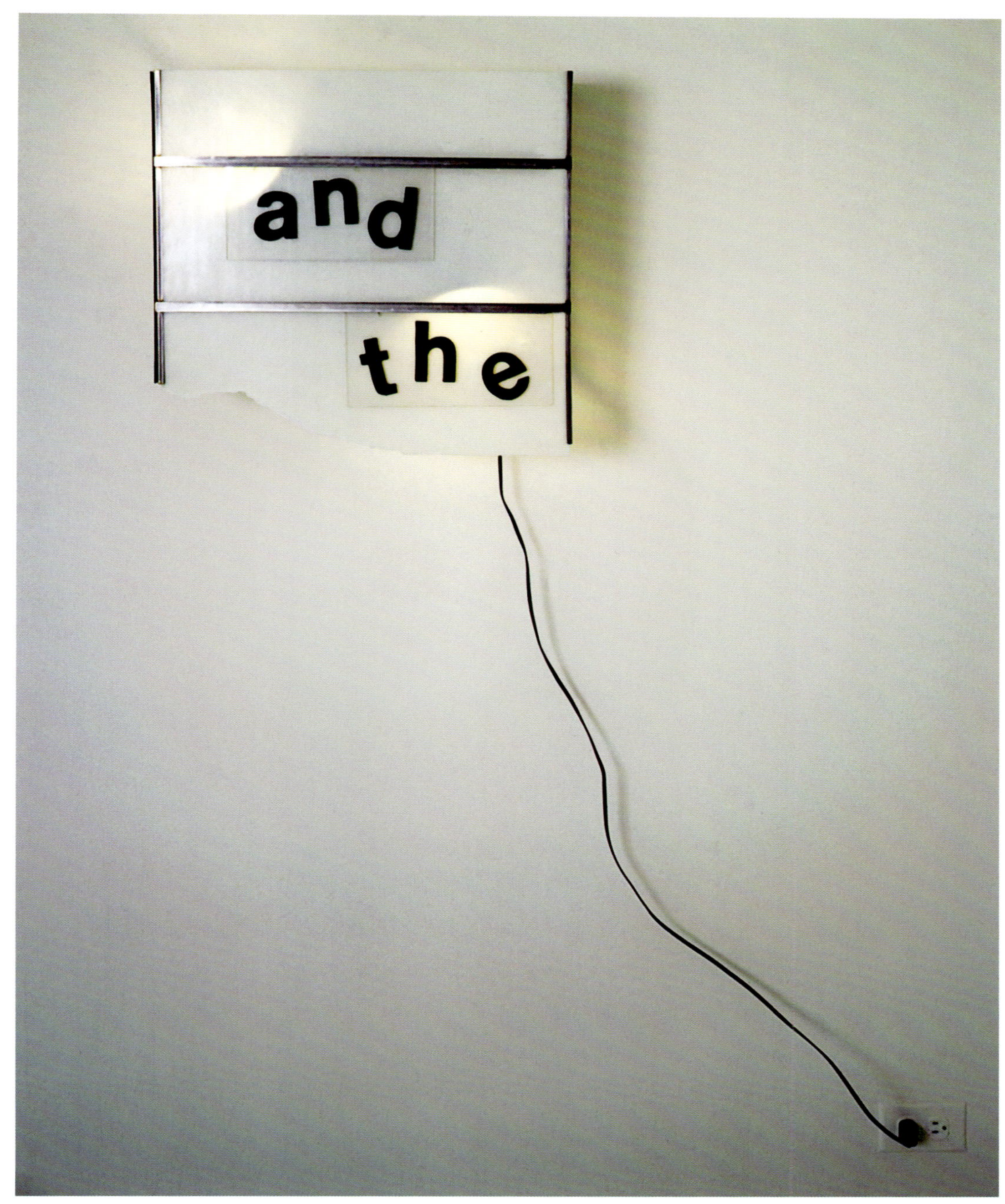

and
the

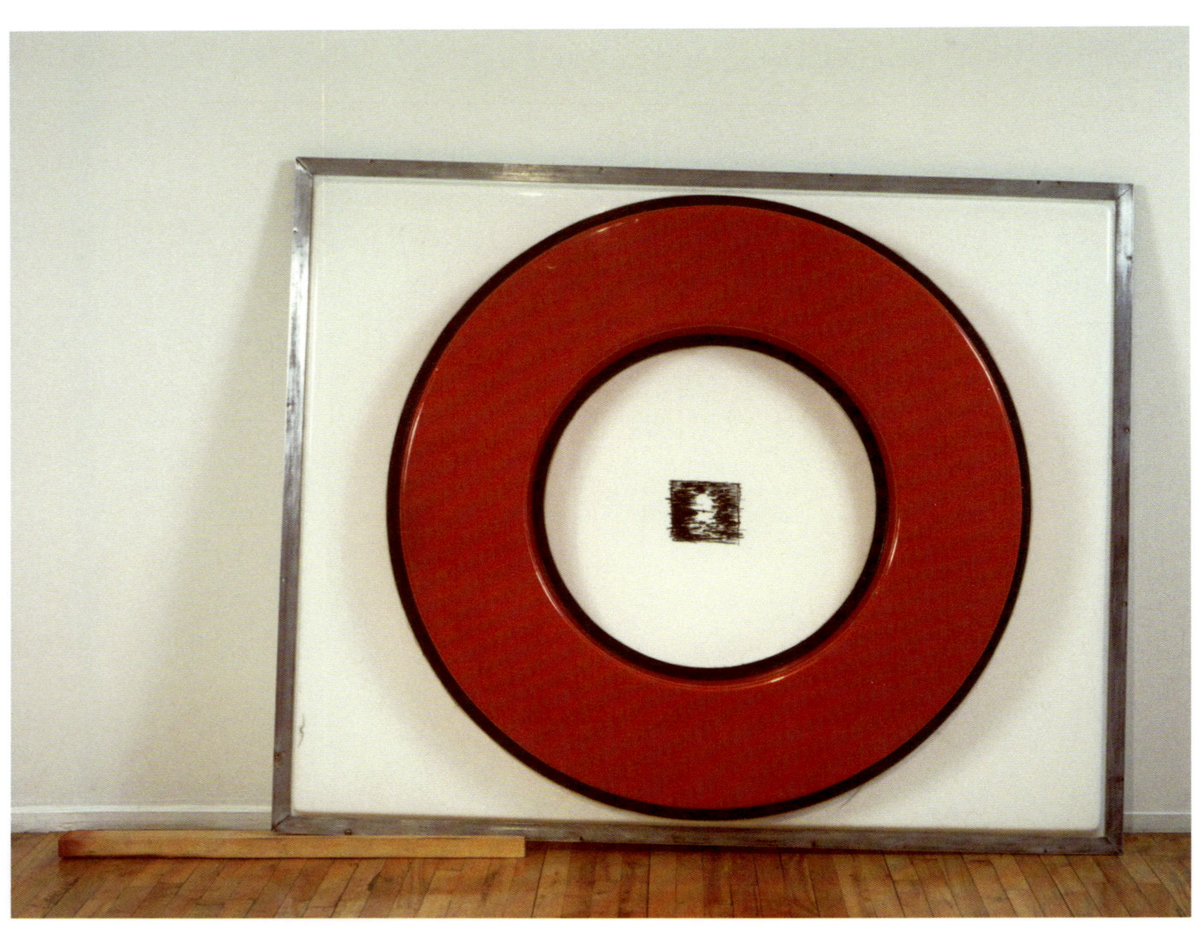

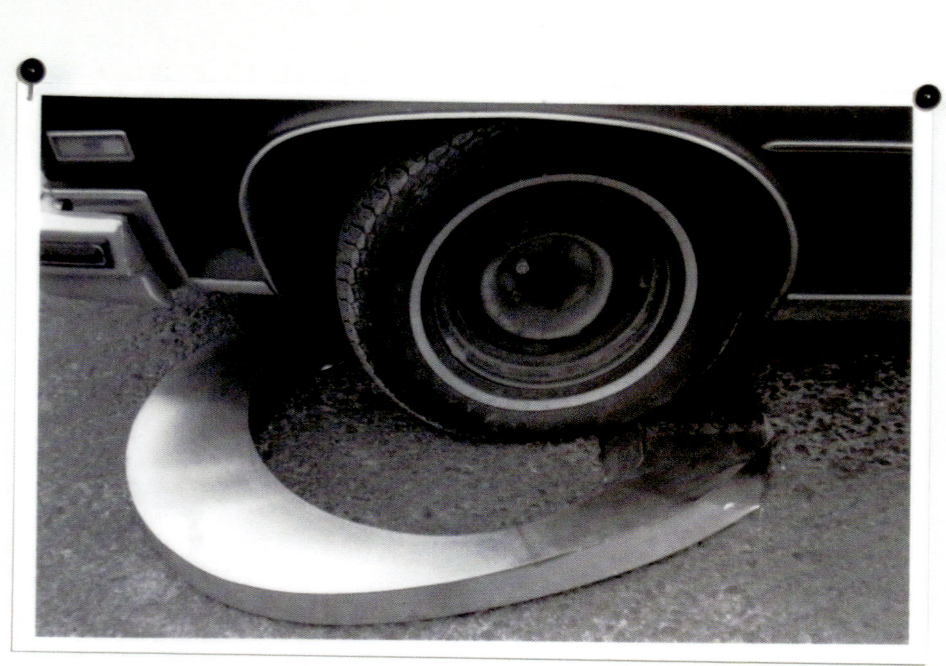

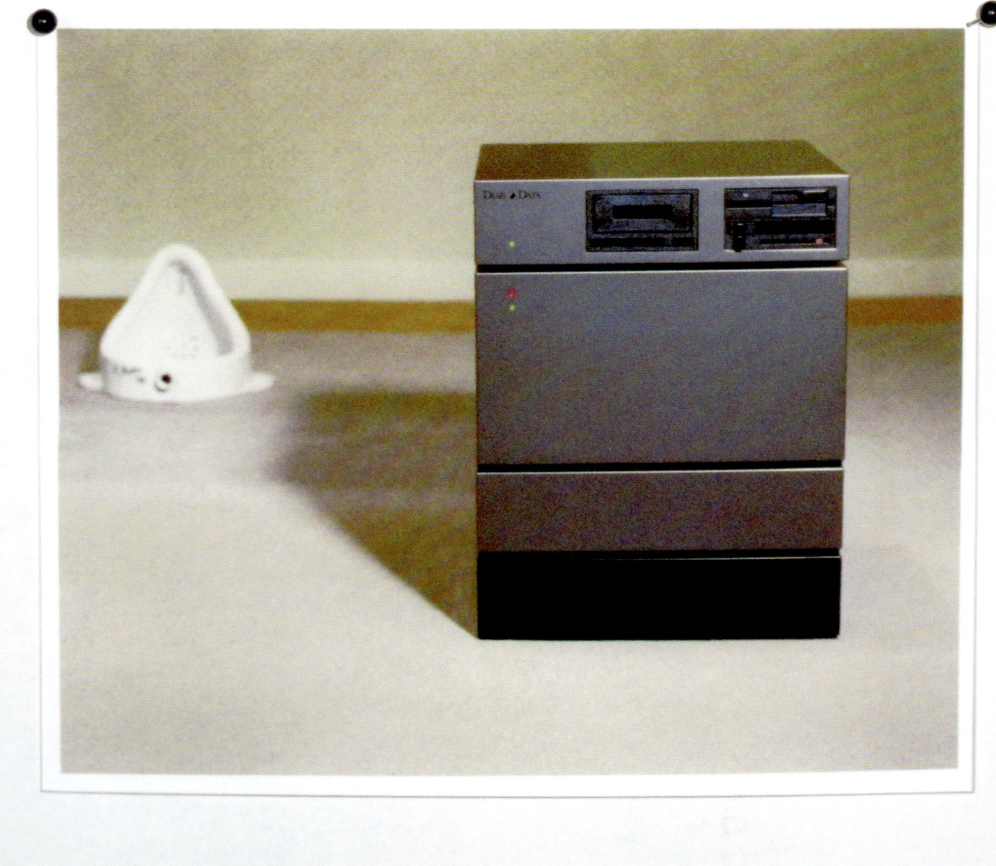

[52] reference: studio wall with photos of Dike's car running over my "O," and Richard Hamilton's *Diab DS-101 computer*, 1985-89

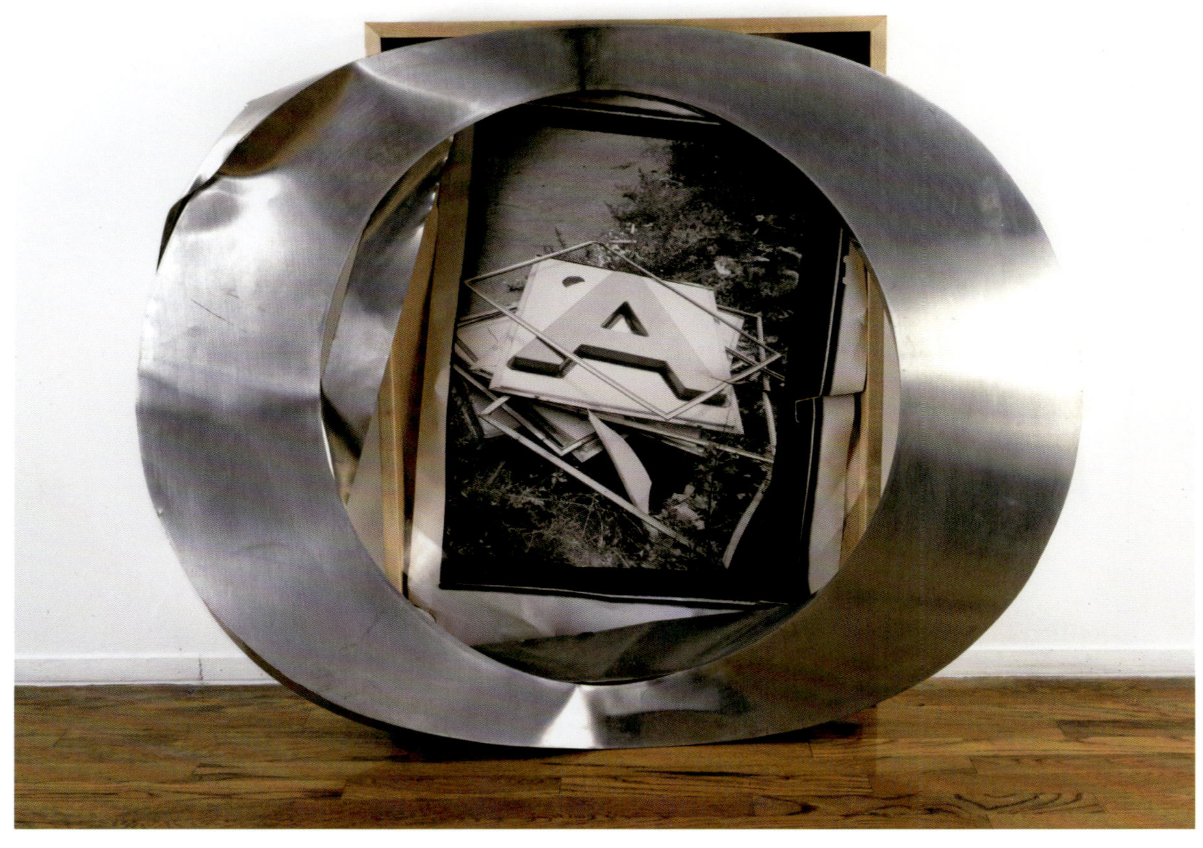

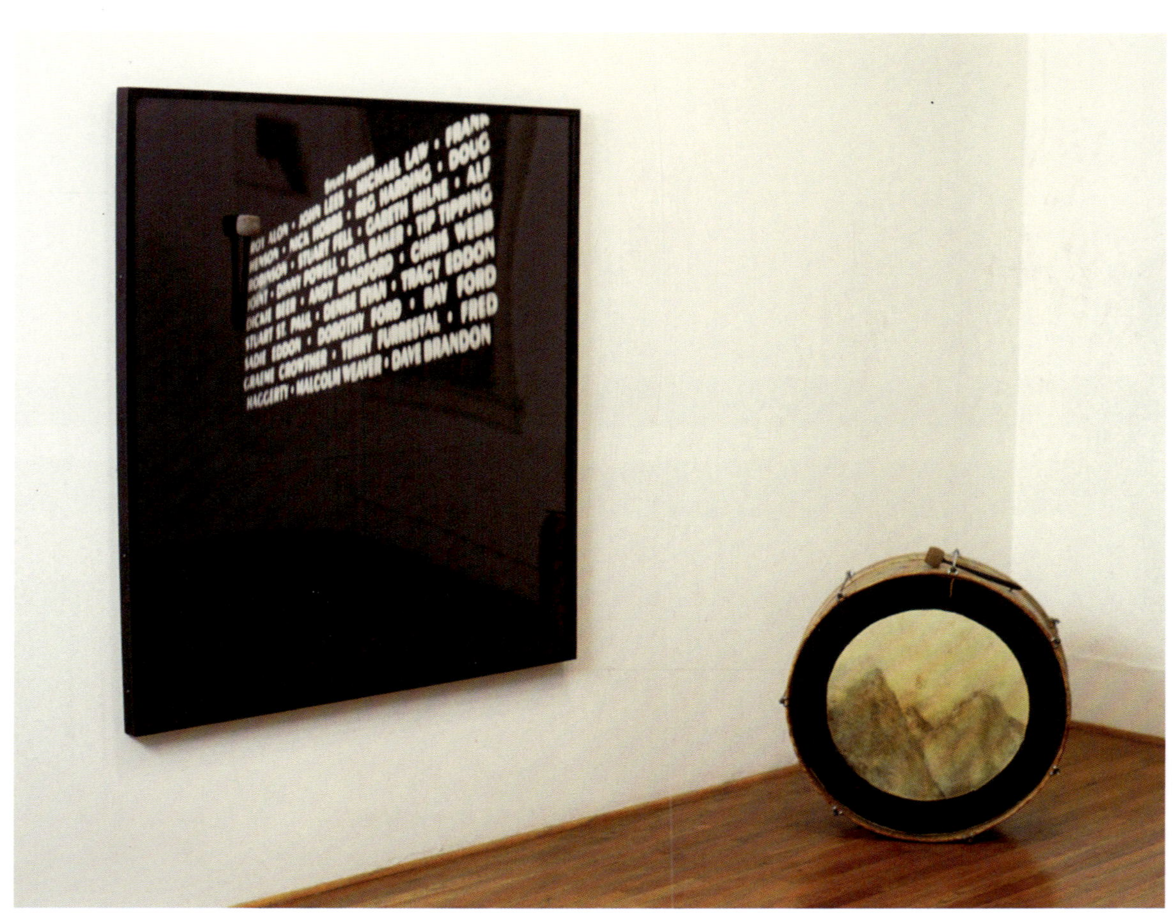
MICHAEL LAW • FRANK
NICK HARDING • DOUG
GARETH MILNE • ALF
DEL BAKER • TIP TIPPING
ANDY BRADFORD • CHRIS WEBB
DENNIS RYAN • TRACY IDDON
DOROTHY FORD • RAY FORD
TERRY FURRESTAL • FRED
CRAIG CROWTHER • MALCOLM WEAVER • DAVE BRANDON

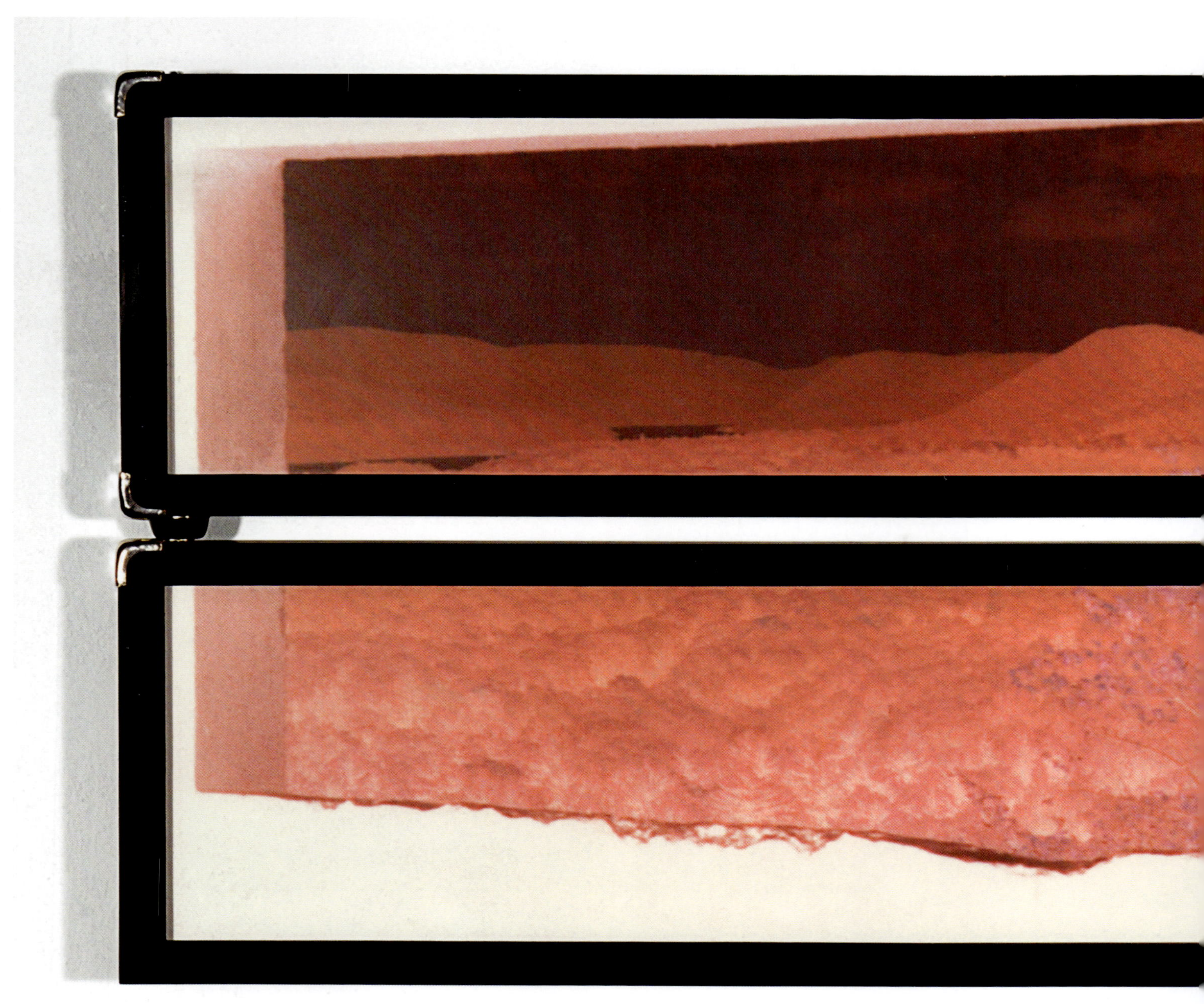

[55] *+/- Landscape*, 1988

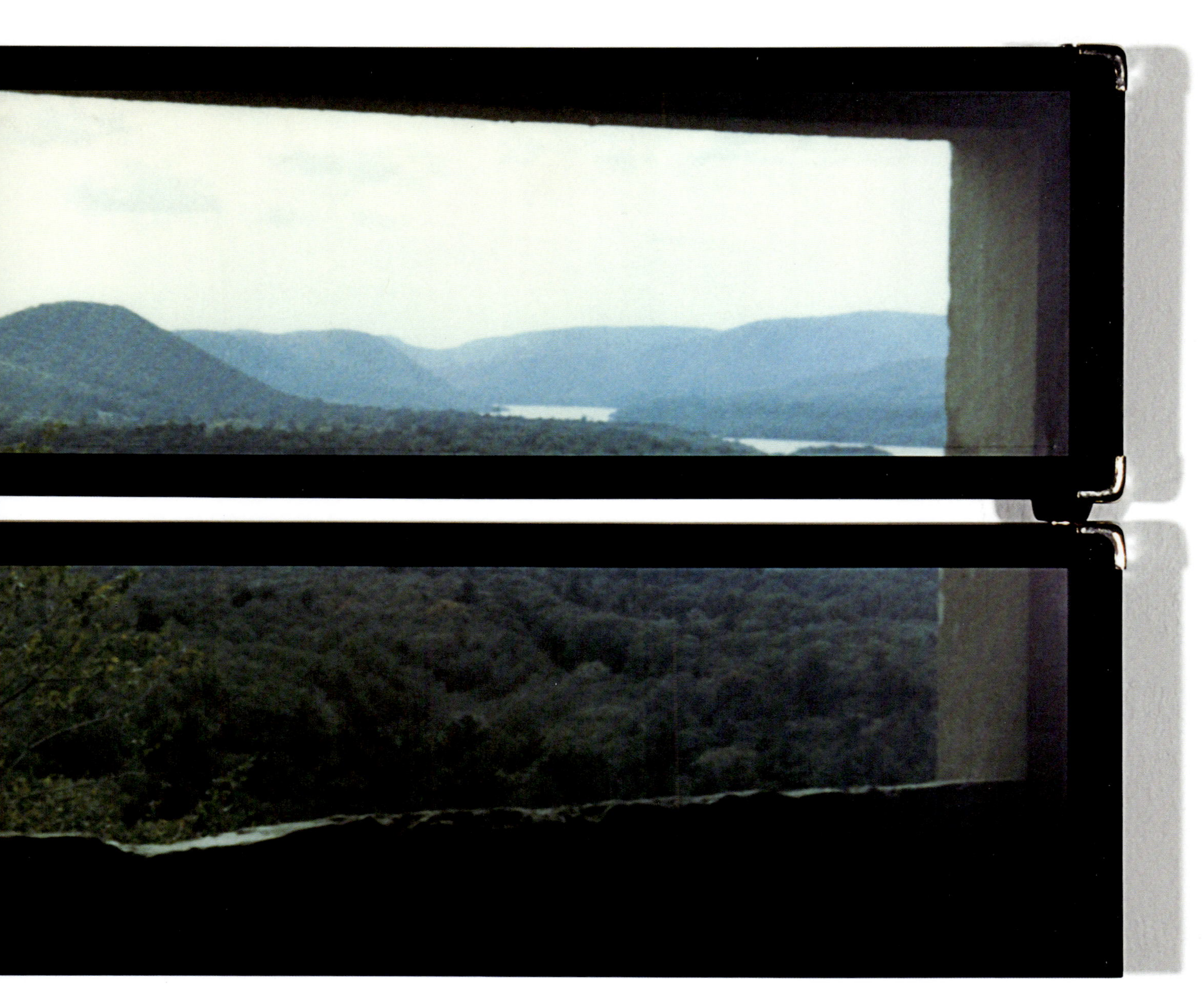

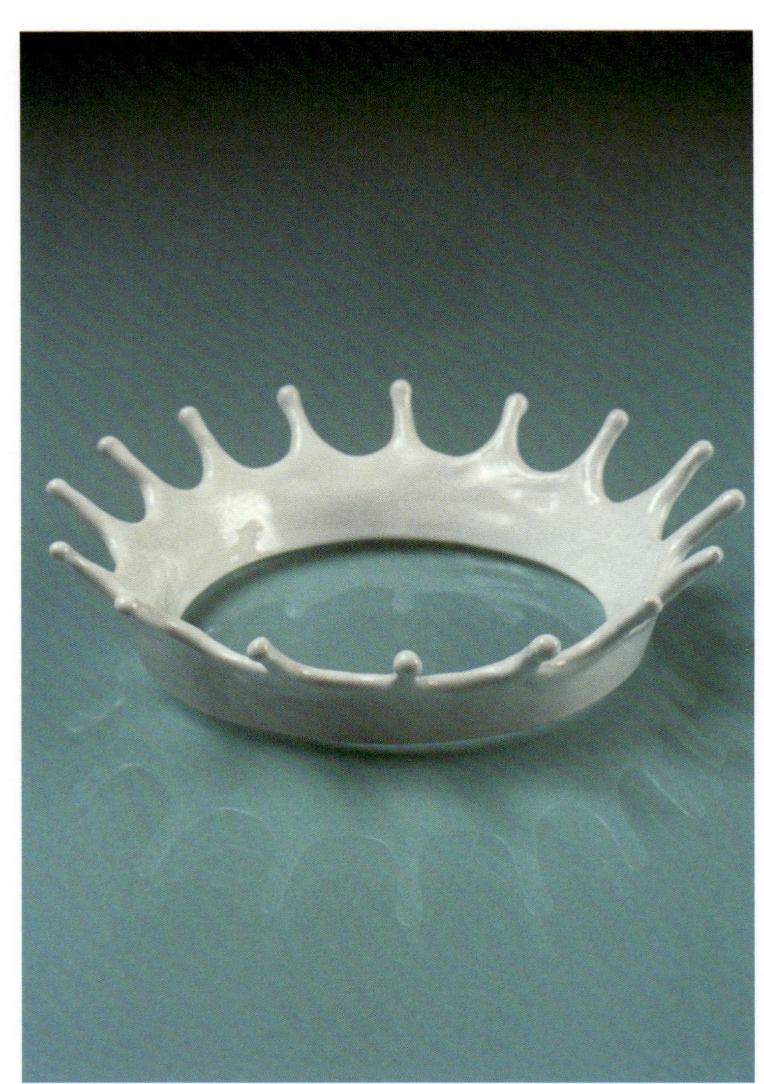

ROSETTA BROOKS

CHRISTINA VALENTINE

THE DEPARTMENT OF LOST AND FOUND

Jennifer Bolande's art persistently implicates images and meanings, signs and signifiers, in the bait-and-switch game of visual, textual, and material codes that pervades our daily lives. Bolande focuses on particular moments of contact when an utterance spirals into a chain of relationships. It is only when these relationships reach critical mass, when they overflow to the point of losing their relevance, that they become her material. Images look differently when they stop meaning what they say. Their original relevance erodes into pastiche and obsolescence; in effect, they shed their skin of daily use, revealing the cogs and wheels that once produced meaning. It is at the moment when an idea begins to empty out its functional value that it can be retraced, reexamined, and reused. Bolande seizes upon these artifacts of social transaction at the moment of their fossilization. In the artist's words, her aim is to locate "cultural artifacts at the brink of extinction or at a point of transition"—which she then weaves into elliptical narratives of new meanings.

Bolande's work hits all the high notes within art discourse of the past thirty years—gaps, dissonance, polyphony. Each piece is a revelation about the illusion of language; what we see and hear is not what we necessarily know or expect. But how do we read these works now? Bolande has mined the language of objects since the 1970s. In the over-whelming landscape of the digital age, where multiplicity is a fact of life and texting has transformed the manipulation of signs way beyond the scope of Roland Barthes, she has left us with a kind of seer's palimpsest. Hers is a narrative that traces the known parameters of, for instance, an object, consumer product or everyday artifact, in a process that both preserves its history and sets it against an entirely new syntax.

In Bolande's work we "hear an image and see a sound," a phrase that seems both absurd and vaguely right, that resonates with the idea of something being possible and impossible at the same time. In the quietest of her pieces, the images we see appear bland, almost inconsequential. But the more you look at them, the more they seem somehow incongruent, until at last you come to believe in their consequences and hear their voices, their storytelling. To shift image and meaning in this way, Bolande selects mute and mundane objects and treats them as something precious, as things with voices.

Milk Crown, 1987 [56] provides a good point of entry into Bolande's practice. The title and the object present us with a kind of riddle: When is a crown not a crown? The white, cast porcelain ring that tapers up to rounded points fits the description of a crown, but the sculpture is also an easily recognizable double of another image—*Milk Drop Coronet*, 1957 by Harold Edgerton [58], the famous photograph of the split second when a falling drop of milk hits a surface (Edgerton invented ultra-high speed and stop-action photography in 1931). Bolande has produced a literal version of *Coronet*. Her sculptural rendition is hyperrealistic; it is the frozen, photo-graphed splash in shiny 3D. This reversal opens up questions of verisimilitude. Which is the real one, the one we can touch or the one we can see only by virtue of split-second photography? Which represents the impossible?

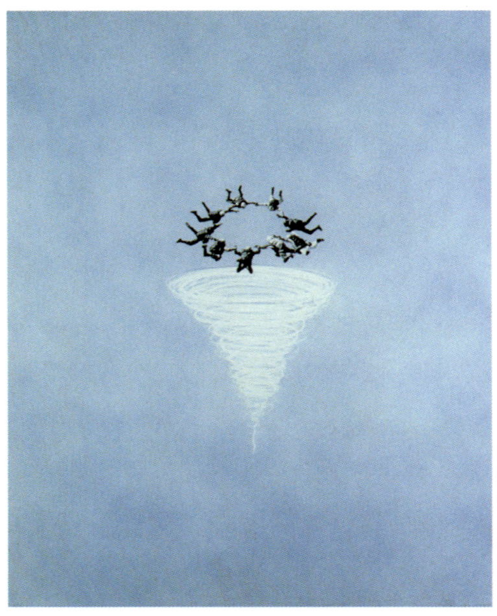

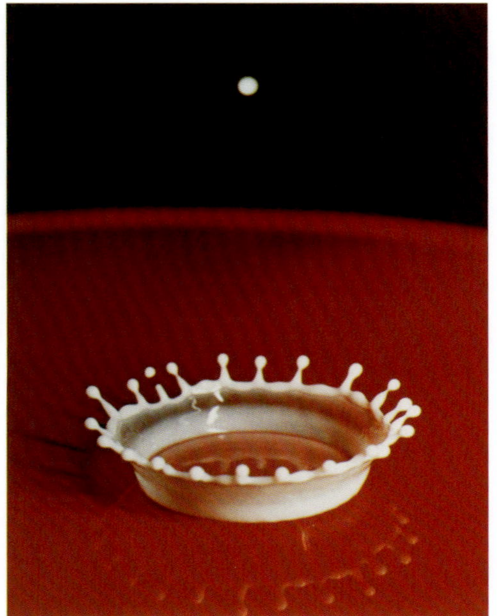

By pushing the reality of the impossible image one step further—from photograph to object—Bolande simultaneously deflates the wonder that surrounds the photograph while inciting the viewer's curiosity about the representation's physical shape and form. This literal treatment of an historic image pushes the boundary of meaning that held the form together culturally. Even the difference between the titles causes a slippage. "Coronet" is a metaphor for royalty and honor, while "milk crown"—a literal description of Edgerton's subject, its material and its form—dispels the regal honor that his title implies. The image, in both the photograph and Bolande's sculpture, is a crown-shape made from a white substance. In the Edgerton it was indeed milk caught in a moment when it took the shape of a crown, while Bolande merely assigns the idea of milk in her physical representation of a white crown fashioned out of porcelain. Here is where the impossible becomes possible—the impossible photographic image is a real document of liquid in action with a metaphoric title, and the real sculpture is a document of the cultural artifact generated by the photograph over time. We are presented with the concept of milk and of fame as it is encapsulated in this particular cultural form. The question, "Which is the real one?" is posed and deferred, elegantly and with humor.

Bolande strikes a delicate balance between semiotic terms with her interventions. In *Milk Crown* the reference to something scientific—something that is purportedly true to reality (high-speed photography)—is slightly skewed in the sense that the technology that makes visibility possible surpasses the capability of the human eye. As representation, it is as unreal—or arbitrary—as a work of art. In effect, the connection between the two images, the photograph and the sculpture, levels the field between artifice and document. The two realms represented by *Coronet* and its double, *Milk Crown*, rock between the natural and the artificial. The fictional crown that the sculpture represents is rendered more real by the palpable physicality of its material, while the photograph retreats into a mere echo of a material that is only referenced and necessarily absent, making the image seem more apparition than reality. The effect of these disturbances and reformulations deepens the longer you stand in front of the work; they slowly unwind inside your head as you begin to forge connections between present and recalled representations.

Another work that moves the viewer from the brink of the literal is *Aerial Phonograph*, 1991 [62]. Essentially a simple record player and a record on a pedestal, the work, upon closer inspection, provokes an amusing yet profound realization. In the place of the LP's label is a picture of a circle of skydivers in the midst of their fall. The placement of the photograph at the center of the record means that the skydivers' falling movement is activated by the movement of the record. One senses strongly that both phonograph, the device that triggers the movement, and skydivers, the image that moves, are passé, remnants of technology and a hobby whose popularity peaked in the 1980s. Now, in this first decade of the twenty-first century, extreme sports such as snowboarding and skysurfing have surpassed the gentler frisson of earlier versions of the sport, which are now merely historic antecedent. The demise of the phonograph with the rise of the CD and iPod has pushed it into similar historical status. Both retain a cultural flavor tied to their original pasts even as, in Bolande's piece, they play off one another in generating new meaning.

Beyond their historic assignations, *Aerial Phonograph* locks machine and men together in the same motion. The movement of the phonograph and the movement of the skydivers leave the two circling together in a state of perpetual motion, in which the skydivers never fall. Of course, should the phonograph be unplugged, all movement stops, but the skydivers are then merely frozen in their circle formation until the machine is turned on again and they can resume falling. Whether in movement or not, the skydivers exist in a heartbreaking holding pattern between earth and sky as the record turns round and round. The hardware of the piece—the photograph, the phonograph, the shiny black base—belies this tenderness. It is doubly tender because this hovering between spaces—on one level between physical earth and sky, but more deeply between cultural relevance and obsolescence—is enacted simultaneously for both skydivers and phonograph. The layering of the technological obsolescence of a thing and the cultural obsolescence of a social activity anthropomorphizes both. This purgatorial embrace between the two concepts (the record player and skydiving) grows out of a shared fragility in the face of their mutual state of expired desirability.[1] In a semiotic sense, they are floating signifiers, no longer attached to a signified that once gave them meaning and value.

To see these types of incongruences so sensitively, if wistfully, joined is to grasp the finesse of Bolande's alertness to that which has lost meaning—or perhaps more accurately, to that which is in the process of losing meaning. Jennifer Bolande reverses nostalgia in her work. Rather than presenting us with a reconstruction of events once lived or of things once possessed, she sets up resonances that short-circuit nostalgia and evoke memories at their source. Through her orchestrations, objects elicit the nostalgia not of themselves per se, but for usefulness, relevance, and desirability. In Bolande's hands "expired" objects connote the lost potency of representing social status or cutting-edge technology. It is in this careful and sympathetic sensitivity to the things we've owned that Bolande's elliptical narratives begin.

In *Side Show*, 1991 [76], a tent stake is carefully lit, as if it were a stage set or an actor on stage. The light source is included in the frame to reveal the rather simple mechanics behind the high theatrics. But the humble nature of the stake and the suggestions that it has been caught in the act of usefulness—it strains against the rope tied to it, whose other end is lost in shadow—again animates the object, here with a sense of eagerness and a display of determination. It is as if the value of the stake is its ability to enact a grand performance of its prowess as a rudimentary tool. The title of the work writes a further narrative in which the stake serves to refer to the activity outside the frame, not just of the sideshow, but of the Big Top, where the real show is taking place. The title, in contrast to pseudo-glamorous lighting, emphasizes the small but significant role the stake plays in the big production, and the shared stake it has in its decline. Again in *Side Show*, there is the underlying pathos of an encroaching fall from use, of something on the cusp of its cultural end. In the midst of the digital age, the fantastic and strange images playing on countless screens in crystalline high definition have surpassed the venial titillations of sideshow curiosities, and what is left of the freak show is not much more than a sense of old-fashioned quaintness. Today, when punks and sales managers alike sport piercings and elaborate tattoos, we live in the sideshow, where we rarely blink and never gawk.

Globe Sightings: Stonehouse Road, Bloomfield, NJ, 2000 [101] offers up a similar kind of personification but through a more forensic method. The information-laden title (object, action, location as street and city) frames the narrative in which we look for the globe. The photograph depicts a school with partially or fully shaded windows. From one of these windows a small globe peeks out, a captive tool of the pedagogical system. This particular photograph is one of a series that Bolande made in 2000–2001. A vocabulary of "globe sightings" builds as we discover the idiosyncrasies of the individual globes ever looking out into the world from their habitations, whether suburban school, high-rise, or store window. In every instance the owners of these globes have placed them by a window, as if to manifest the difference between the map and the real view, the encompassing totality of one (however small) and the limited frame of the other (however vast). Looking at these photographs, it is hard not to feel a sense of irony when every inch of the planet has been digitized and is available for us to see any hour of the day or night in topographic or minute scale. To own a globe today is a bit like holding on to a souvenir of superseded representation. In vivid blues, greens, reds, and yellows, a globe is a cartoonish illustration compared to the pinpoint accuracy of the scalable digital map.

The globe now represents a romantic idea of an organic unity, an ideal Gaia. Once it represented the ambitions of imperial expansion, as Europe sent ships in search of gold and the untapped riches there for the taking from heathen savages. In our age of late-capitalist globalization, both the reach of corporate entities that know no loyalty to any nation and the instantaneousness of the transmission of information that knows no geography have re-flattened the Earth. In the process, the planet has been put under the very real threat of irreversible environmental degradation. As the old image of an infinitely fruitful and exploitable planet collides with the consequences of geopolitical realities, the representation of the cartoon-globe takes on new poignancy. At the core of Bolande's practice—which witnesses the transformation of old certainties into wistful yearnings and posits the reclamation of objects that have lost their usefulness—is an awareness that there is never an end to our unsated longing. What she presents us with is the illusion of our very desires and dreams of satisfaction. The thread of progress's castoffs that moves throughout her work points to this facet of our society. Bolande's semiotic analysis of the romanticism of the lost reveals us in our illusory and persistent occupation of salvage.

Cast of Characters, 1999 [59] is a summary of the accumulation we hope will somehow protect us from change. A Bolande family portrait of sorts, the image is a visual algorithm of not only her work but of our acquisitiveness. At its most basic, the photograph is a grouping of rectangles. The tallest, in the background, is a group of skyscrapers; the smallest, in the foreground, a group of boxed and unboxed refrigerators. In the middle, two stacked speakers, a refrigerator, washer, and dryer sit within the rectangle of the open back of a delivery truck. These objects are not to scale, but positioned like figures arranged from tallest to shortest in a group picture. In *Cast of Characters* we have it all: the buildings we live in, the appliances we furnish them with, and the culture we consume. The linchpin to this piece is the classic Marshall Stack speaker. Musicians from The Who to Jimi Hendrix made "the Stack" an icon of hard rock, and it has come to be a symbol of rock's rebellion and its aggressive sound. Over the years bands would set up banks of dummy Stacks as stage props, even if nonfunctional. The material became immaterial as the symbolic use took on the more palpable reality and desire superseded the technological. In *Cast of Characters* the Stack, in the midst of new and vintage refrigerators, represents the cycle of desire that precipitates the technological commodity.

Bolande enforces no hierarchies of currency or significance. She operates within the totality of signs and their waxing and waning; however, the relationships that she creates in her concocted narratives maintain a constancy of significance, whose richness matches the urgency of our desire. She gives voice to images, and images to match our murmurings.

1. The "purgatorial embrace" is both material- and language-based, as the title reads and sounds like "aerial photograph."

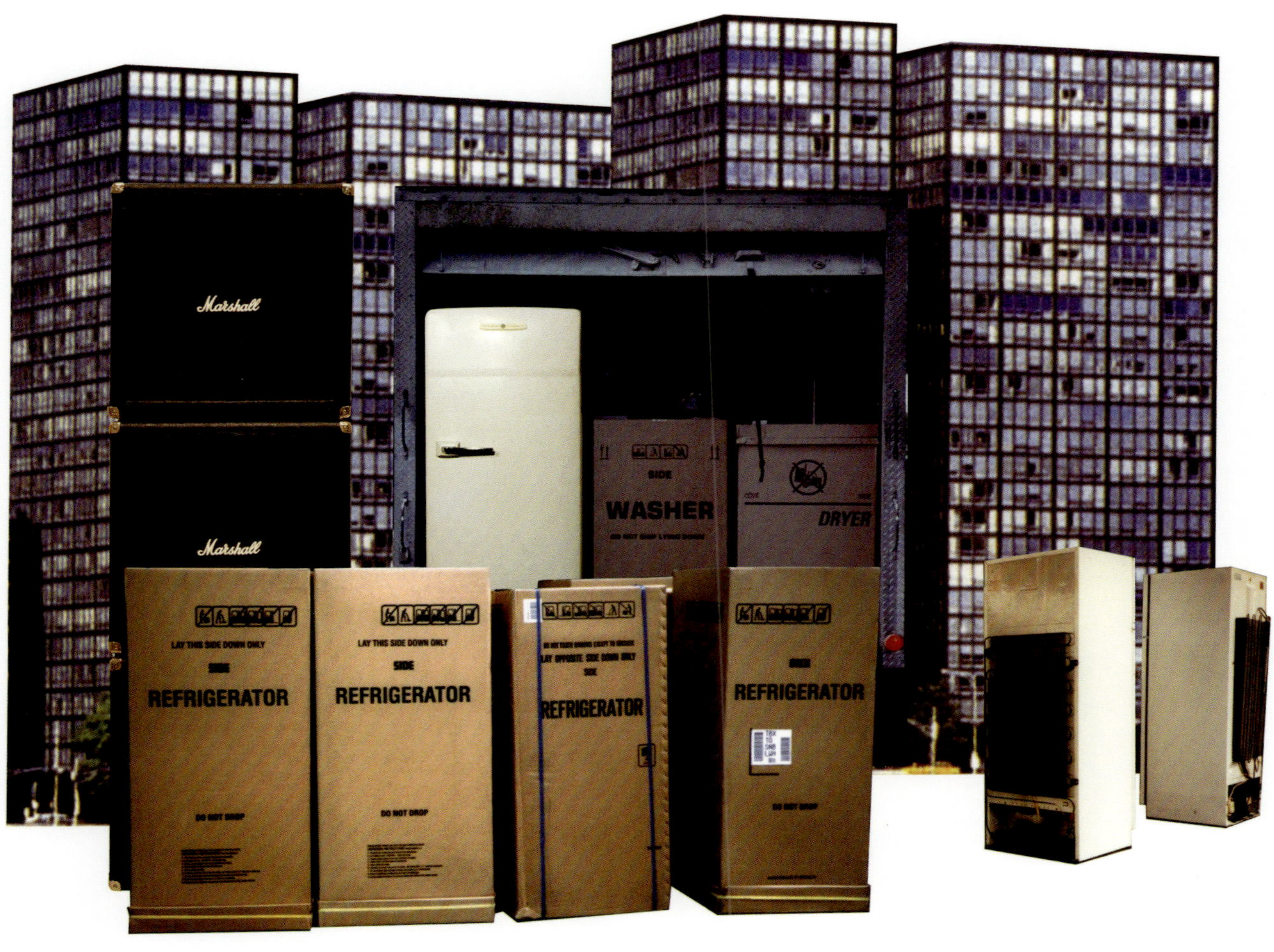
Marshall
Marshall
REFRIGERATOR
LAY THIS SIDE DOWN ONLY
SIDE
REFRIGERATOR
DO NOT DROP
LAY THIS SIDE DOWN ONLY
SIDE
REFRIGERATOR
DO NOT DROP
REFRIGERATOR
SIDE
WASHER
DRYER
REFRIGERATOR
DO NOT DROP

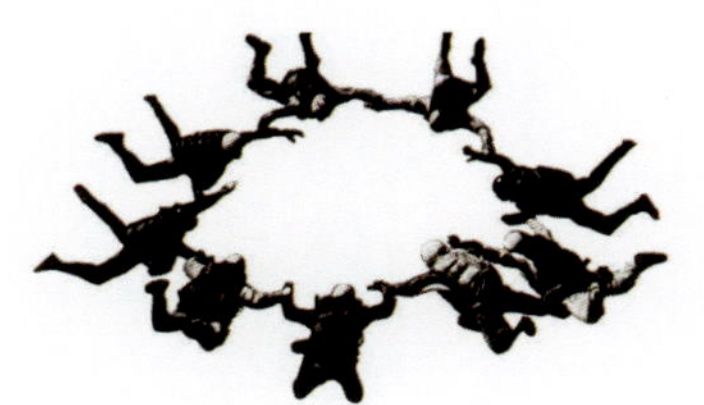

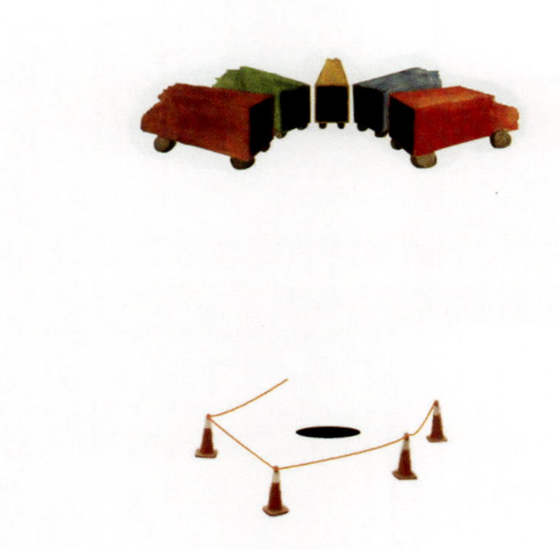

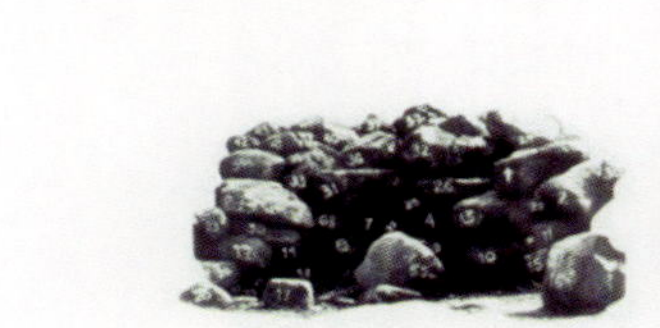

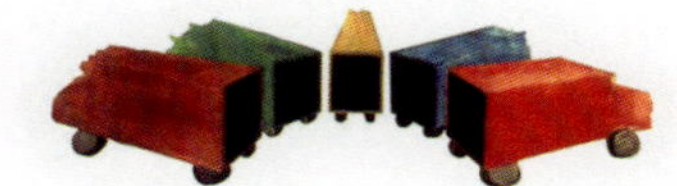

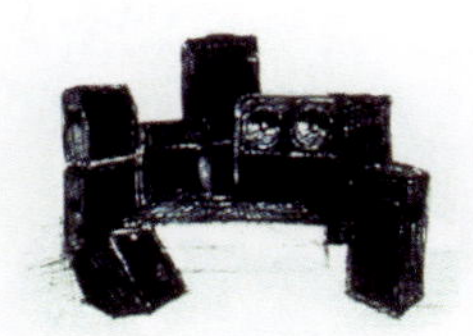

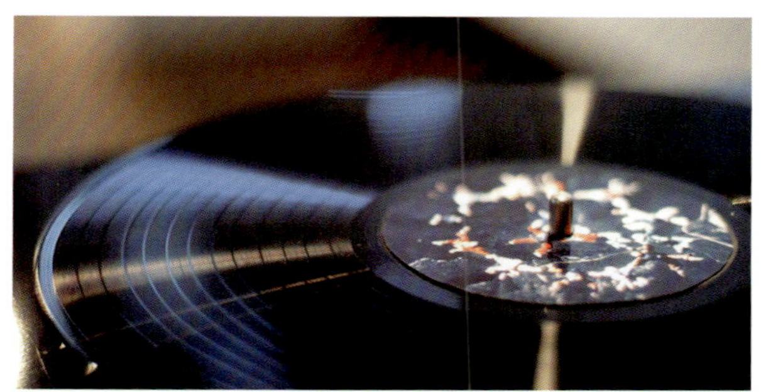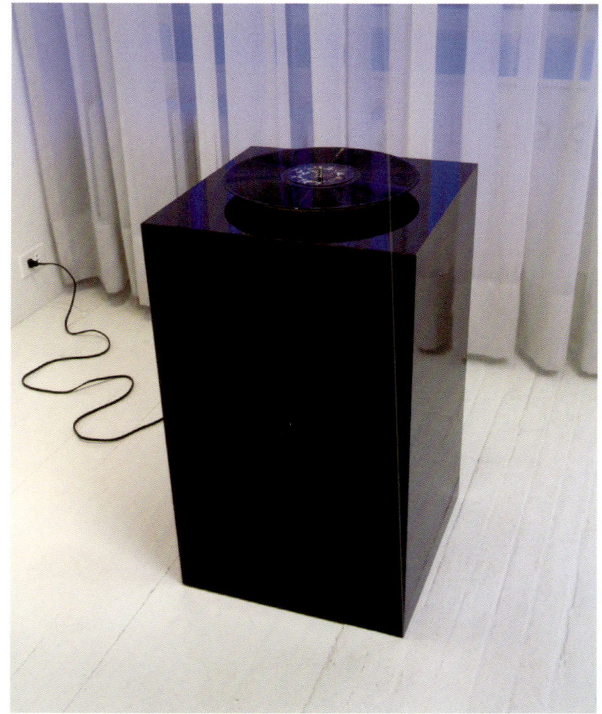

[63] *Holding Pattern*, from the series *Road Movie*, 1995

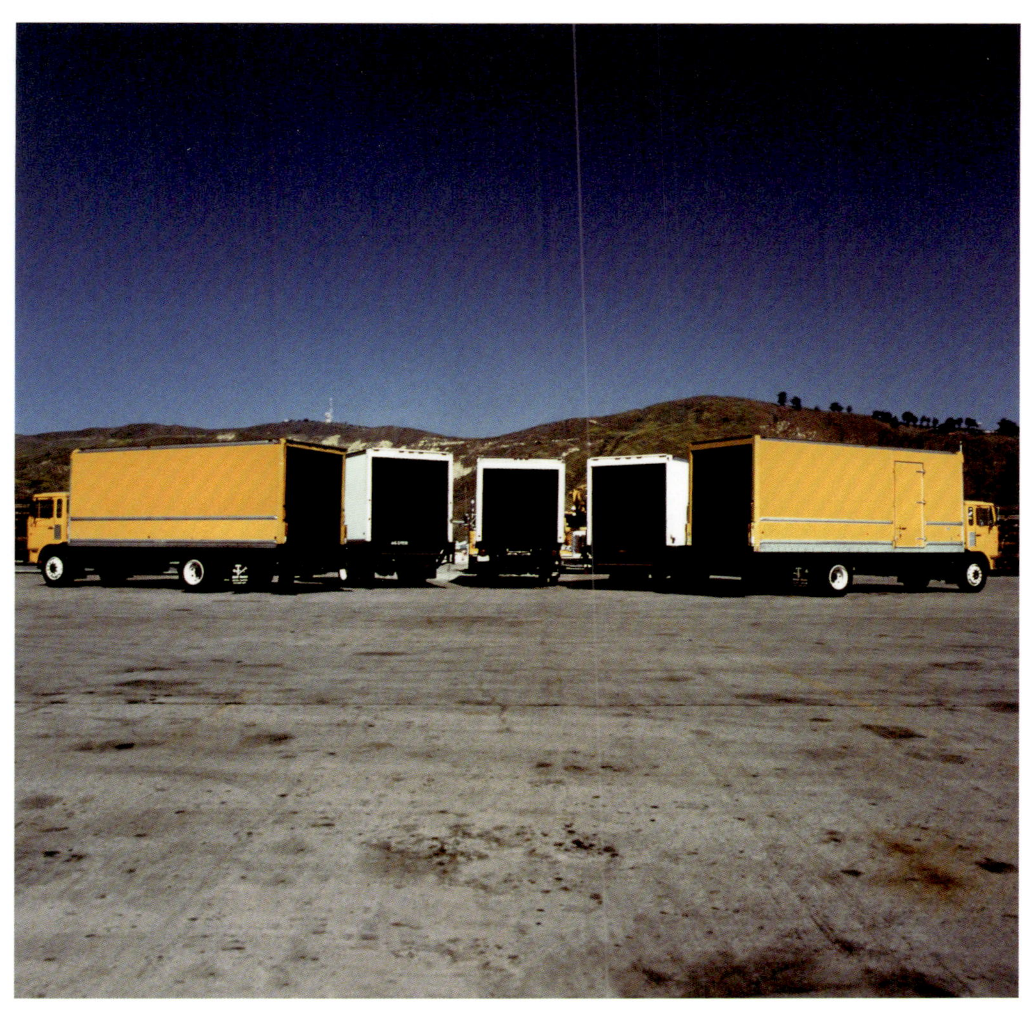

[64] *Steering Wheel*, from the series *Road Movie*, 1995

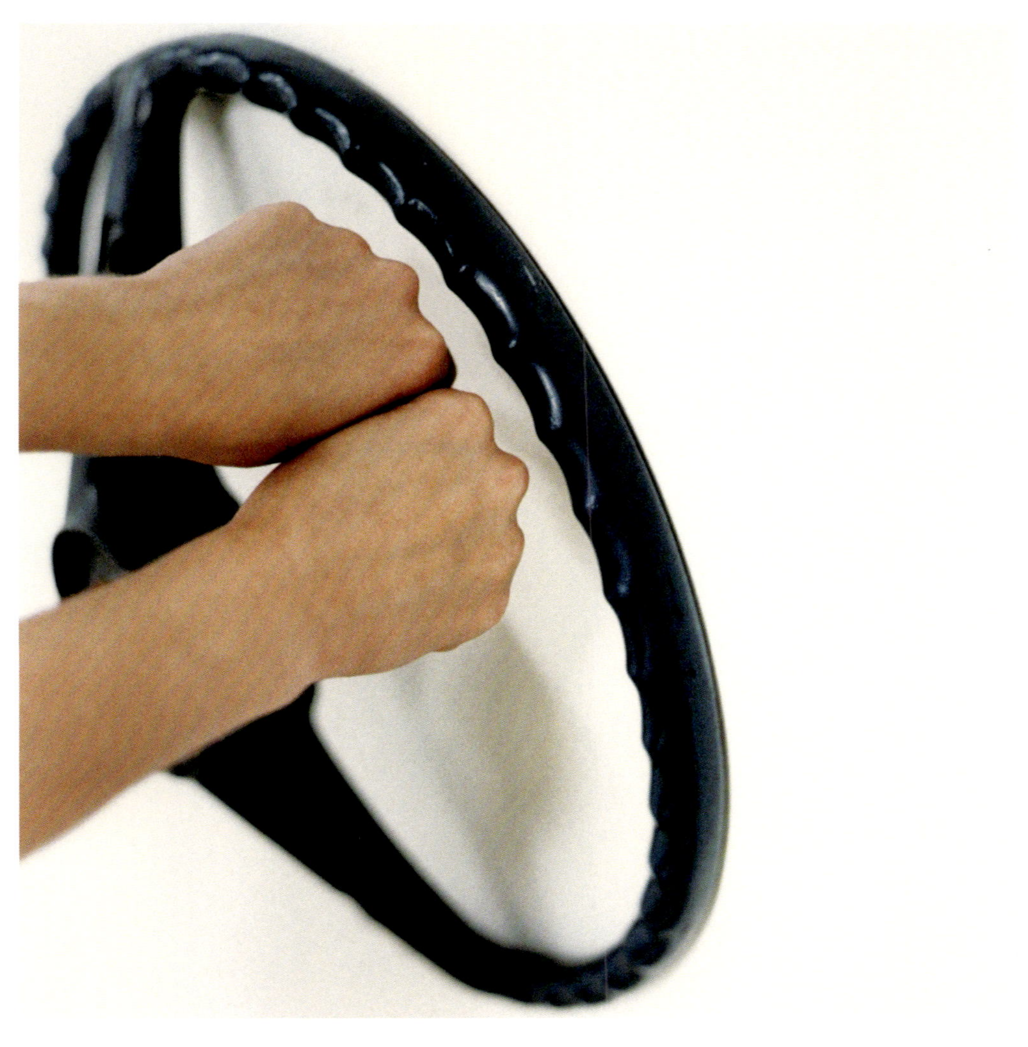

[65] *Glove*, from the series *Road Movie*, 1995

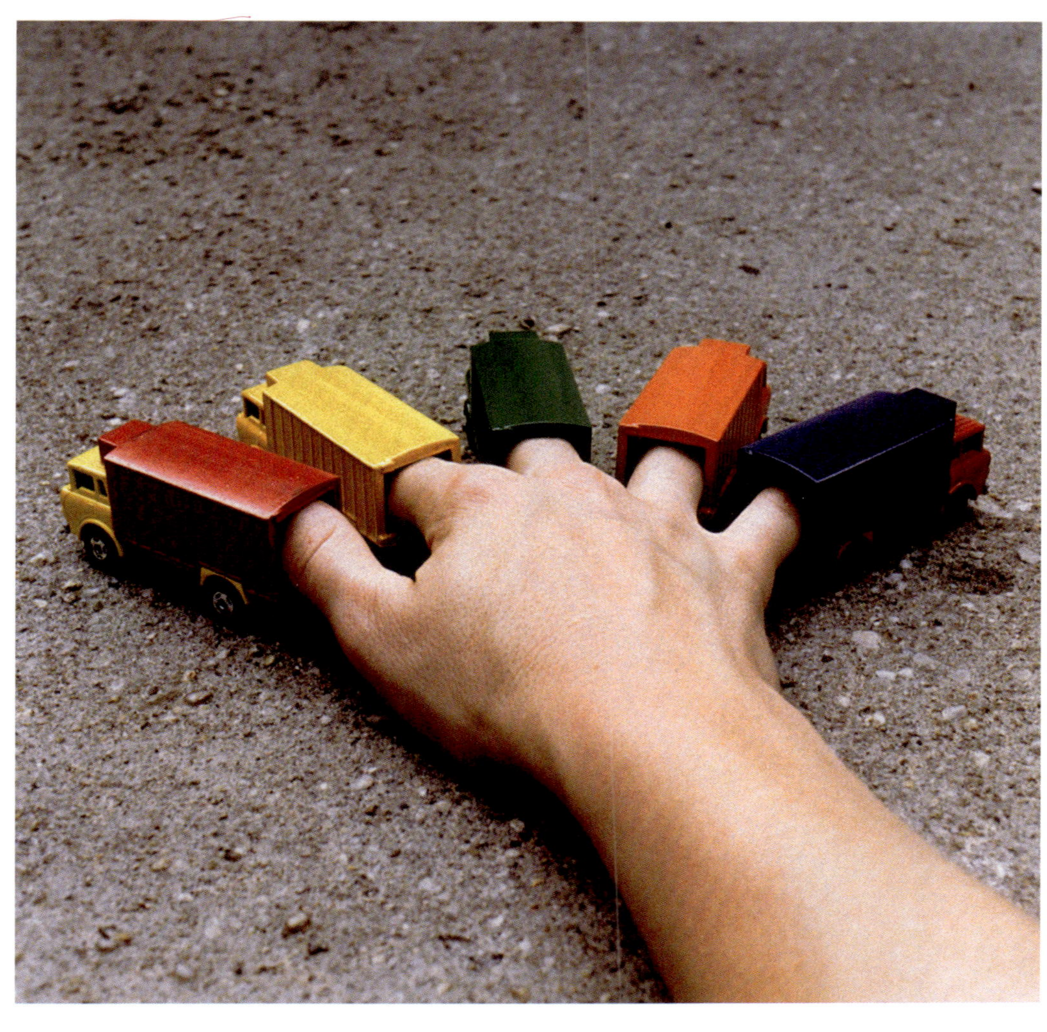

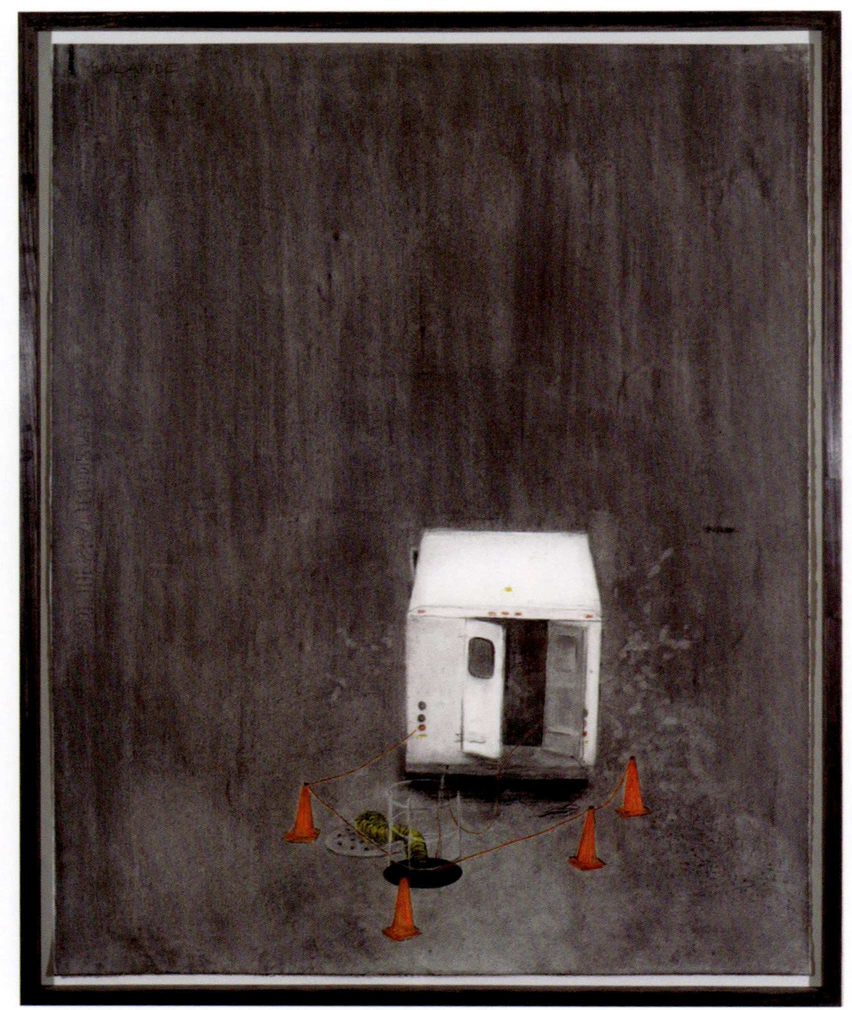

[66] *Held Open Space*, 1991

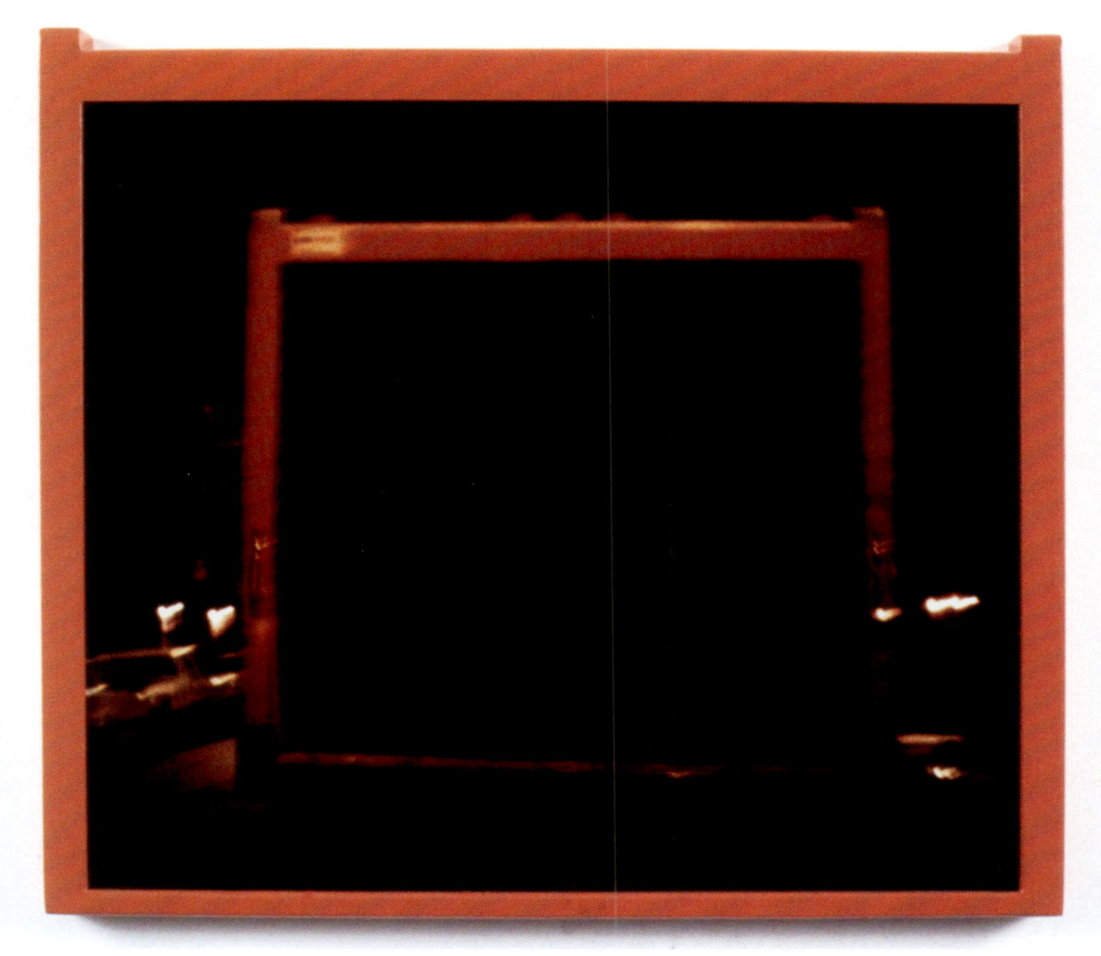

[67] *Orange Threshold*, from the series *Road Movie*, 1995

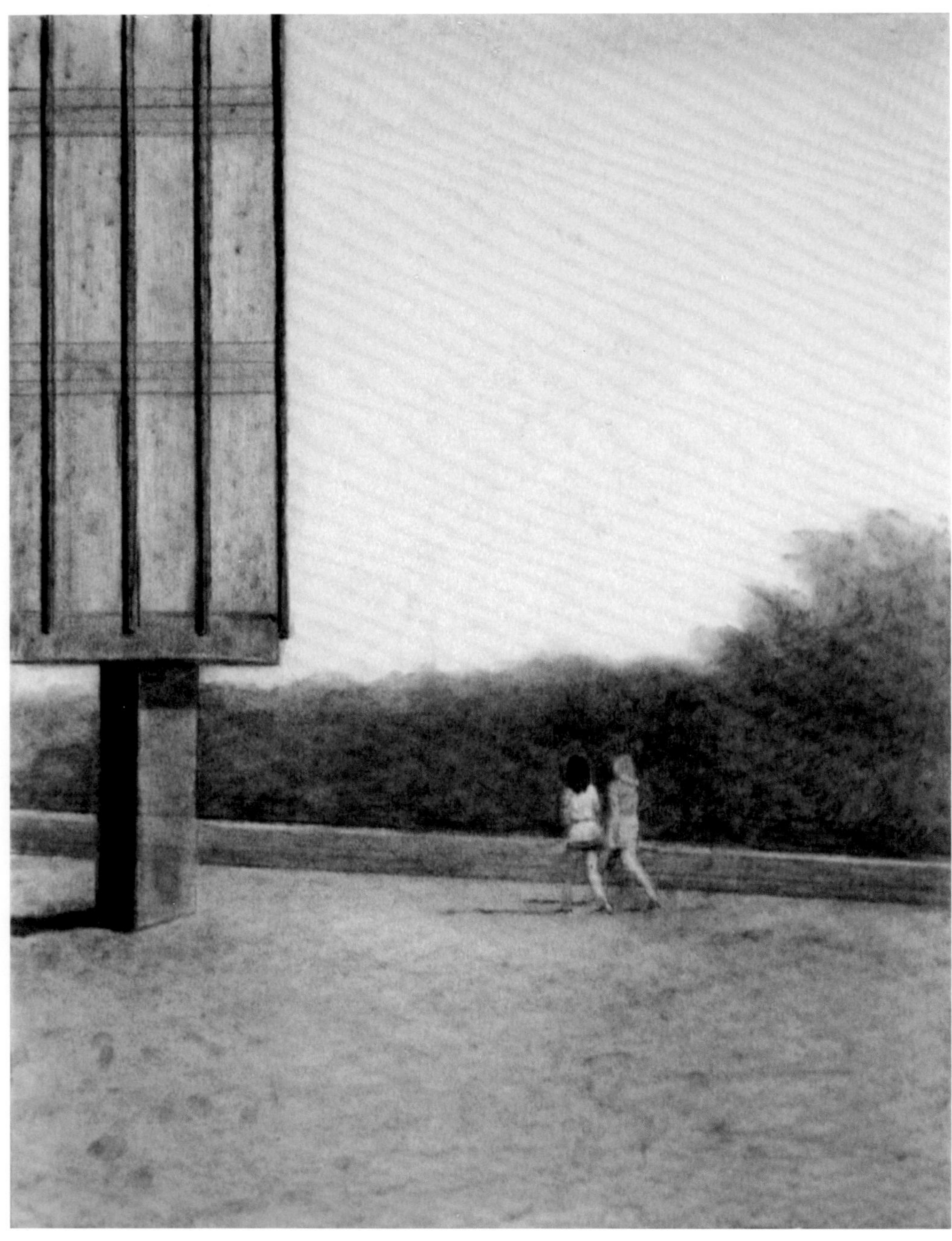

[68] *Industrial Park*, 1999

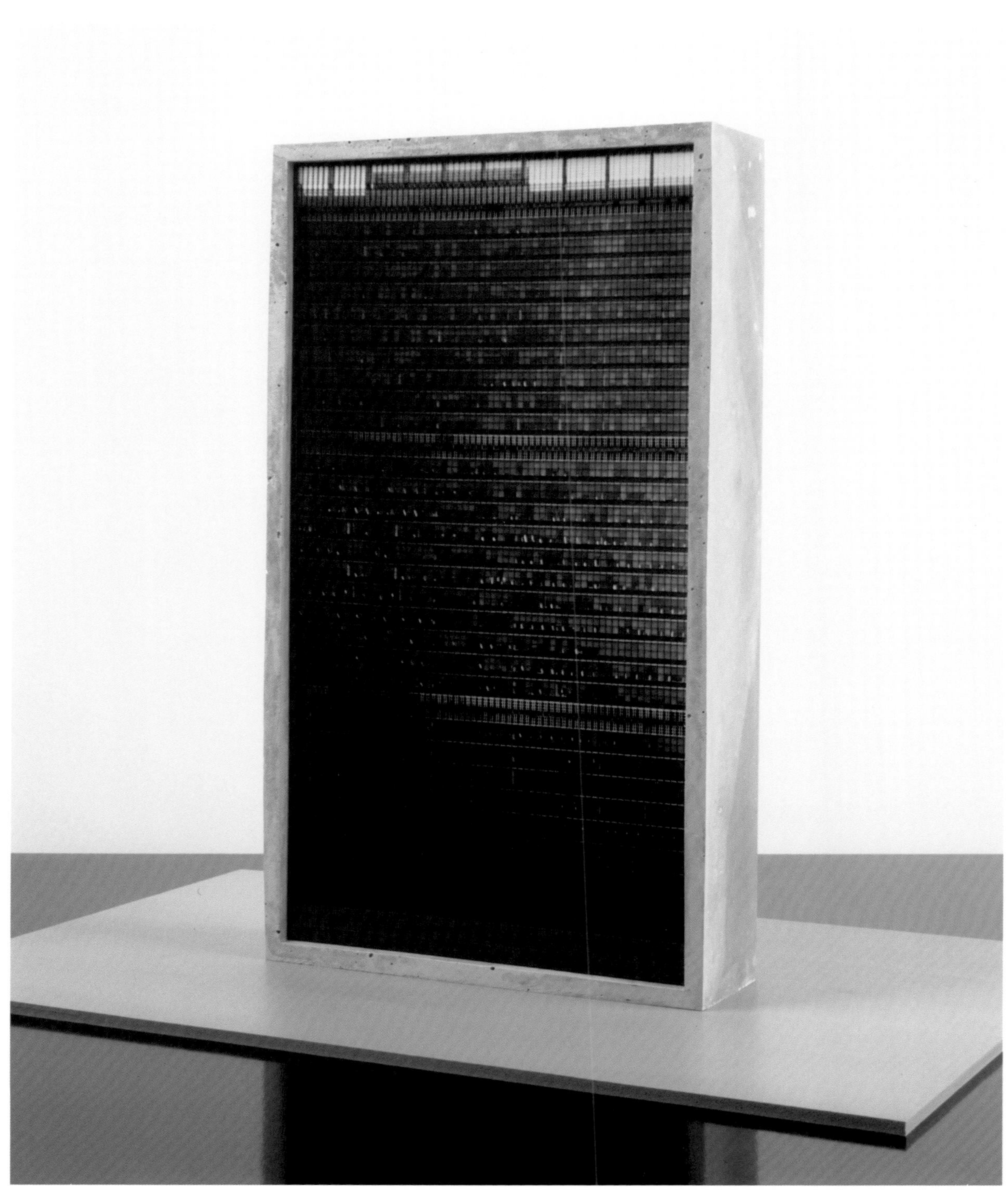

[70] *Mountain*, 2004

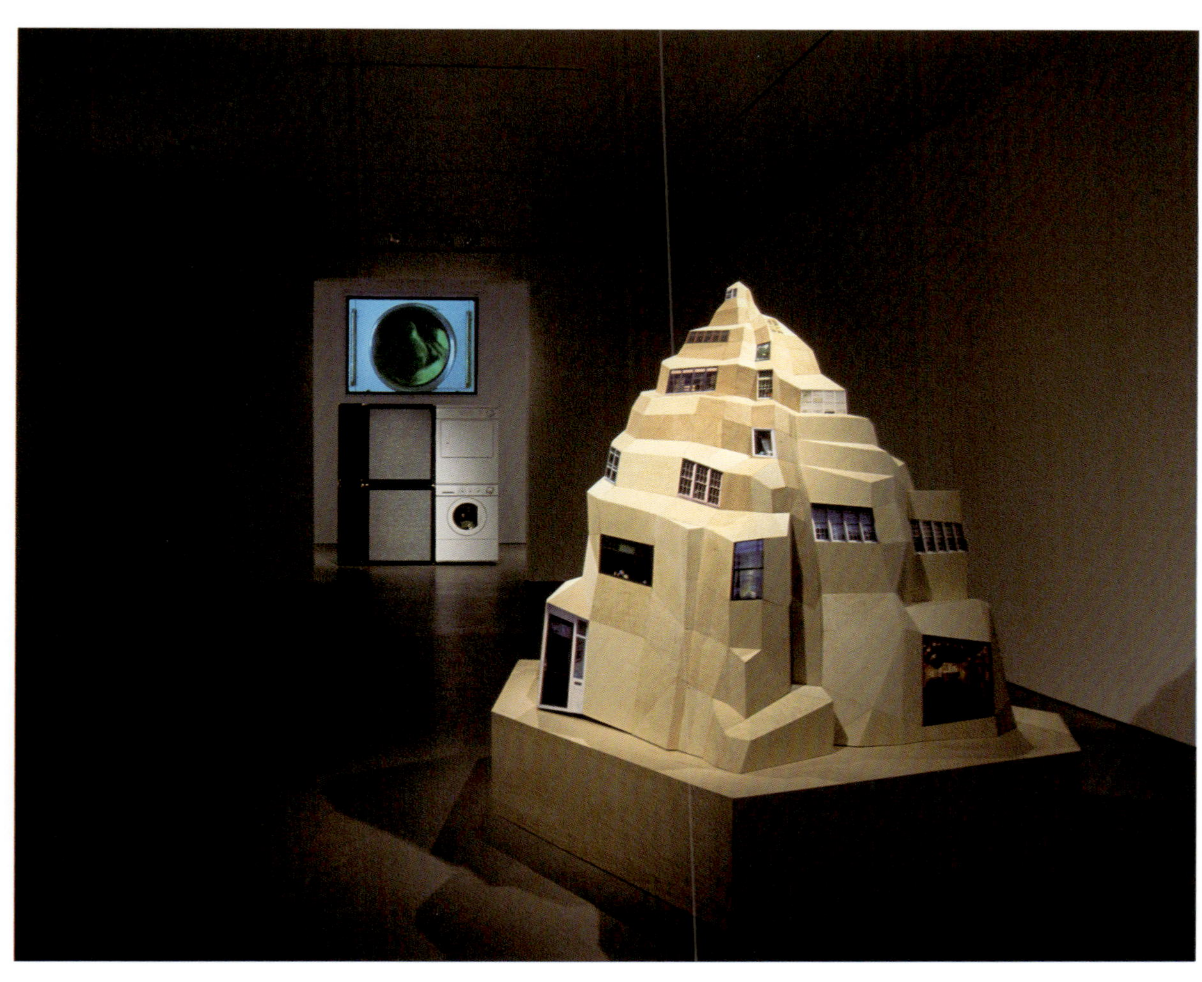

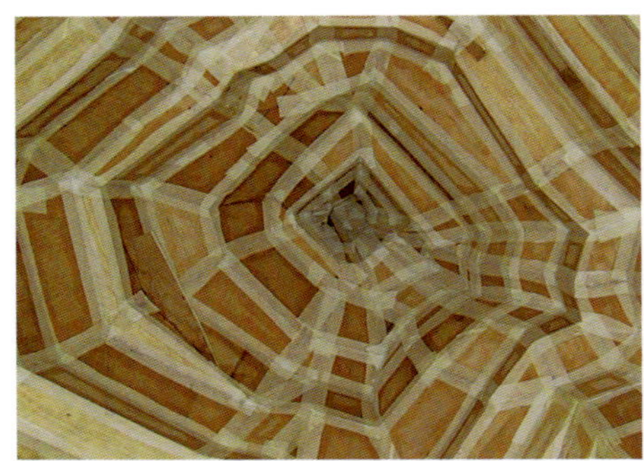

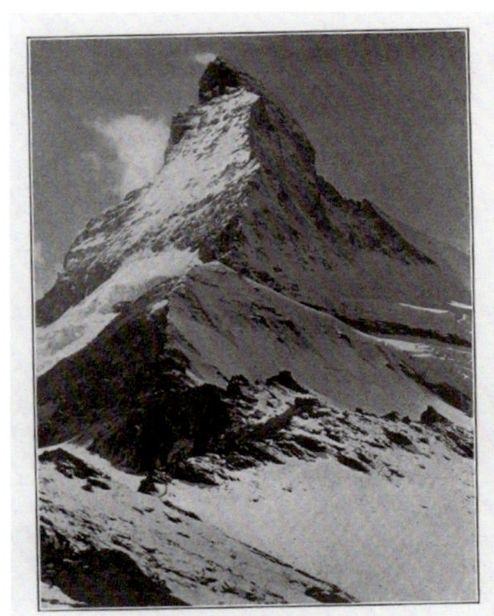

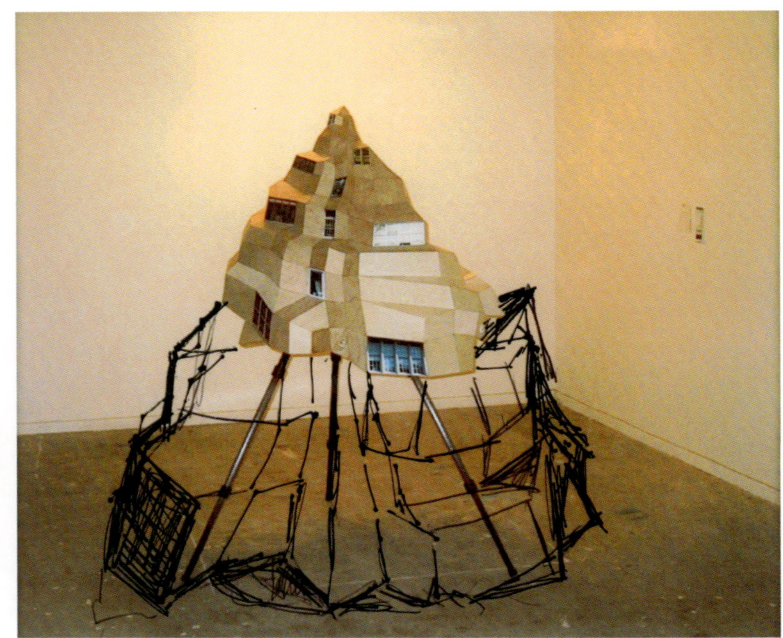

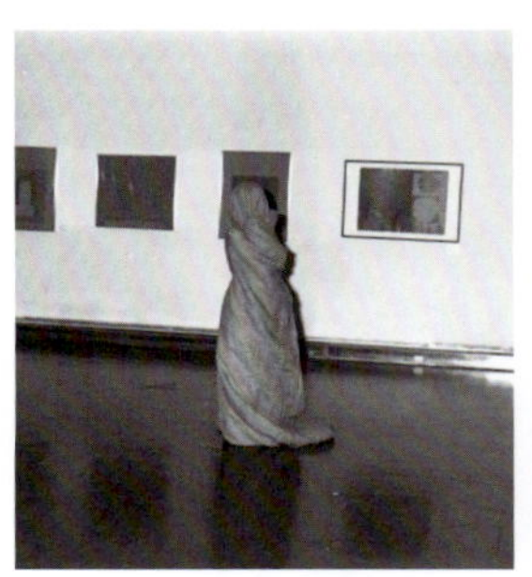

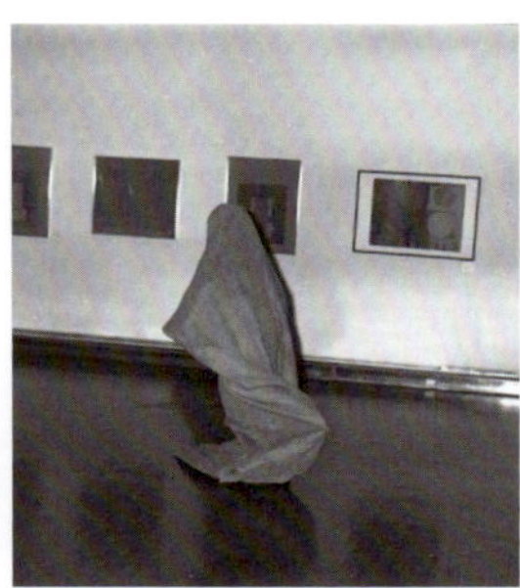

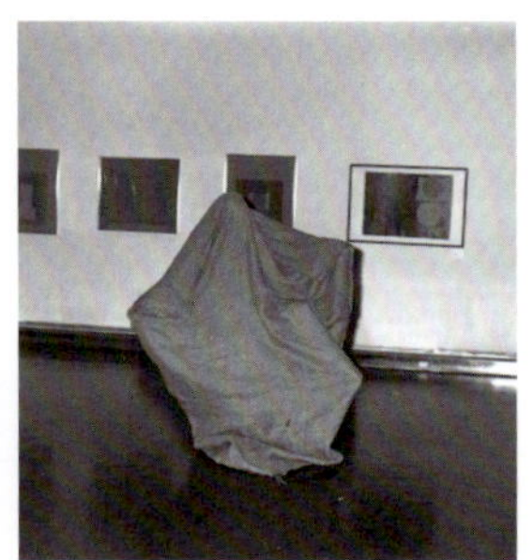

[71] interior of *Mountain*, 2004   [72] *Mountain Study #1*, 2003   [73] reference: Matterhorn   [74] *Bag dance*, 1976

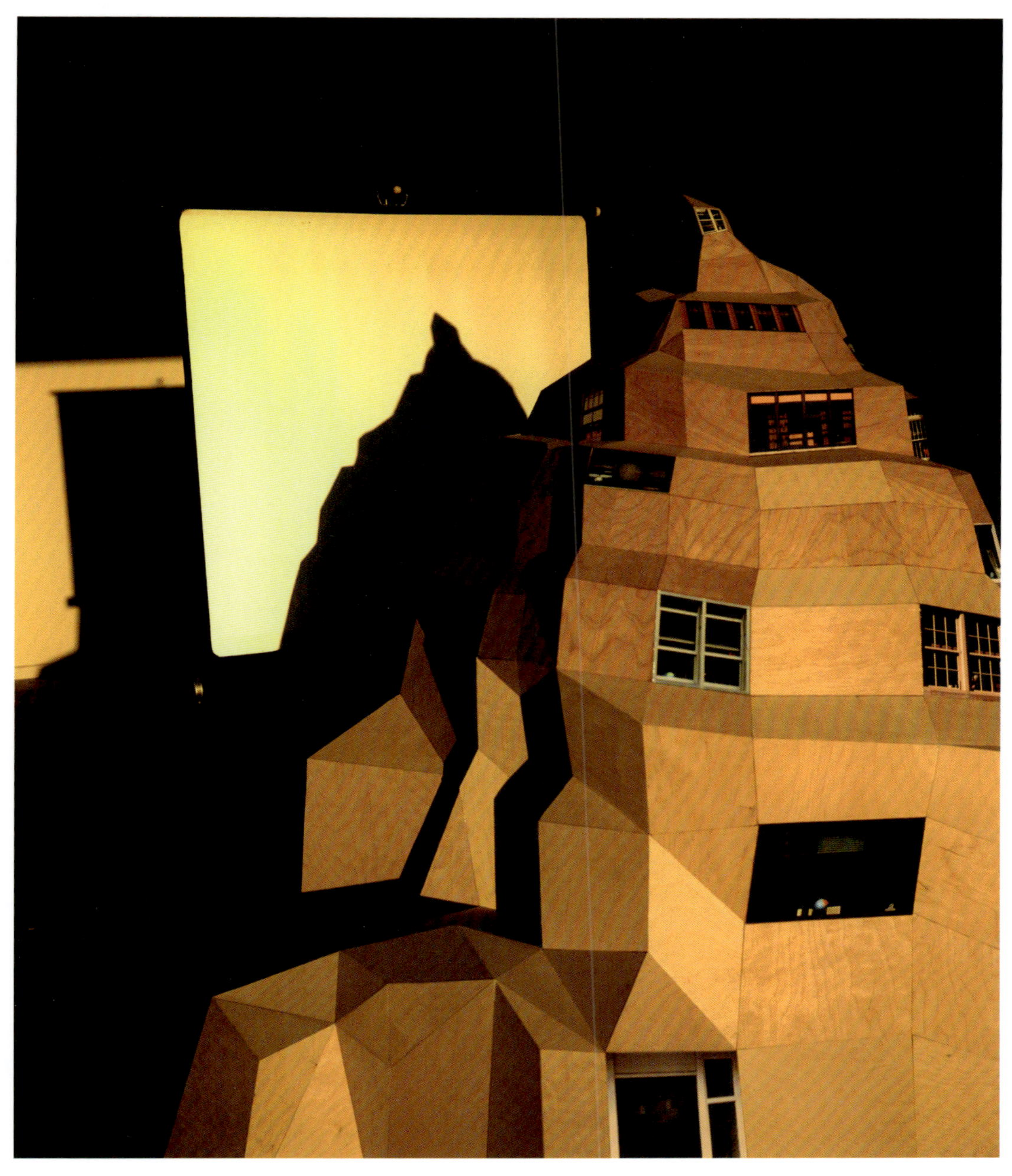

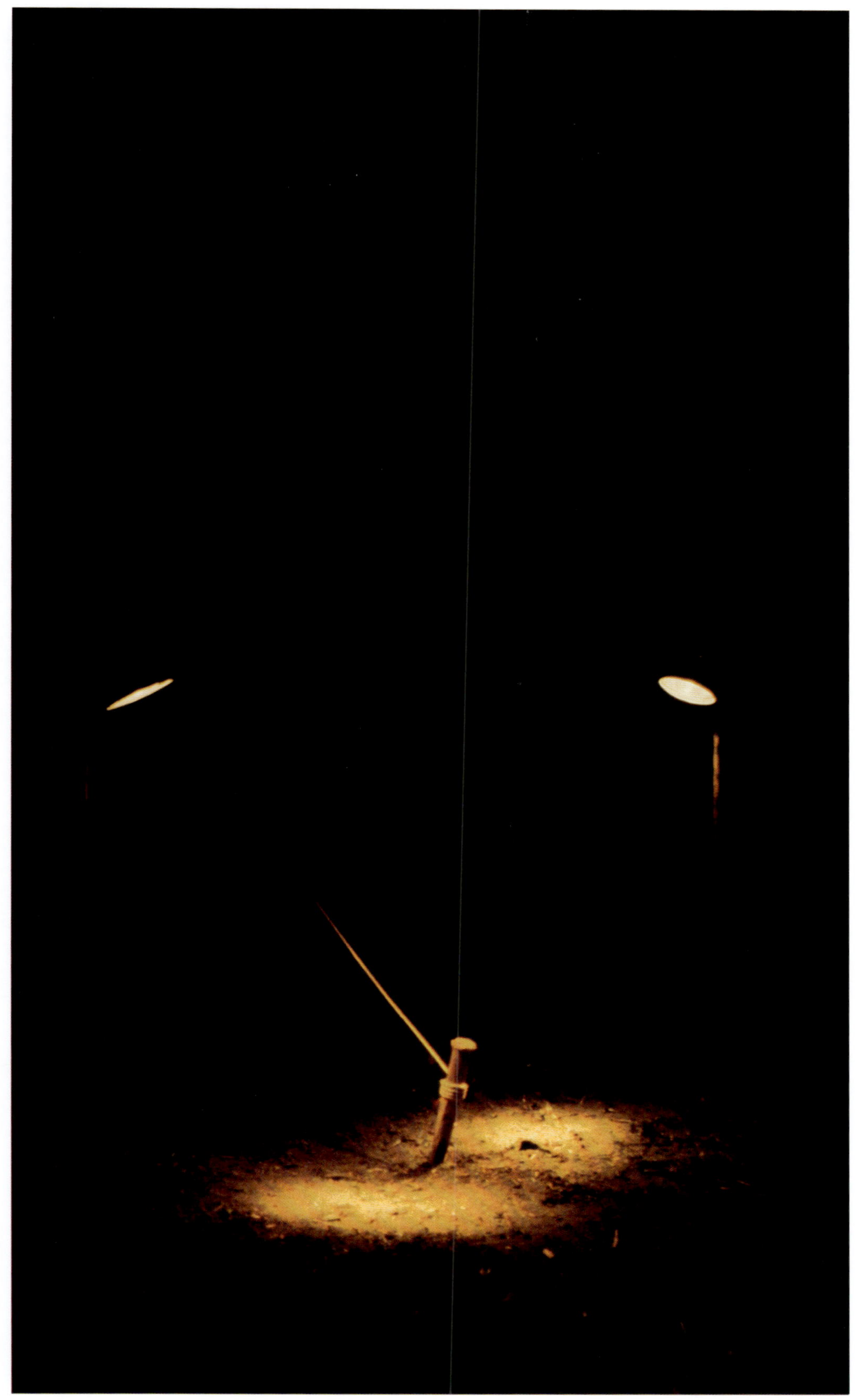

[77] *Movie Chair*, 1984

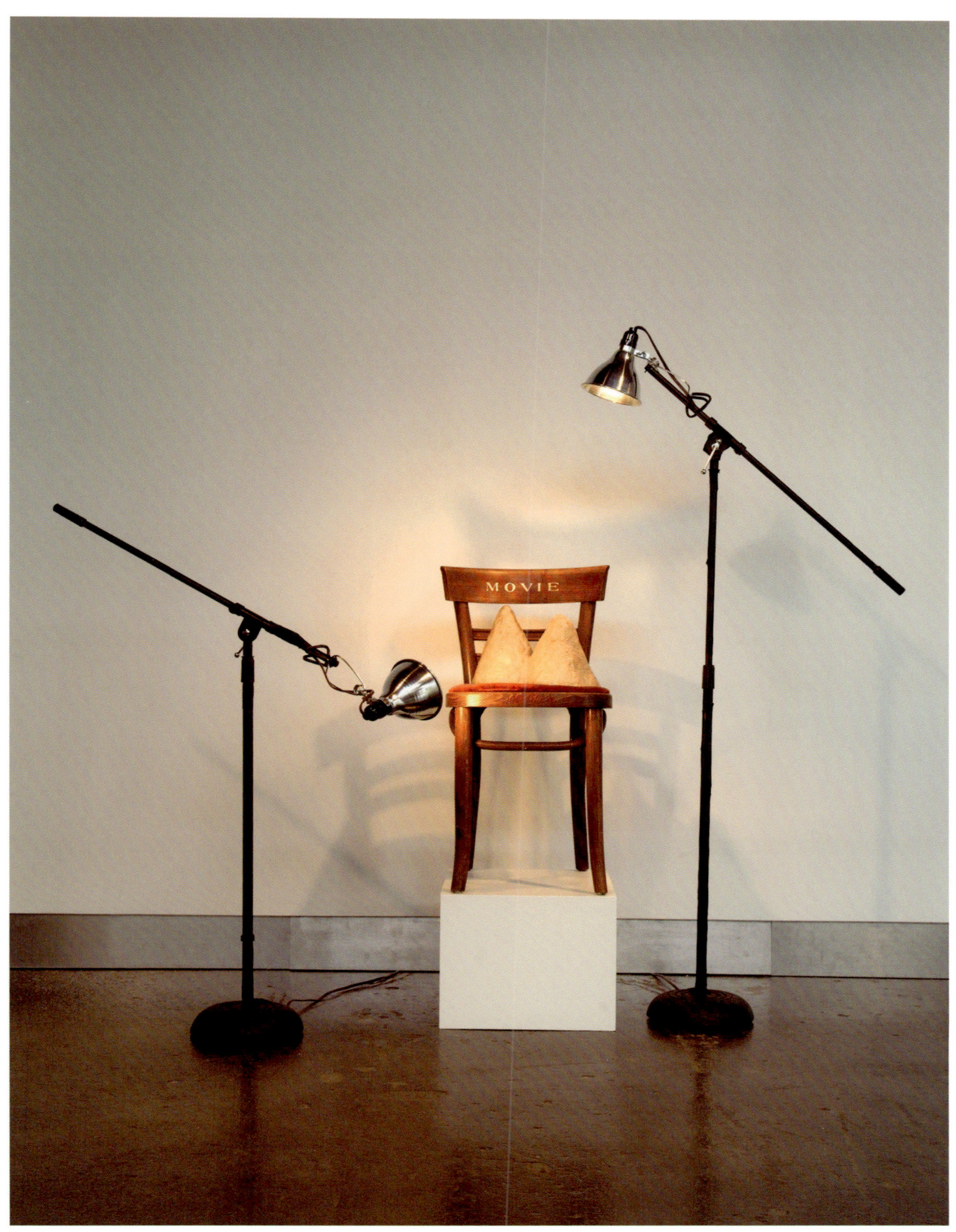

MOVIE

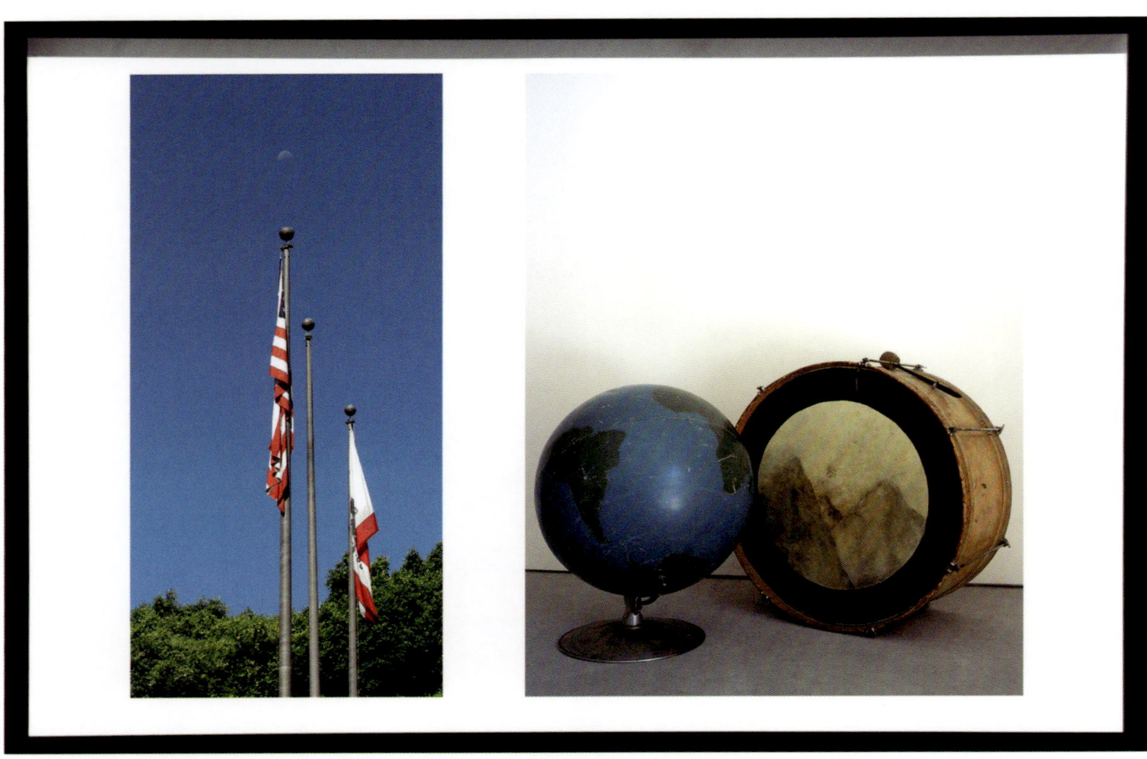

[78] *Diptych #8* from the series *Space Photography*, 2009   [79] *Map Folding Incident #1*, 2001

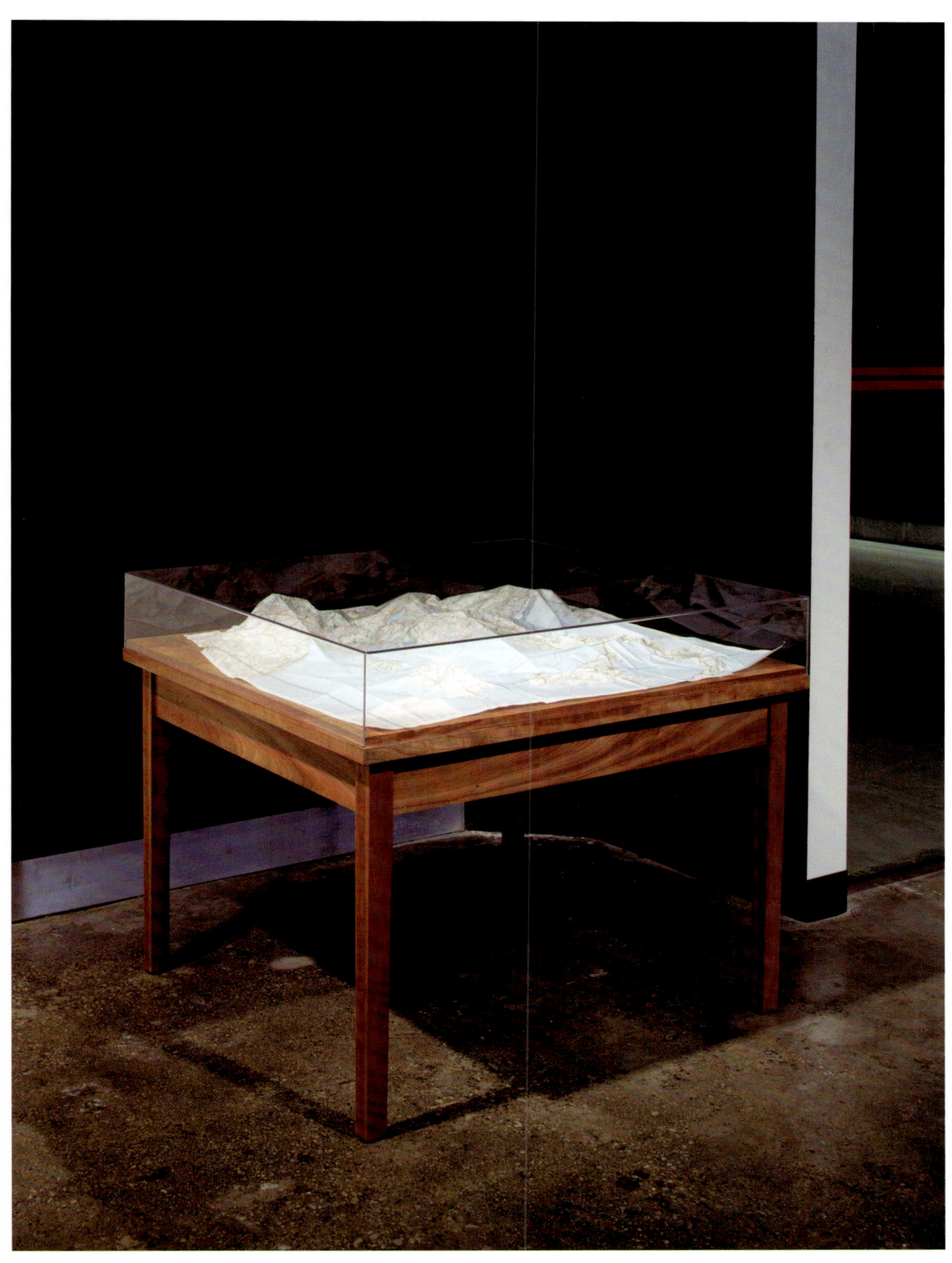

[80] *Caruso Group*, 1985

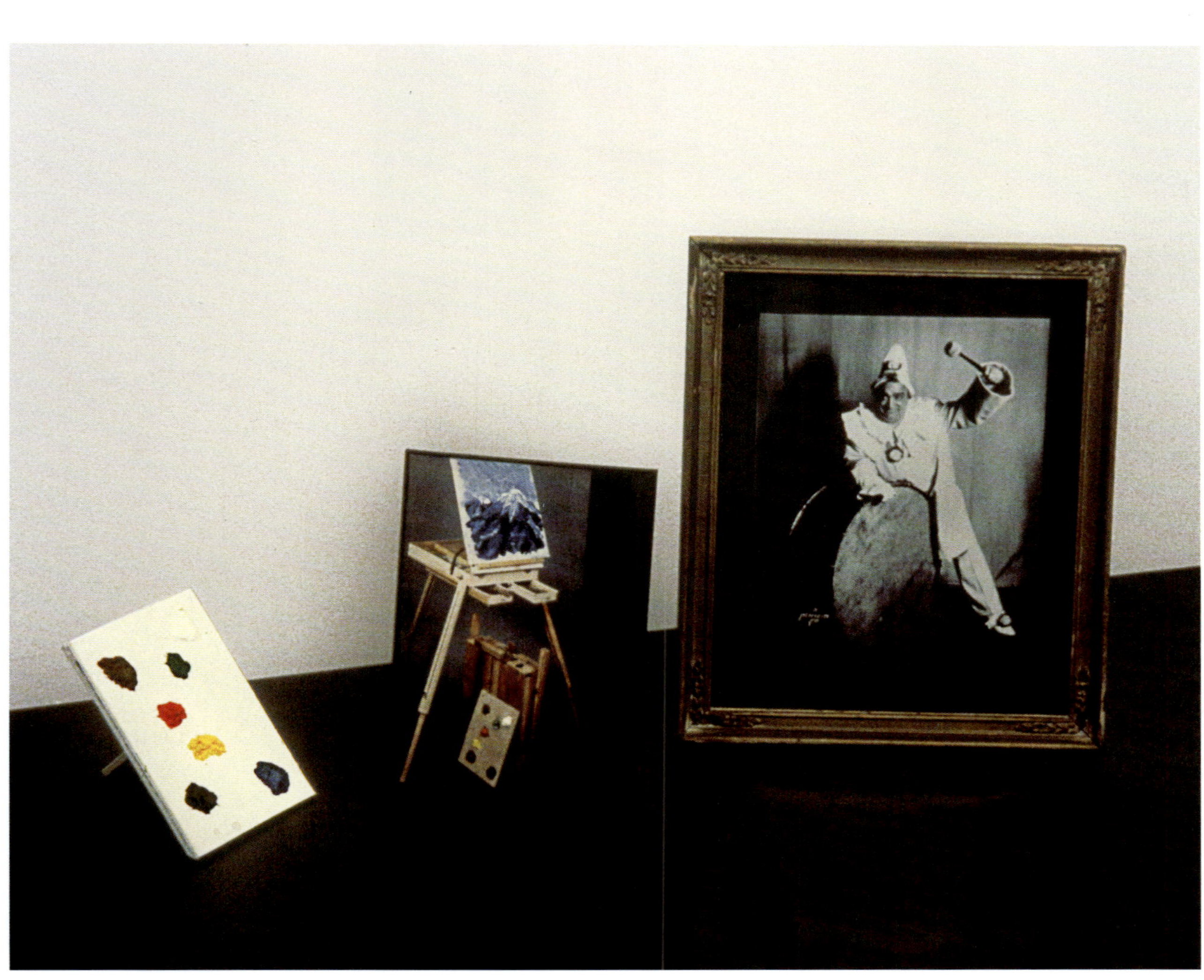

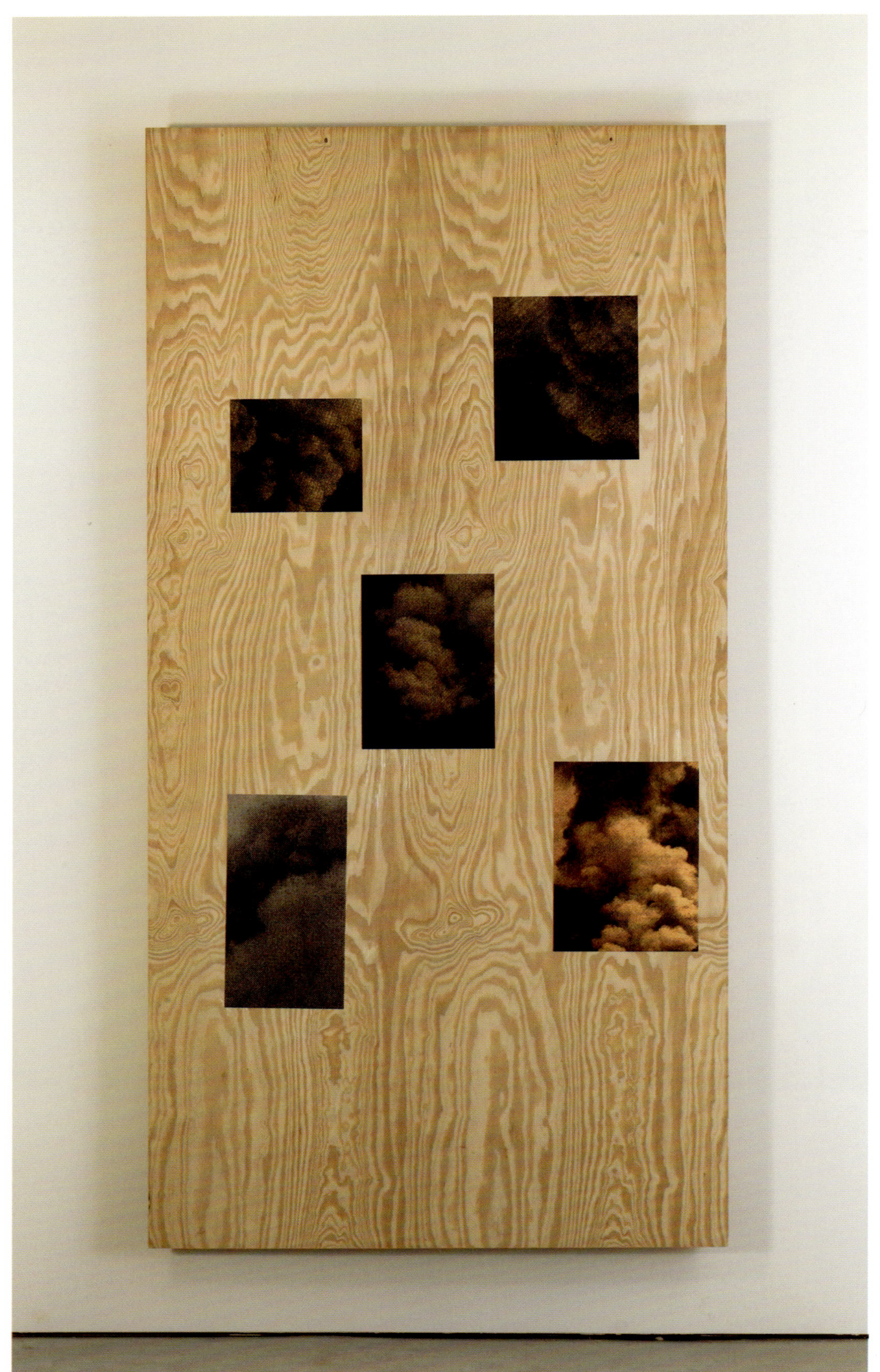

SPEAKING PHOTOGRAPHY

Jennifer Bolande's art is so fluent in the language of photography that we may learn to speak it just by surveying her work. *Jennifer Bolande Landmarks* offers occasion to do just that. With much to say about the development of Bolande's work over the past 28 years, this exhibition is equally conversant in photography, not only as a medium but also as a mode of address, a language with it own grammar and intelligence. As practiced throughout contemporary art, this language is present even when actual photographs are not. And what more productive place for learning photography's language than this show? Like any good classroom, it even has a globe on the windowsill. Make that 25 globes on 25 windowsills, for that is the number that appears in *Topology House*, 2002 [100], a sculpture constructed from photographs of windows, like a greenhouse made of salvaged frames, each one taken wherever Bolande spotted a globe in a window from the street.

Photography's materials and techniques are everywhere on display in this exhibition. We see all kinds of color photography: from standard C-prints (printed like any commercially developed snapshot and as fugitive over time) to cibachromes (archival prints, which use dye-soaked plastic and look as sharp and saturated as slides). Scrolling down the wall and crashing to the floor, where it curls up like a wave, is *Cascade*, 1987 [8], a duratrans (named for an obsolete Kodak plastic that was used when this printing technique first became popular). The printing and papers of photography are variously deployed and commemorated throughout Bolande's art, right up to the present. In the *Smoke Screens* series of 2007 [81], photographs of smoke are affixed directly onto sheets of plywood that hang on the wall like giant sheets of paper, supporting images of the stuff that all vestiges of the darkroom have gone up in. This smoke is, of course, printed digitally.

The gesture of the curl—curling smoke, the curl of *Cascade*—seems deeply embedded. We encounter it again, for instance, in *Stack of Shims, (with wire photo)* 1987 [89]. A photograph of trees downed in a tornado hangs above a stack of wooden slats that stands against the wall. This picture of an aerial view of disaster is a re-photographed newspaper image [83] that has yellowed, crinkled and curled at the corners. (And in case you wondered, as I did, about the title, note the illuminative wire service photo-credit.) The artist says the clipping was pinned up in her studio for a long time, like a peripheral point of reference, flagging exactly what, she was not sure. It's as if it actually took the process of disintegrating, of slowly yellowing and peeling up from the wall, for the image to become an object, a thing that Bolande could pick up and use. And it is this thing-ness of photography that wires the gaps that are so much a part of Bolande's art. *Stack of Shims* is riddled with them, gaps, between paper and wood, between trees seemingly at rest and shims resembling newspapers, between the spiraling distance to the ground in the aerial view and the abrupt immediacy of the object in front you, between your head and the picture and your body and the stack of wood, between time captured in a photograph (which is always in the past) and time embodied in sculpture (which is always in the present). Nowhere is this last gap more efficiently collapsed and constructed at once than in *Milk Crown*, 1987 [56], Bolande's iconic rendition of Harold Edgerton's milk splash (captured

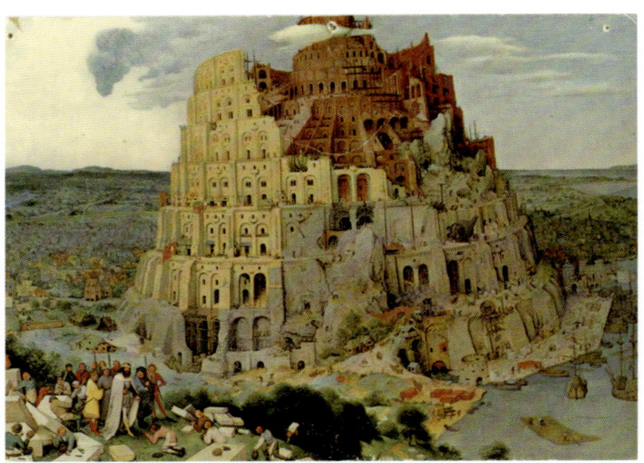

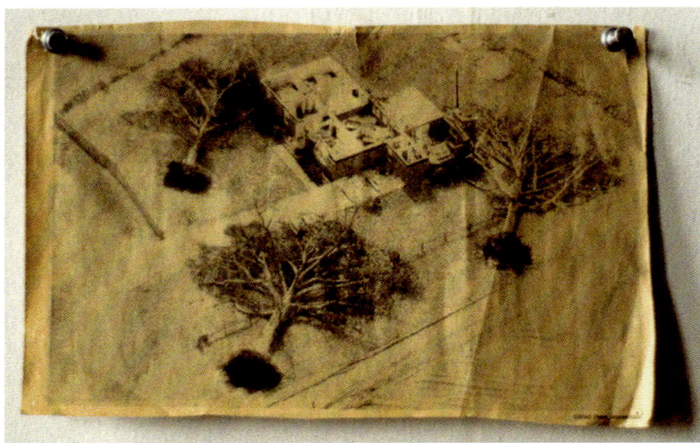

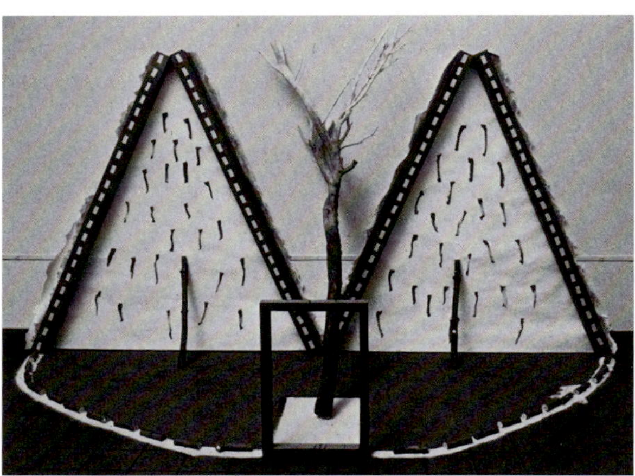

with a stroboscopic camera)[58] into a sculptural piece of porcelain. As a thing, photography takes many shapes in Bolande's work. There are framed and various forms of mounted photographs (mostly medium to small in scale), photo-objects, light-boxes, postcards. Photographs stand alone as iterative objects. In *Side Show*, 1991 [76], for instance, a photograph of a spotlight on a tent peg is so succinct a pictorial statement that there might as well be a spot lit tent peg in the room.

However, when photographs are assembled with other objects, their function appears to be more reiterative, underscoring that which surrounds them. *Conjunction Assemblage*, 1988 [38], is a wall relief composed of a refrigerator door with a Marshall-stack speaker on top of it, plus a framed photograph of the same. The photograph abuts the objects, like a weirdly flat echo. Alternatively, in *The Rounding of Corners*, 1991 [41], the pictorial content of the photograph appears enlarged by the objects that surround and modify it. A photo of a woman's torso cradled by shoulder pads is bracketed ([woman as object] [precious body] [this is what framing feels like]) by a beefy cardboard box of a frame that is packed at the corners with clumps of shoulder pads. The photograph in *Orange Threshold*, 1995 [67], of the back of a truck is perfectly parenthetical to the frame around it: both are orange and square.

A grammar takes shape around Bolande's use of photographs as subjects, objects, punctuation, verbs. This grammar leads us into a realm of language that is articulated by photography even when there are no photographs in sight. As if reaching for terms by which to understand it, photography has been known by its metaphors ever since its invention: "light writing," "light drawing," and most poetically, "the pencil of nature" as Henry Fox Talbot, one of photography's originators, defined the "character of truth and reality which that art so eminently possesses." Keeping these metaphors in mind, consider these works by Bolande: *Movie Mountain*, 2004 [75] is a photograph of props and objects in a constructed tableau, a sort of Philip Guston night studio, in which an anthropomorphic mountain poses in front of a blank screen, casting upon it the perfect shadow. The screen, in turn, casts its silhouette onto another screen, making for a double portrait of mountain and movie. Hence, one supposes, the title, since this

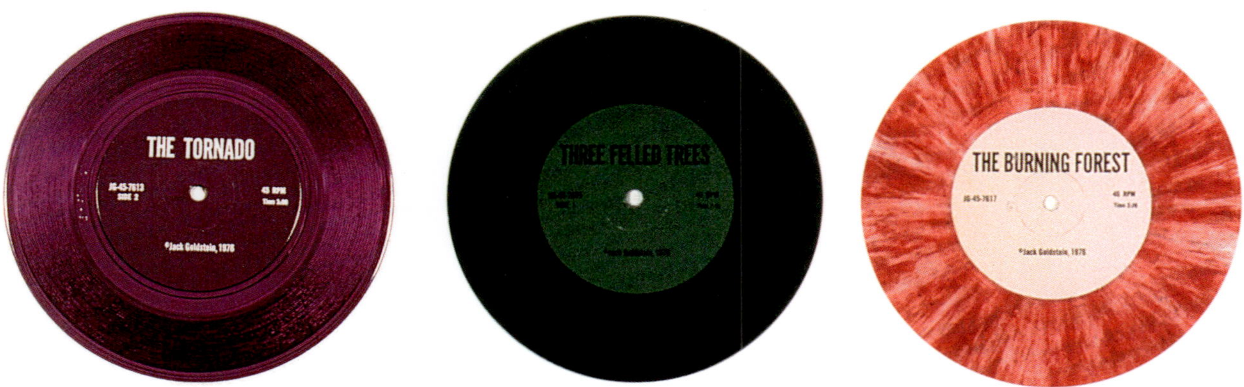

is no film. Nor, for that matter, is *Movie Chair*, 1984 [77]: a sculpture of a mountain plopped on a chair, posing under bright clip-on lights, the accoutrements of every photographer's studio. Bolande's art is ever encompassing of shadow plays and moving pictures, just as photography's history is bracketed by them.

Working like a postmodern Maid of Corinth, whose classical legend is to have made the first drawing when she traced her lover's shadow by lamplight, Bolande uses photography to draw and drawing as a kind of photography. *Central and Mountain*, 1985 [5], is a sculpture made from a big marching-band drum with a drawing on the skin. The drawing shows three mountaintops that seem to crouch, cautious and curious, in view of a mallet that is strapped to the drum, ready to strike. (This striking, of course, transpires in the mind's eye—or ear—where the thunder rolls around and around them there hills.) So where's the photography? Sepia in tone, soft to the eye, tentative yet certain in touch, the drawing can be seen as photographic in a pictorialist sort of way. More importantly, there is something about Bolande's drawings in general that makes them, like spirit photography, appear irrefutably part of the world as she sees it. They don't seem so much drawn as developed on paper.

Unlike a depiction or rendering, the drawing on the drum appears to be the thing itself. Because image and object are equivalent in Bolande's art, each is interchangeable when it comes to cobbling together and transmitting a sense of pictorial intelligence. To spark a similar gap, Alfred Stieglitz titled his small photographs of clouds "Equivalents" because he saw no difference between photograph, cloud, and their mutual capacities for experience and meaning. Another Modernist, Edward Weston, deemed it

photography's goal "to render the very substance and quintessence of the thing itself, whether it be polished steel or palpitating flesh." Temperamentally on the cool side, Bolande once made a series of photographs that study her hand and its reflection flatly hovering over an aluminum elevator door.

This photographic notion of "the thing itself" seems key to the simultaneously straightforward and elliptical nature of Bolande's work. As she told the artist David Robbins in an interview, "I study things over time, sometimes for years, to understand what it is, and what its attraction is for me."[1] Accruing over decades, these things have been theater curtains, movie marquees, mountains, globes, speakers, microphones, flags, pictures of the planet Mars, the moon, tornadoes, smoke. And while each subject yields a specific understanding that can only be gleaned from the individual work, collectively they may be understood as follows. Abstracted from the sphere of the public domain—which is her elected terrain— Bolande's things all seem to evoke a sense of encroaching obsolescence. Whether it's due to technology, the weather, the end of the space race, or beginning of a new global era, this vision of things falling under scrutiny even as they fall from view is as emphatic as touch in Bolande's art. She works in order to grasp her own understanding and in the process creates a gulf in comprehension, a gulf filled with such intensely focused time and study that it is as sublime to behold as the reach across any great distance.

Everything is touched in a photograph: touched by light. This is what makes a photograph an indexical object, a conceptual proof of something that is not really there. Like the sound of that bass drum, for instance, and sound in general, Bolande's

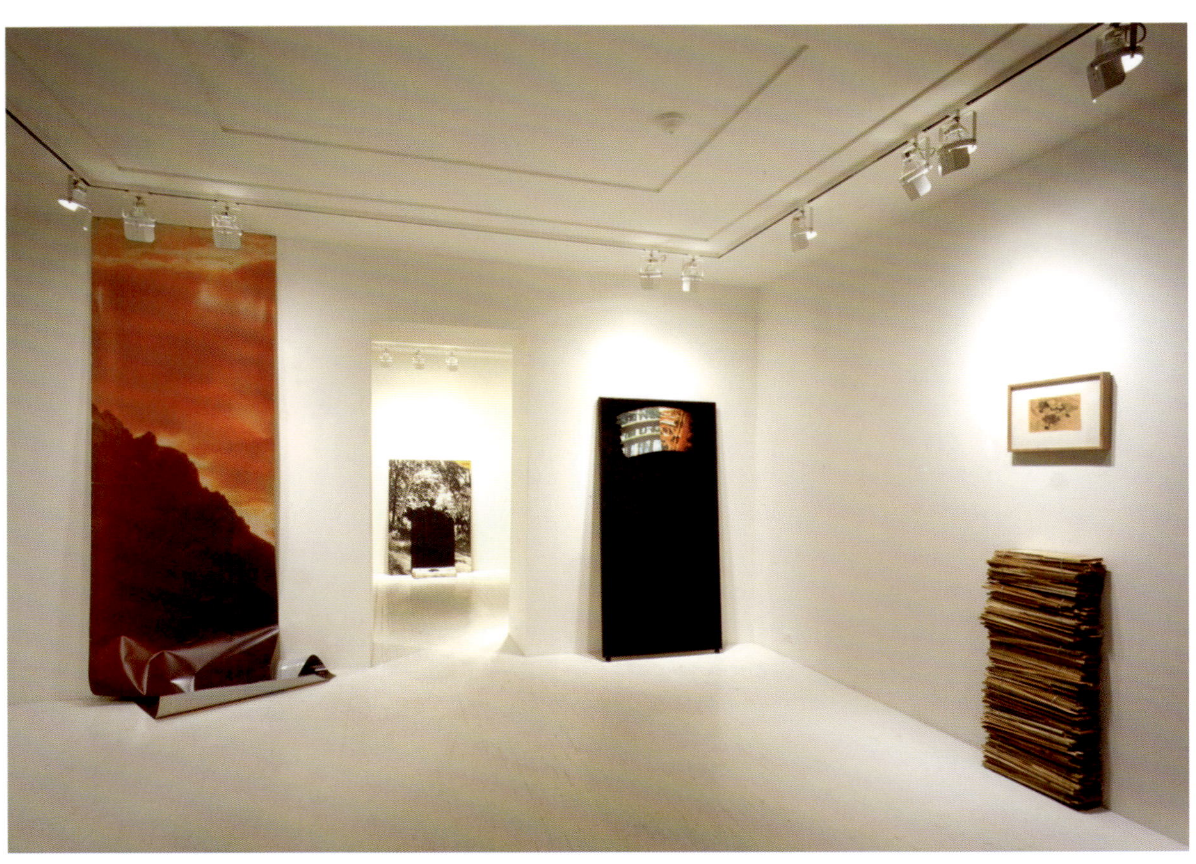

[86] Installation view: Robbin Lockett Gallery, Chicago, 1987

work is filled with images and objects that make noise or amplify. The opposite of symbolic, indexes embody. And so does Bolande, who comes to art by way of choreography and dance, seek to embody forms of understanding through her work. Thus I have come to see her index of circling and conical things— traffic cones, tornadoes, cones of light (which could also be cones of sound, sight), *Milk Crown*, skydivers holding hands to form a circle in the air—as funneling the power of concentration, which is also essentially invisible and yet profoundly physical.

Bolande's work is also consistently filled with apertures and chambers; these loom as empty as the darkroom, the negative, the camera obscura of photography itself. Take for instance, the five gaping big-rig truck beds in *Holding Pattern*, 1995 [63] (a masterful piece of semi choreography, conducted in a parking lot); the open van and manhole in *Held Open Space*, 1991 [66]; the filmic frames of *Green Towel Sequence #1*, 2004 [7]; the filmstrip construction of *Appliance House*, 1999 [20]. Each chamber stands ready to be filled, like the slots in an empty slide carousel, or the frames of an incipient picture collection.

Turning from the exhibition *Landmarks* to this book, one finds clues throughout as to what pictures might be slotted into these chambers. Bolande has already inserted a few. Spotted amidst the flow of her own works of art, these pictures signal various uses. There are historic paintings as pictorial points of reference: Bruegel's *Tower of Babel*, 1563, [82] with its craggy profile and Magritte's *Time Transfixed*, 1938 [10] (the original title of which, *La Durée Poignardée,* or "time stabbed by a dagger," resonates disturbingly with Bolande's embodied sense of language). A postcard of Times Square [106] and NASA footage [9] appear as source material. Finally, nothing less than commemorative of an artist she knew and deeply regarded is a picture of a set of 45-record albums [85] by the conceptual artist Jack Goldstein, who died in 2003. Of the night they met in 1976 (at a performance by Jack Smith who threatened that he had to mount a mess of slides on stage before he would begin), Bolande, who was deeply immersed in performance and questing her way through the downtown scene, wrote, "That night changed my life. I knew what was possible and I was inspired to be an artist."[2] She describes going back to Goldstein's studio and seeing his looping 2-minute film *Metro-Goldwyn-Meyer*, 1975, in which the appropriated lion logo grew stranger,

more detailed, and finally by Bolande's estimation, "irretrievably suspect" with each repetition. He gave her a set of records, since lost; represented in this book, they appear to hold a key place in Bolande's picture archive. (Just read the titles: *The Tornado, Three Felled Trees, The Burning Forest.*) Another artist, whose work Bolande memorably encountered in her early days in New York is the sculptor Ree Morton; her untitled assemblage of 1972 maps emblems of mountains into just the sort of theatrical terrain that Bolande has come to so readily inhabit.

Like most contemporary artists, Bolande speaks of photography as a tool. "Photography is generally my first line of approach to any subject," she recently wrote in *Artforum.*[3] And while making photographs is not her object—Bolande actually considers herself a sculptor—the language of photography has proved instrumental to the understanding of her work. This understanding, in turn, grants one a great deal of fluency in the bigger conversation emerging around photography today. Significant expressions of which can be engaged through work of such artists as Trisha Donnelly and Erin Shirreff, as well as *The Original Copy: Photography of Sculpture, 1839 to Today,*[4] a recent survey at the Museum of Modern Art, New York. All expound on photography's language as we have gotten to know it through Bolande's art. Her work also shows us that, no less vital for being already partially dead, this language grows increasingly historical, critical, and expressive with each new entry into the digital lexicon. Of all the obsolescent things that Bolande's art points to, photography is the most paradoxical. Even as the thing itself vanishes, the language remains rich and widely spoken.

This essay synthesizes and builds on two past curatorial projects, Constructing Images *(1991) and* The Photogenic *(2002). Both group shows featured work by Bolande, whose work continues to shape my own.*

1. Robbins, David and Bolande, Jennifer, "A Conversation..." *Milwaukee Journal Sentinel*, May 25, 2010.

2. Bolande, J., "Remembering Jack Goldstein," *Afterall* #7, Spring/Summer 2003, republished on June 30th, 2011, www.EastofBorneo.org.

3. Bolande, Jennifer, "Jennifer Bolande Talks About Plywood Curtains," *Artforum*, New York, Vol. XLIX, No. 3 (November 2010), pp. 210–213.

4. *The Original Copy: Photography of Sculpture, 1839 to Today,* curator Roxana Marcoci, took place at the Museum of Modern Art (MoMA), New York, August 1–November 1, 2010.

[87] *Globe Sightings: St. Mark's Place, NYC*, 2000

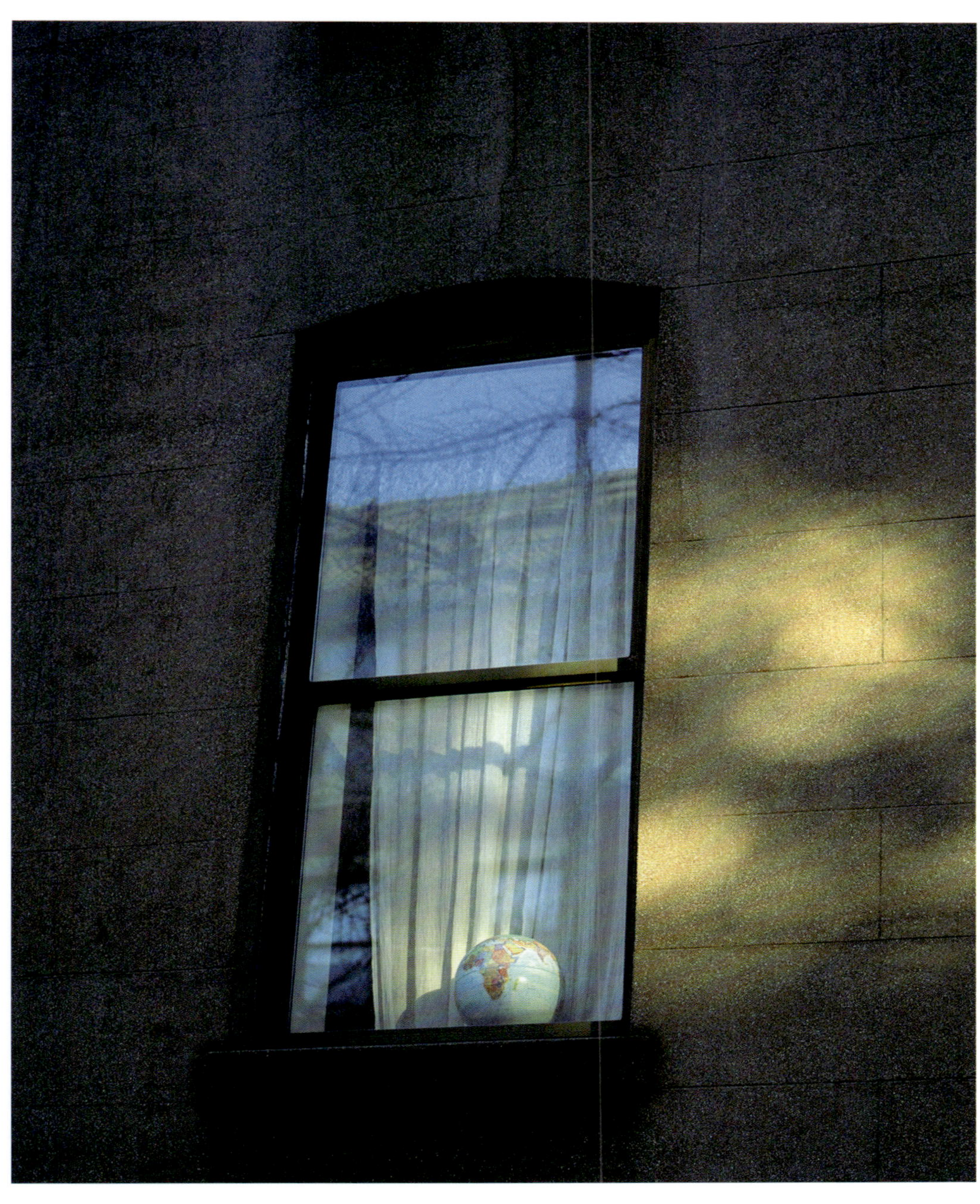

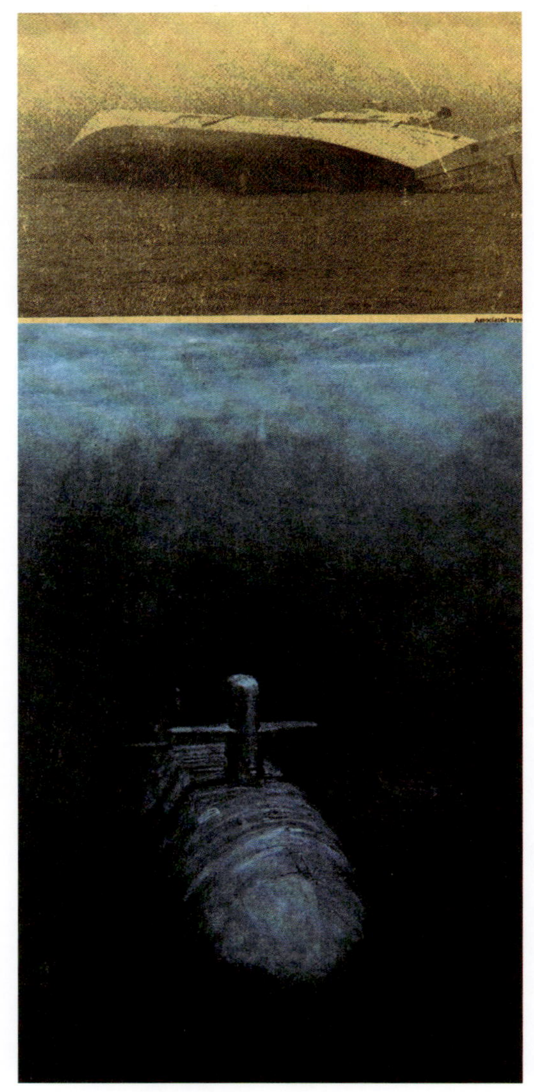

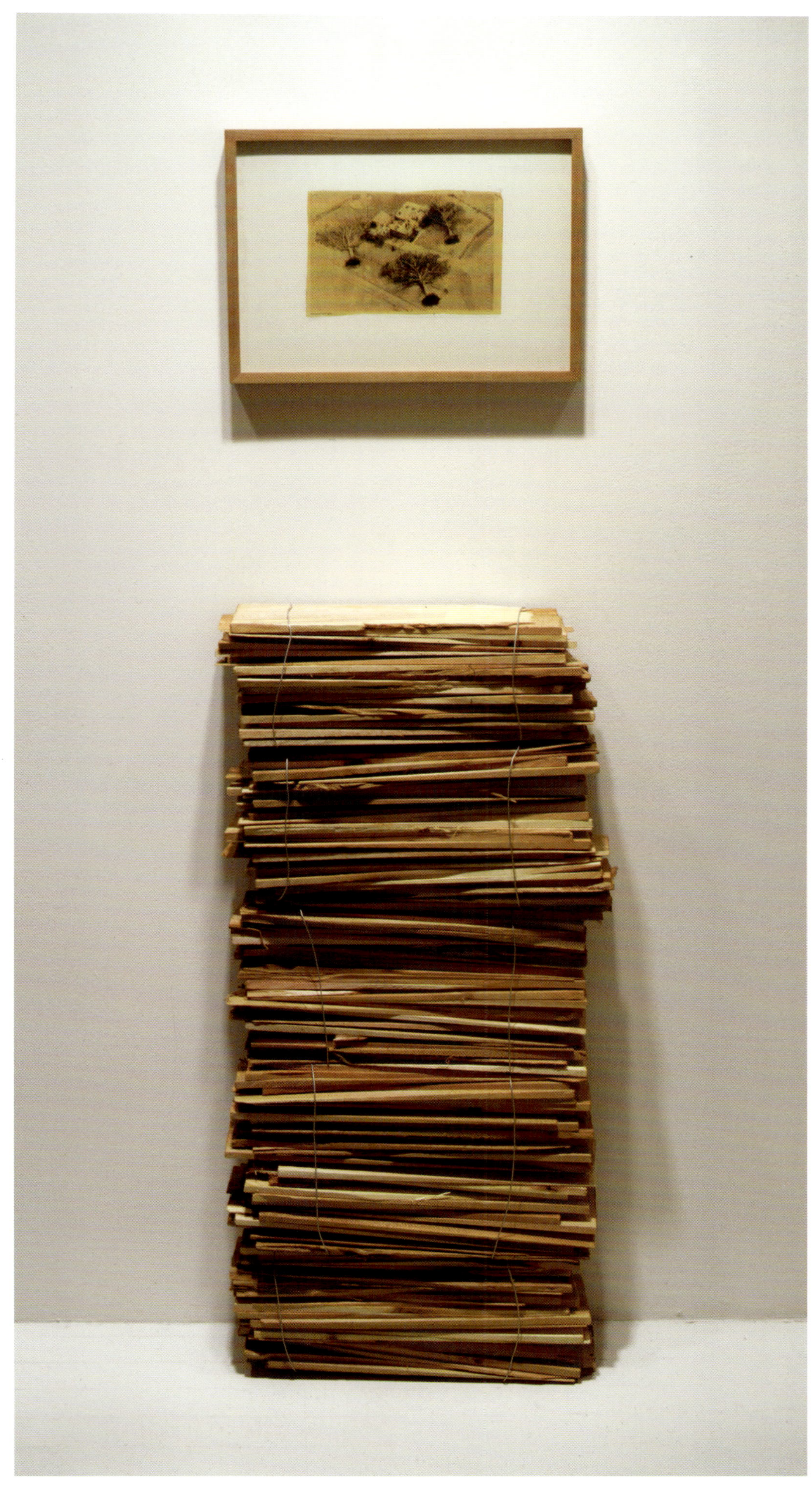

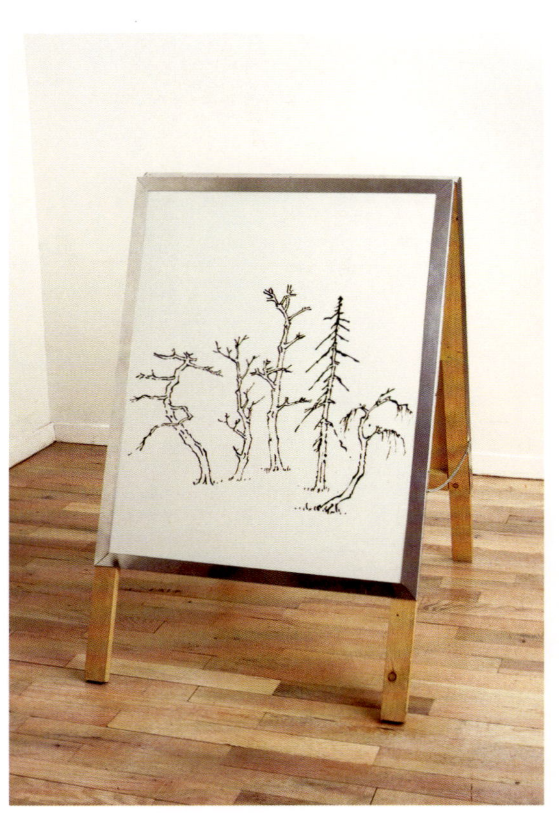

[90] Sandwich Board, 1983

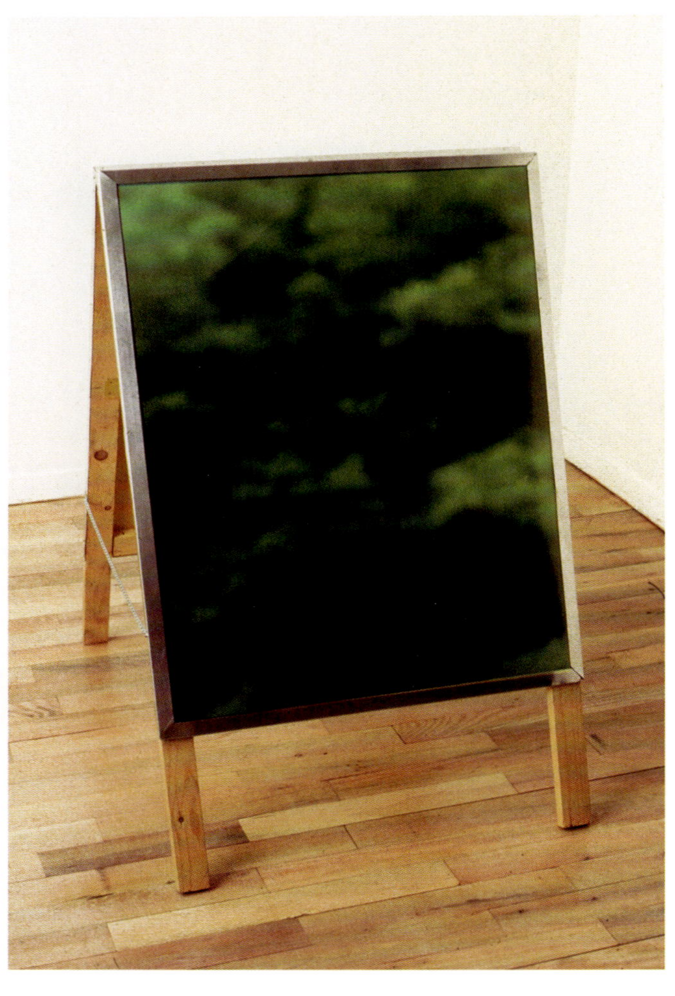

[91] Smoke and Snow, 2010

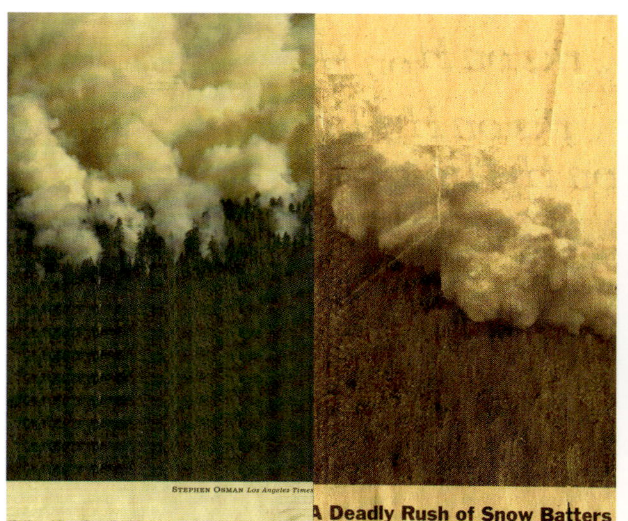

STEPHEN OSMAN *Los Angeles Times*

*National Forest south of Lockwood Valley. The nearly
and continues to grow.*

A Deadly Rush of Snow Batters

An avalanche swept through forests near
Evolène, Switzerland, yesterday, killing

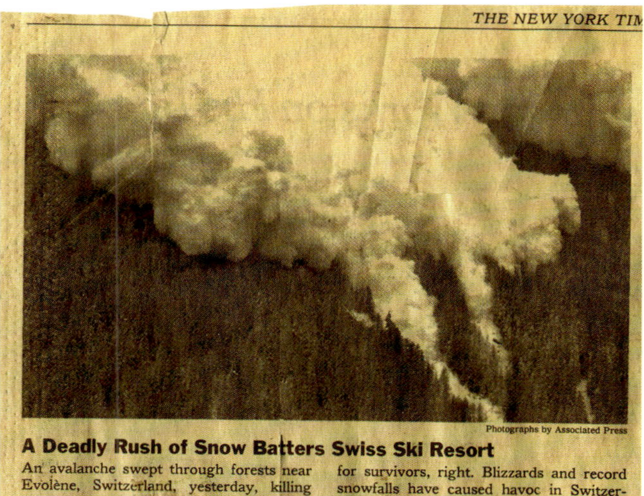

Photographs by Associated Press

A Deadly Rush of Snow Batters Swiss Ski Resort

An avalanche swept through forests near
Evolène, Switzerland, yesterday, killing
two people at th   ort, in Valais Canton,
on the south fac   he Alps. Workers dug
for survivors, right. Blizzards and record
snowfalls have caused havoc in Switzerland,   France and in Austria, where
20,000 tourists are trapped in ski resorts.

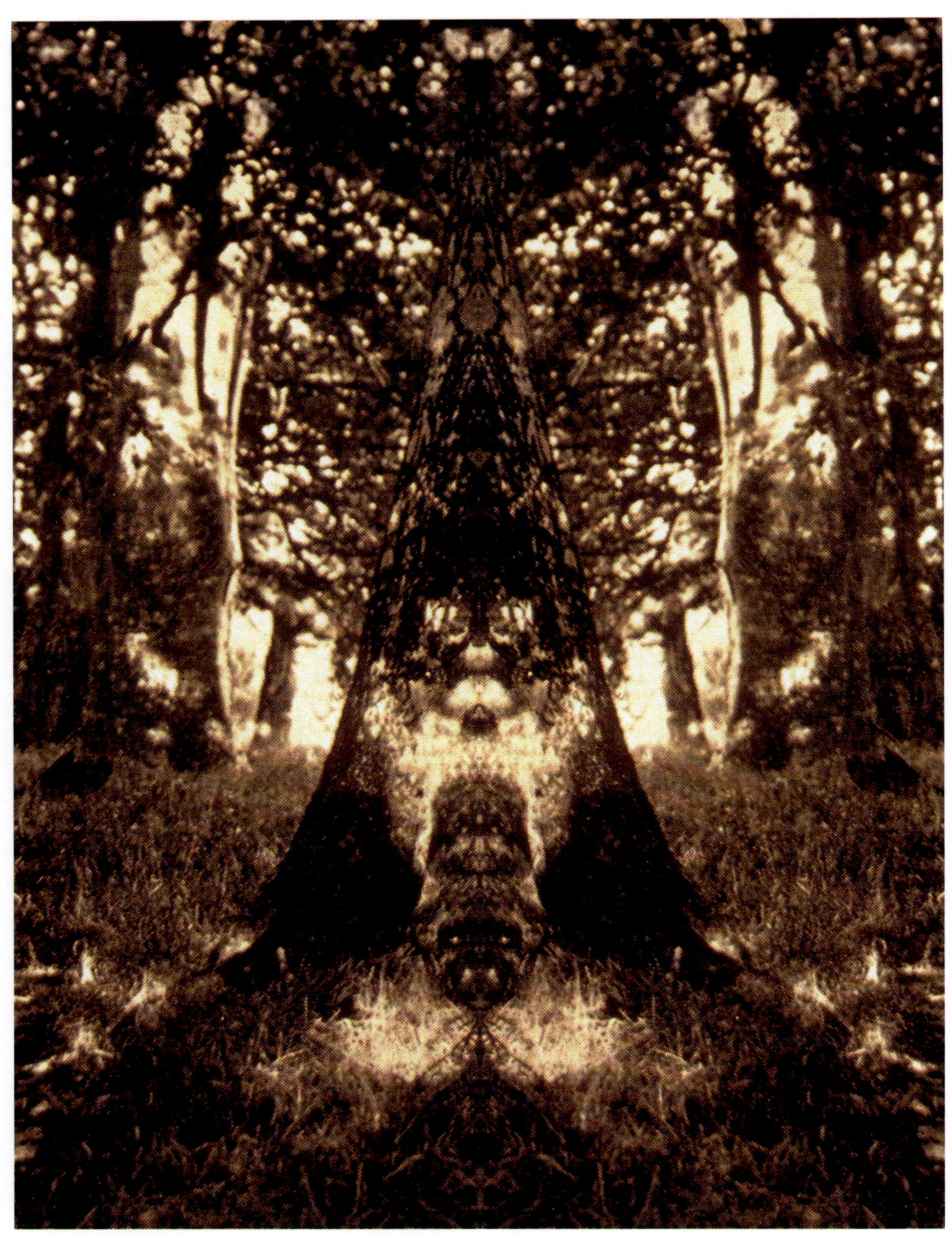

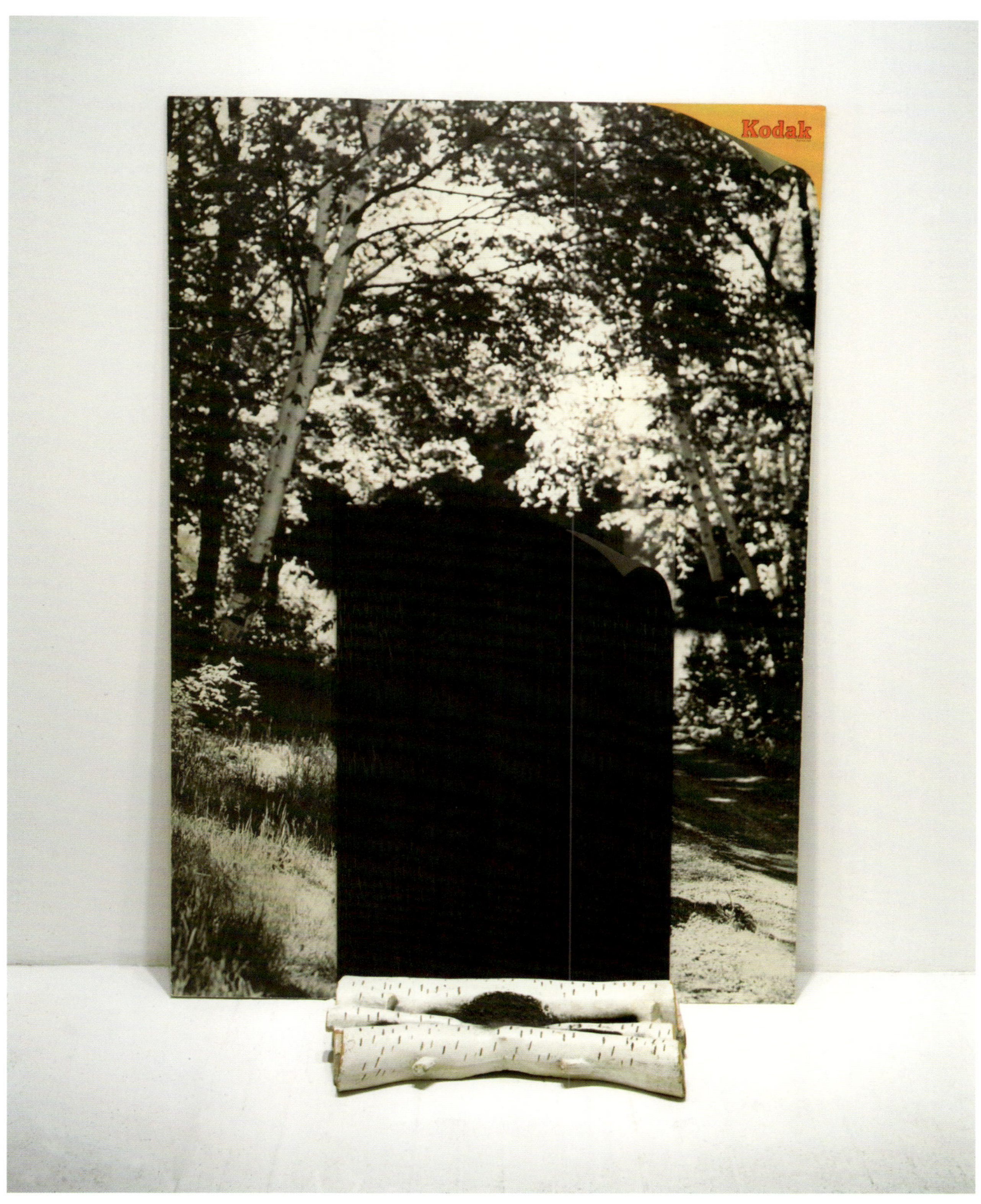

Kodak

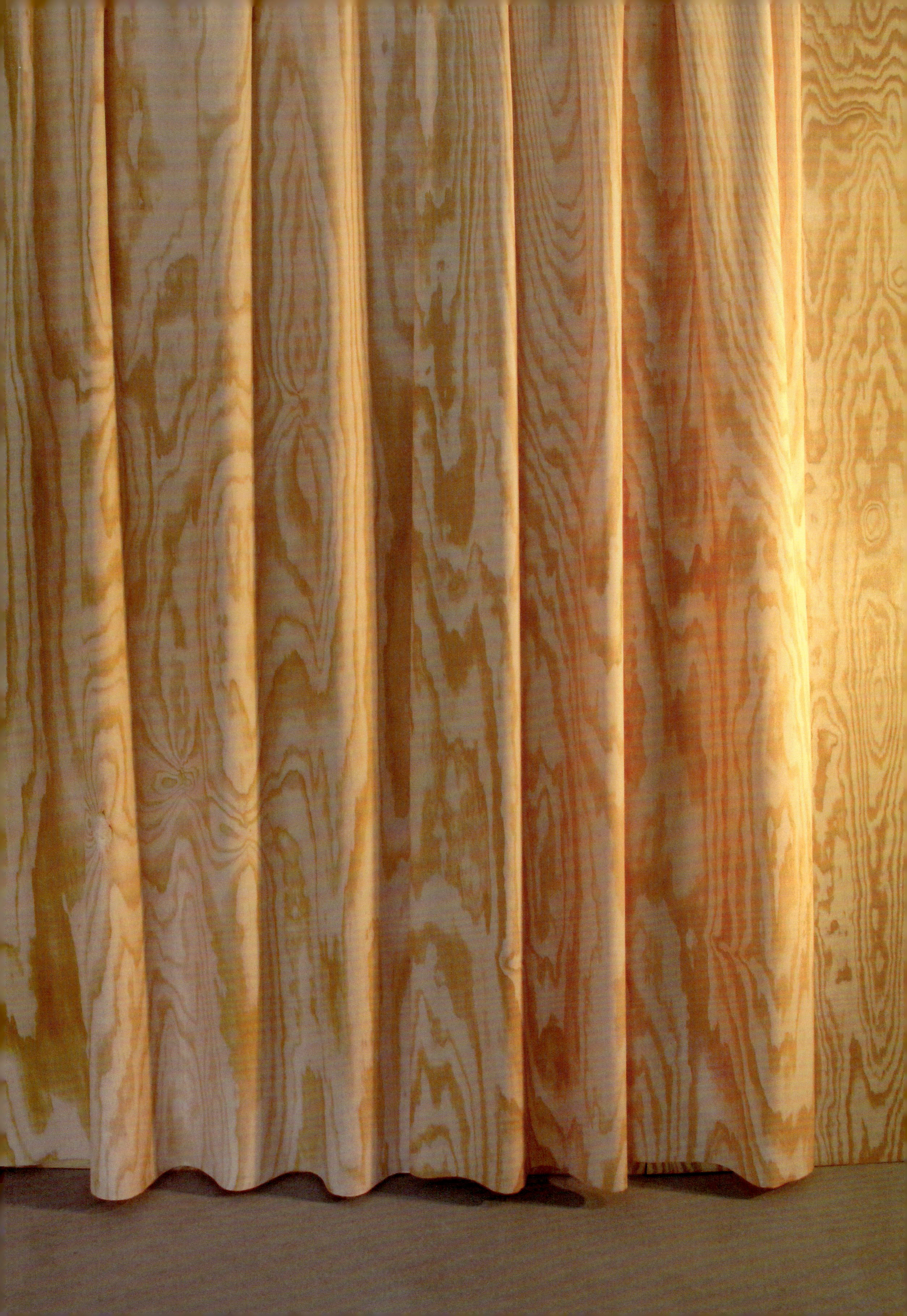

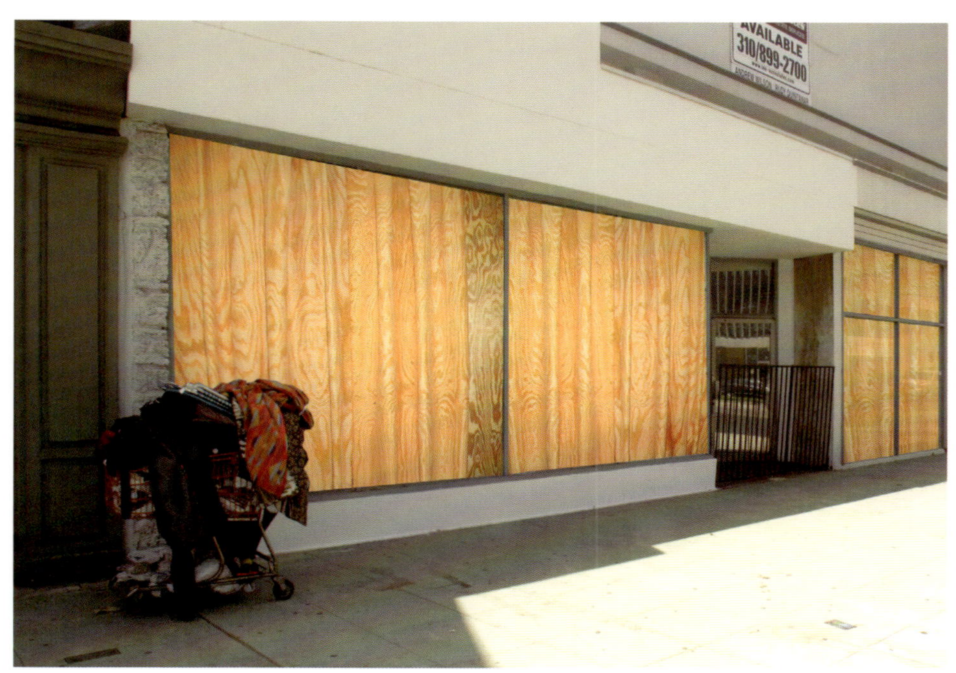

[94] detail: *Plywood Curtains*, 2008   [95] *Plywood Curtains with Shopping Cart, Wilshire Blvd.*, 2009

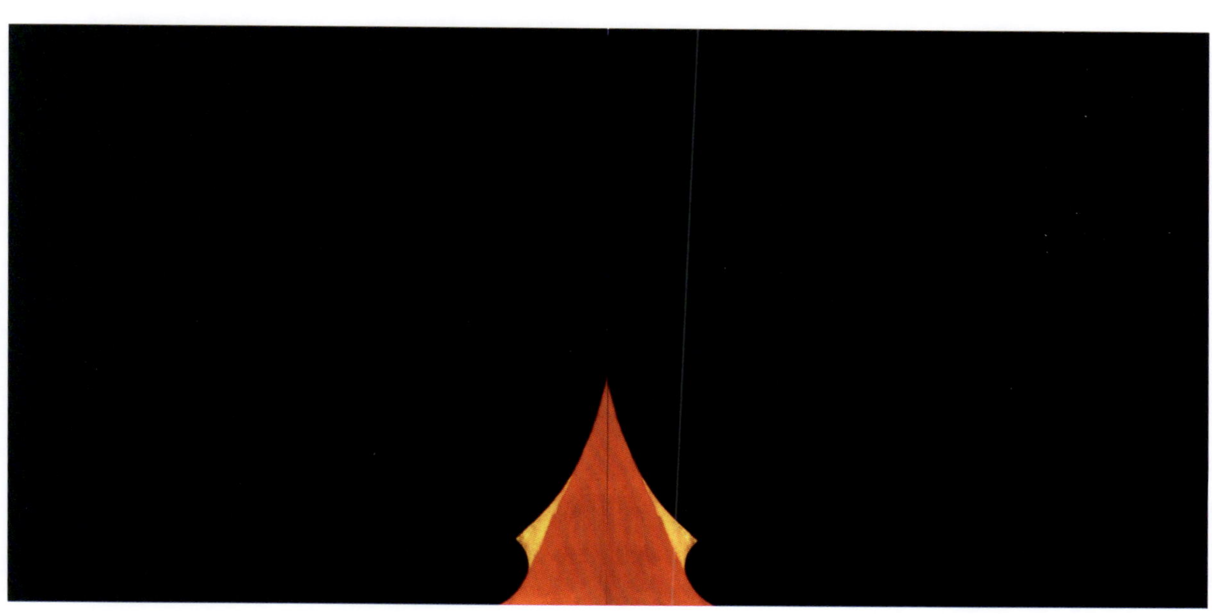

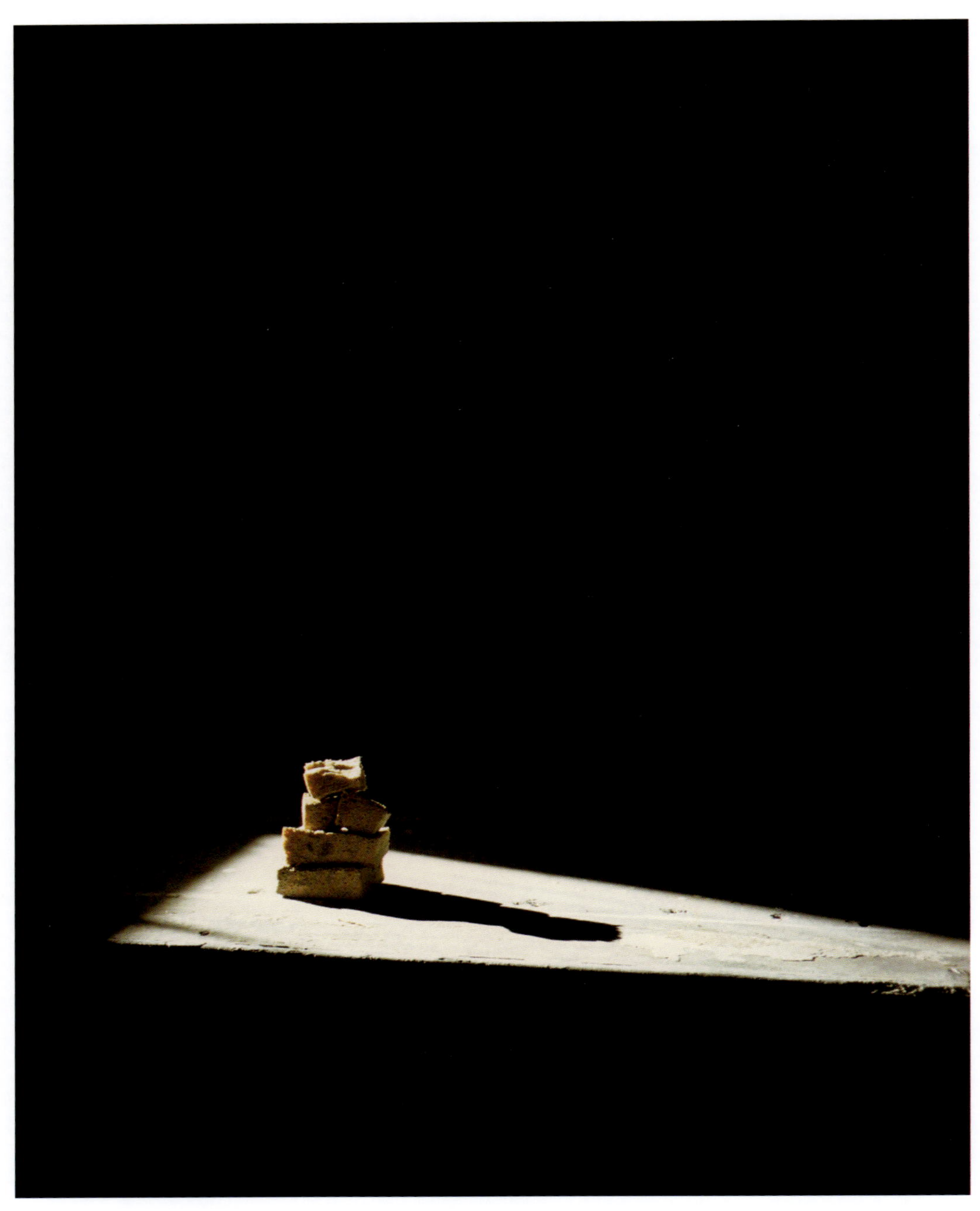

NICHOLAS FRANK

CONCENTRATED SPACE

... the difference between something and nothing is nothing...
—Paul Bowles

Existential contemplation of the vastness around us, by which I refer to the utter cold and dark abyss of endless space, has not been much in fashion lately. We're all far too busy attending to our own affairs to much wonder on the smallness of our existence. Away from the lights of cities, intrepid voyagers will certainly gaze up at the night sky, hoping to catch a glimpse of a shooting star or two, but without really recognizing that they're witnessing the fiery end of some anonymous scrap of cosmic debris, evaporated by contact with the thin cover of Earth's atmosphere after what might have been a journey of many millions of years. To us unconcerned with the details, the atmosphere isn't particularly thick or thin, it's invisible. In his masterwork *The Sheltering Sky*, Paul Bowles saw the sky as an impossibly fragile membrane, barely separating us from the crushing void surrounding us, providing us with at best a temporary shelter from the incomprehensible storm of the universe. But Bowles wasn't concerned with supernovae, black holes and other violent cosmological phenomena, he was thinking about scale.

Witness the stack of sponges in one of the photographic diptychs comprising Jennifer Bolande's 2010 series *Space Photography* [97]. Really only small sponge-pieces, the stack sits forlornly alone within a vast space that has the empty feel of an attic. A triangle of bright sunlight illuminates the tiny stack, simultaneously exposing it and the universe outside. Its little shadow stretches out on the dusty floor, as if portending the spectre of eternal rest. Paired, as it is in one particular

diptych (images are repeated and paired differently among the various diptychs), with the reflection of a semicircle of window-framed sunlighton a mirror, the piece takes on the "cuspy" tone Bolande is so expert at generating. In her work, things are always teetering on the point of their disappearance or dissipation, but forever stuck by the peculiar permanence of photography in an intractable state of immortality. The present is a fragile, transitory condition that defies reflection and denies its temporal context. This concordance of fragilities—of events, of images, of memory, and, most tellingly, of photographic scale—is where Bolande's work begins.

The Globe Sightings photographs (c. 2000–2001) are the product of chance encounters with a fading relic of our educational past, the spherical-map globe.[1] An effort to give at least some accurate-to-scale sense of the world's shape and continental dimensions, globes are being made obsolescent by screen-based digital maps that give us access to nearly every corner of the "real" globe, with alternate map and satellite views, street views and dimensional renderings. The world has, somewhat ironically, been re-flattened. No simple case of video killing the radio star, as both the spherical globe and the Google map are virtual renderings, but the *vérité* of one species of rendering has clearly supplanted the earlier one. Photography has triumphed over the object. However, Bolande points out that in a sense—in her sense—maps are really another kind of photographic rendering.

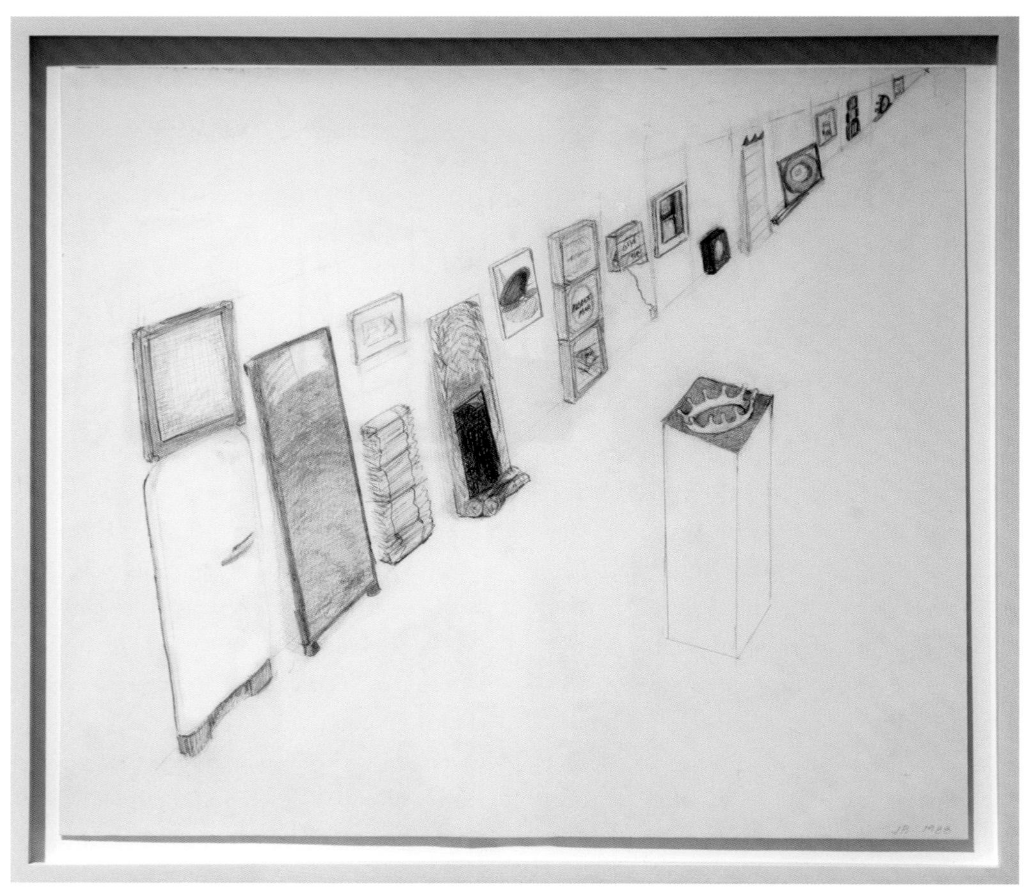

[98] *Retroperspective*, 1988

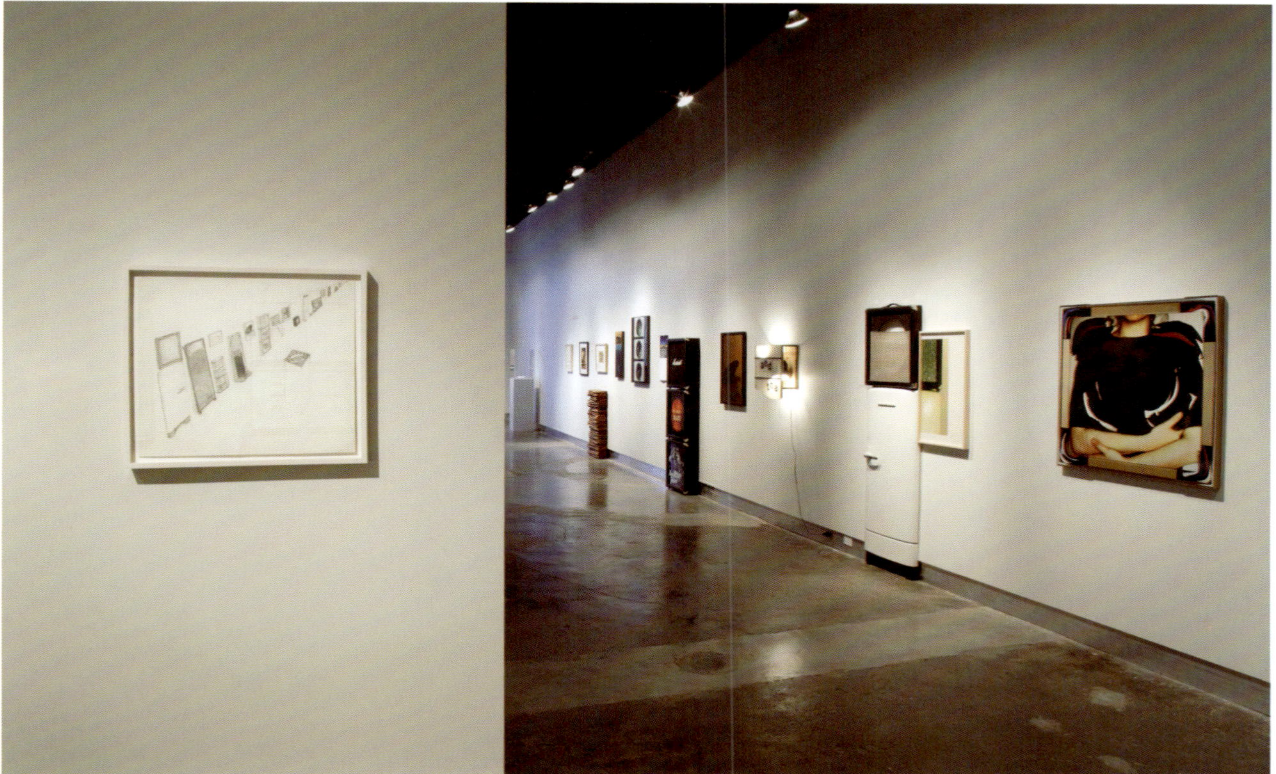

Ever sensitive to the cultural processing of images, Bolande communicates the phenomenon by photographing it. Her globes are seen through the windows of classrooms, apartments, and stores, captured from the natural distance of a wandering photographer pointing her camera here and there. For me, the most affecting of the series is *Globe Sightings: Stonehouse Road, Bloomfield NJ,* 2000 [101]. A red-brick two-story school occupies the image, fronted by a tidy, trim-treed lawn. Shades are pulled down in each of the sixteen visible windows, and in one first-story center window we see the unmistakable sea-blue color of a school globe peeking out. Bolande positions us at her camera's viewpoint, within the shot, and simultaneously in the more traditional role of viewers of her photograph, outside the frame. It is her particular skill to call forth the history of images with a single gesture, and in this case we are reminded of the famous Moonrise shot, the first view of Earth from the firma of another heavenly body, notable for its depiction of our lonely fragility within the vastness of space. There the *Stonehouse Road* globe sits, alone in its own dark void, perhaps aware of its impending obsolescence (as the artist surely is). Uncannily, we are inhabitants of the real globe and the fake one, observers of ourselves, like the astronauts peering down on the whole of humanity and its history, which will all, too, expire, along with the schoolhouse globe.

The wall-sculpture *Topology House,* 2002 [100], collects the various "globe sightings" photographs into one assemblage. Multiple photographic perspectives converge, lending the sculpture its oddly angled architecture. Each section is the size and shape of the windows framing the globes, so it is a glass house, the kind you don't want to throw stones at. Our real "globe" is our house, and we needn't look far to be reminded that more threatens its stability than asteroids being flung our way (though that certainly worries some people, too). The idea of a global map as a kind of collective self-portrait is amplified, even exponentially multiplied, as so many perspectives are bumped up against each other. The piece is also a rare, actual self-portrait: there Bolande peers out, visible in the curvature of an oculus hanging alongside a globe in a store window. She's looking at herself in the mirror and at us through the photograph at the same time. The store reads as a second-hand or antiques dealer, whose sole purpose is to defy and amplify obsolescence in the same gesture. These multiple ironies cannot escape Bolande's attendant gaze, which in keeping with the concordance of contradictions, is at once coolly detached and warmly considerate.

There are yet further layers. For instance, she conflates the globes-within-windowed-rooms with the camera's box, also a dark, walled interior with a glass aperture that lets in light and renders the visible. The rewards of Bolande's work reveal themselves dimension upon dimension, and there is a clear reason why a mere two will not contain the scope of her ideas.

Jennifer Bolande Landmarks finally allows us to see these things all together in one room.[2] The artist and I worked closely over a year and a half to choose photographs and sculptures for their representative stature within her body of work, and for their remarkable thematic consistency over time. Pieces were arranged to build time-bending resonances throughout the installation. At Inova, the flagpoles in a *Space Photography* diptych [78] were hung directly across from *9-foot Pole,* 1989 [102], reflecting and refracting its position within her constellation of concerns. Set near *9-foot Pole,* the *Central and Mountain,* 1985 [5] bass drum boomed with currency, in the room and also in a photograph paired with a globe and those diptych flagpoles. Inova's 70-foot-long wall afforded us the opportunity to realize in three dimensions the funny *Retroperspective* drawing of 1988 [98], a charmingly sketchy rendering of important pieces from the artist's body of work to date, lined up along a single wall and vanishing off into single-point perspective in the far distance. (That far distance from 1988 is, of course, now.)

Throughout the exhibition, past, present and future converged, and in doing so complicated and confused such time-based distinctions with a multiplexity of simultaneities and directions. No nostalgiac, Bolande refuses to let the past settle into a comfort zone of easy definability. She wants the older works to remain firmly in the present, even as that present slides along from year to year. A curator's goals align with this intent. This would be only one element of her work, but I am convinced that the artist has knowingly constructed a picture of the entire process of what it is to think, to make art, to show it, to see the work go out into the world to multiply and comment on itself and become the subject of commentary, to be brought back together in a gesture of solidarity and contemplation, and to have its relevance measured and re-measured again and again as it and its maker proceed towards history. Even before *Retroperspective,* I think she knew this was coming.

1. *The Globe Sightings* series is comprised of over 200 photographs taken at various locations in cities around the world (which adds layers to the 'global' concerns of the subject).

2. The exhibition title is itself an echo of Bolande's first New York solo show, at The Kitchen, in 1982, titled *Landmarks.*

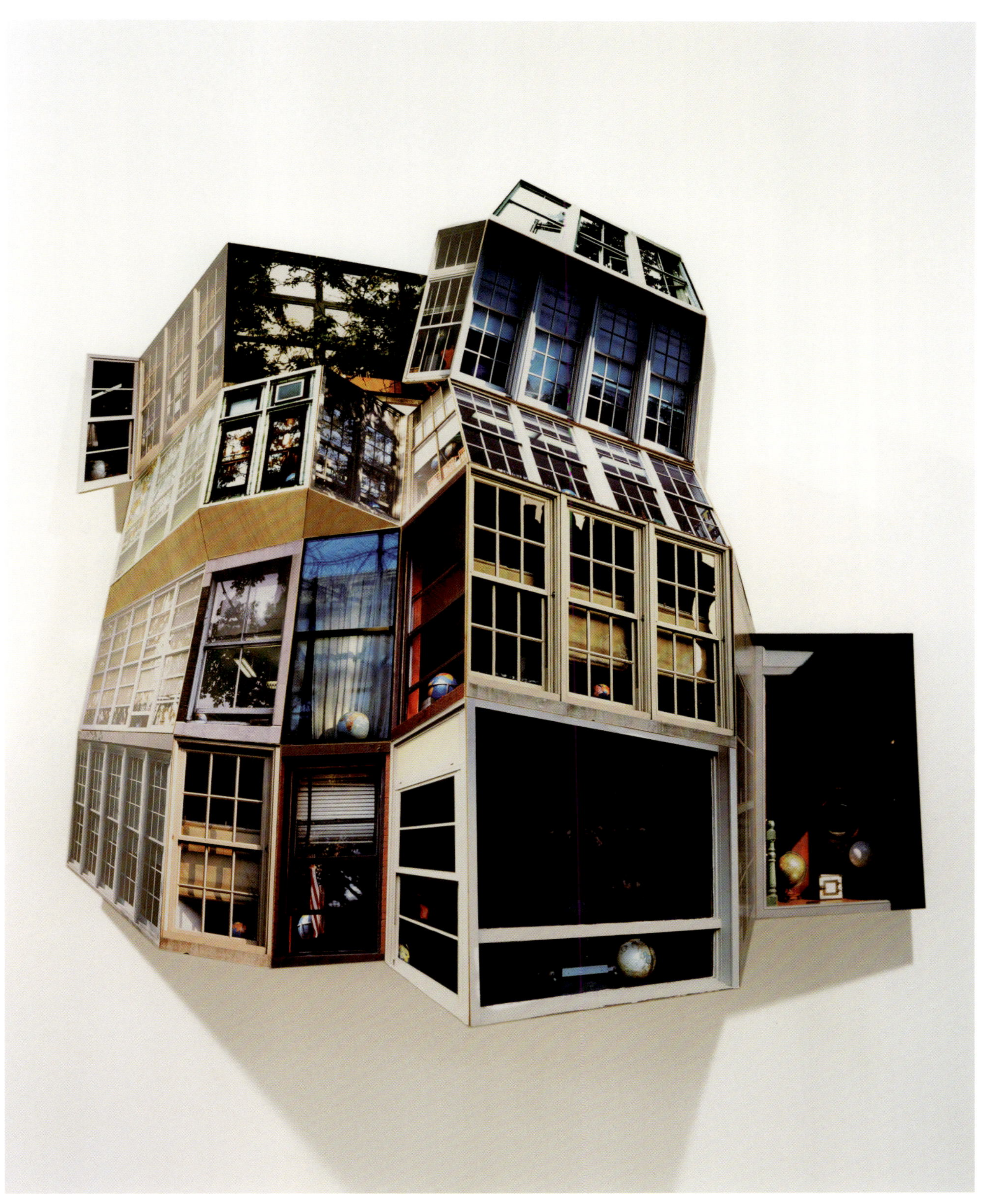

[100] *Topology House*, 2002   133

[101] *Globe Sightings: Stonehouse Road, Bloomfield, New Jersey, 2000*

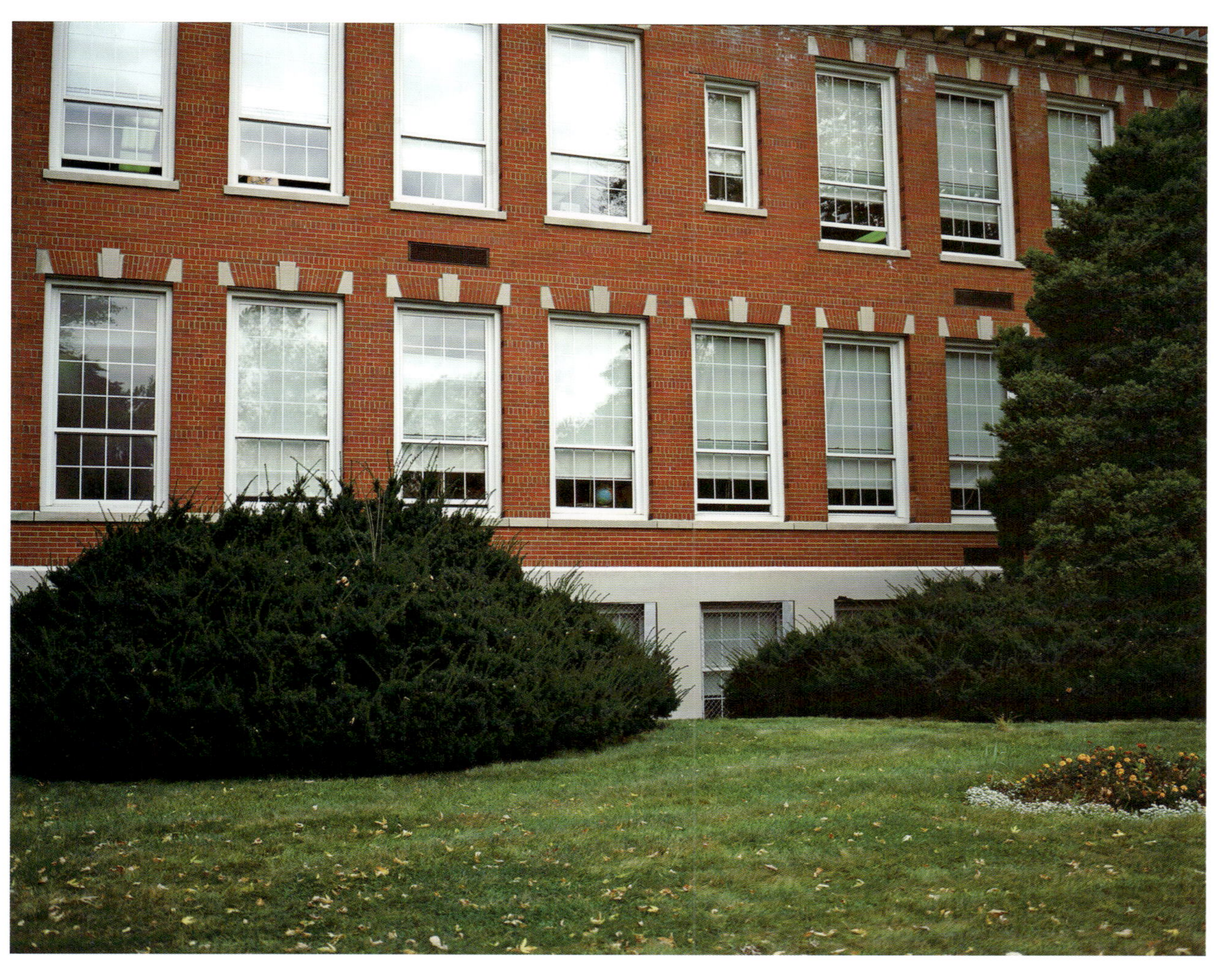

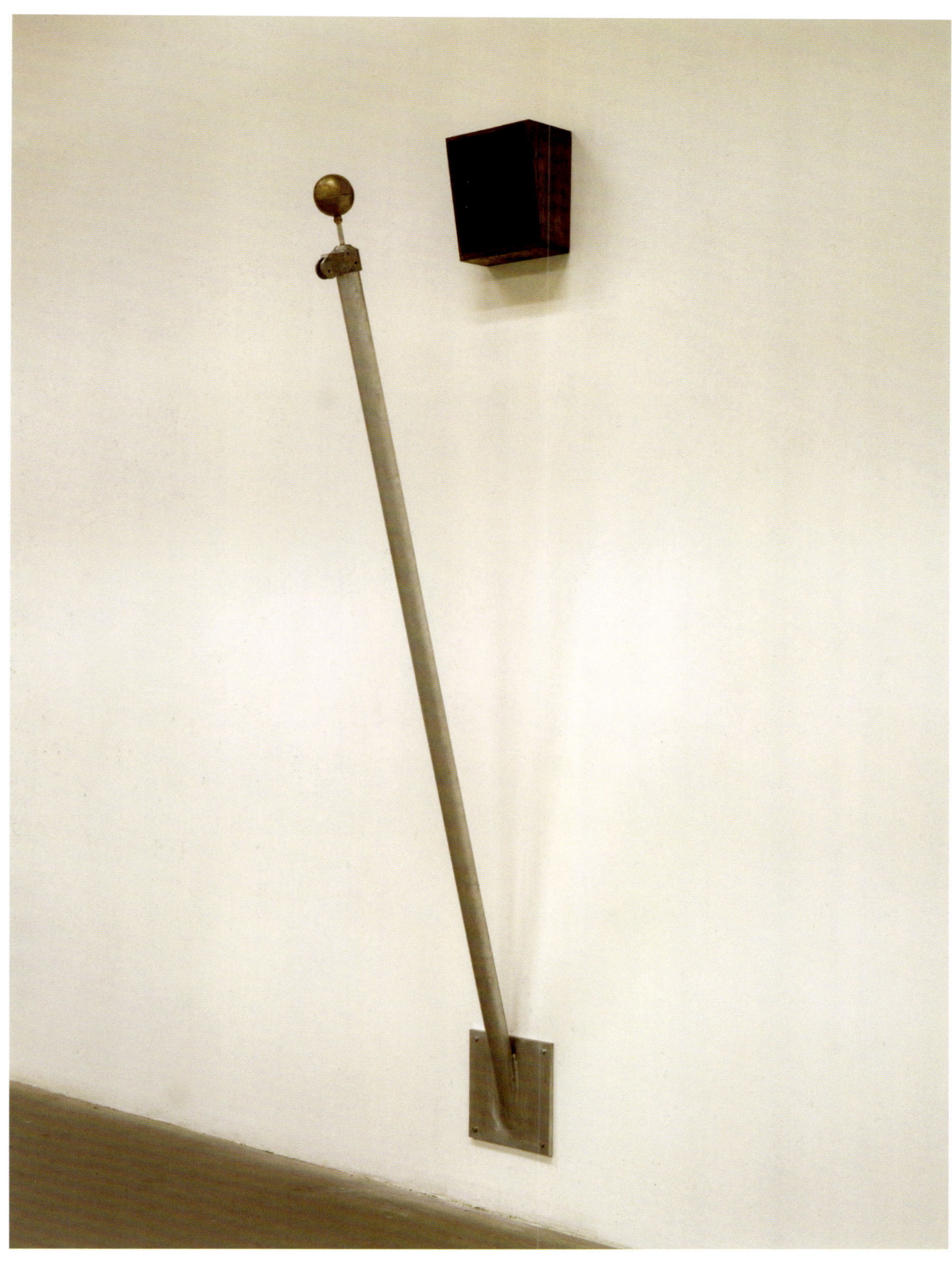

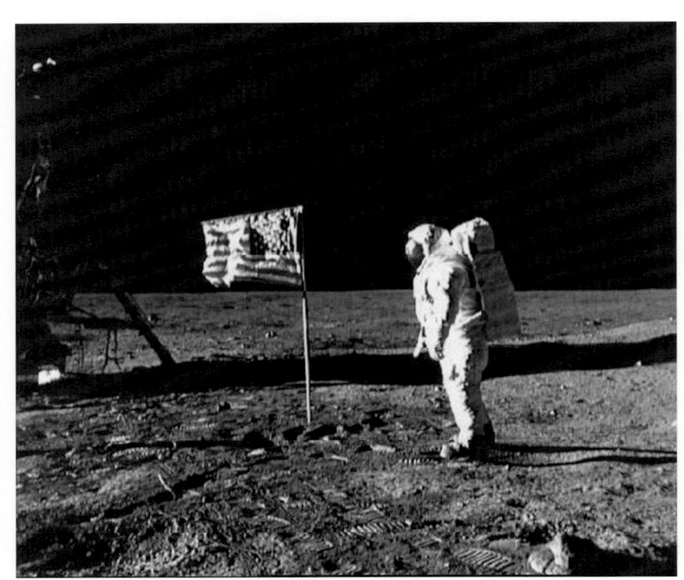

[103] reference: *Buzz Aldrin and the U.S. flag on the Moon*, 1969

[104] *Flagship Episode*, 1985

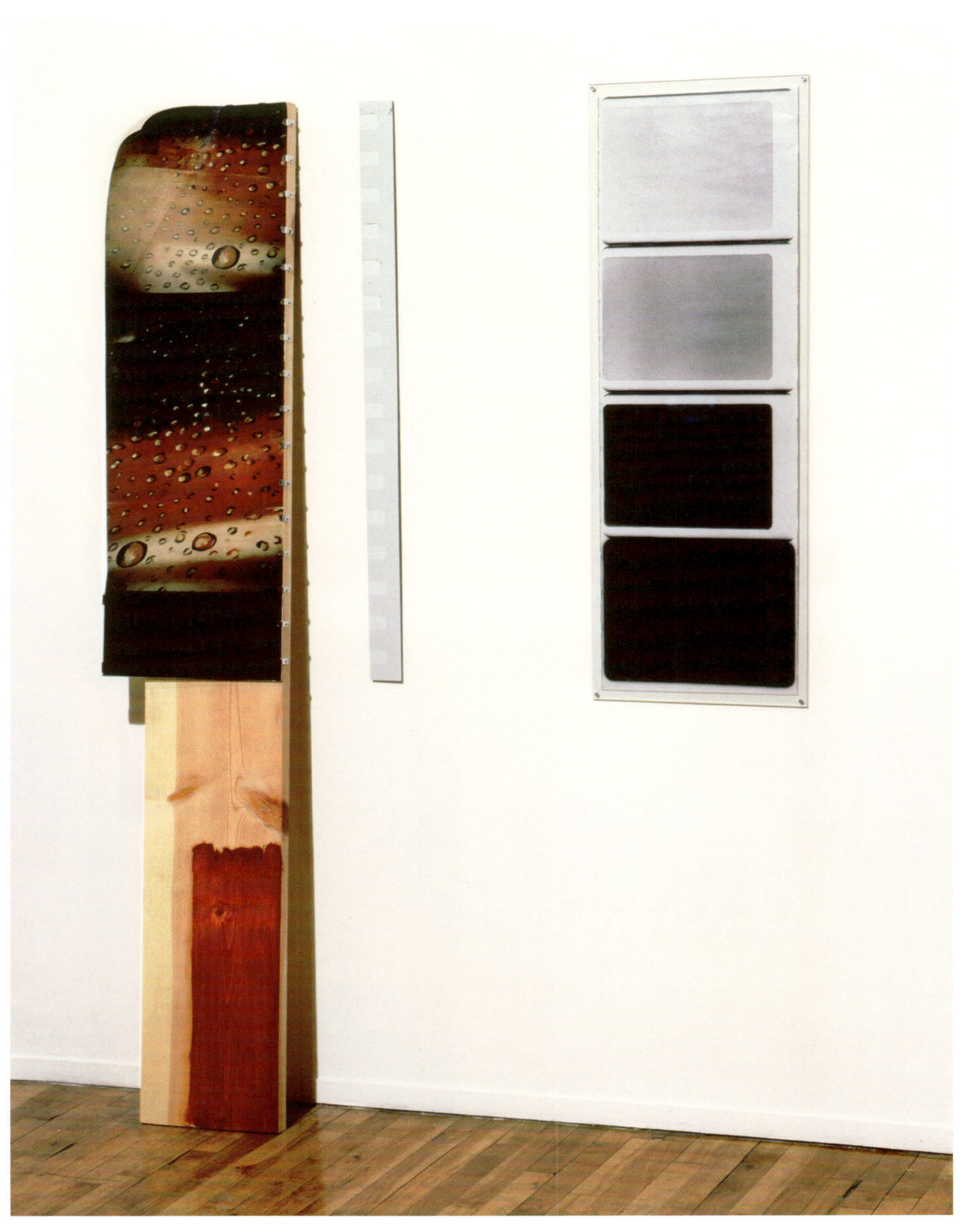

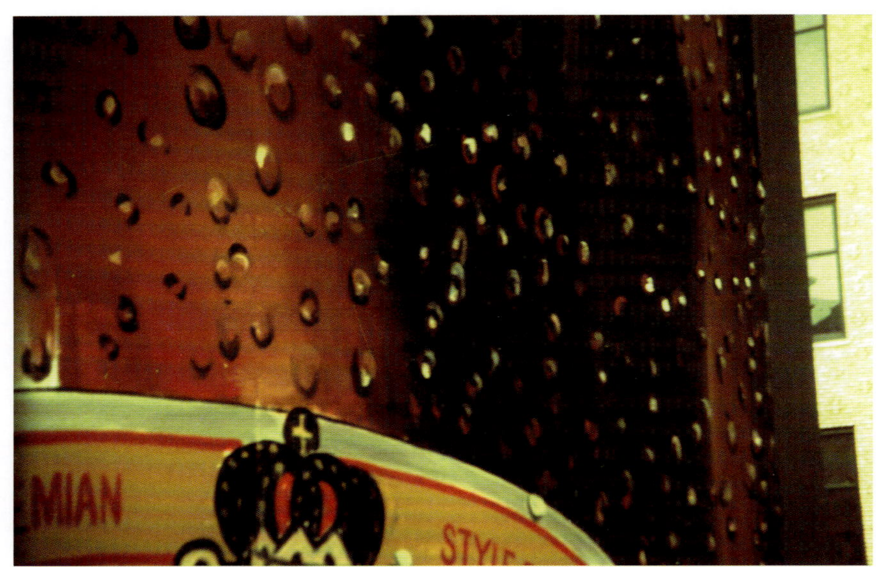

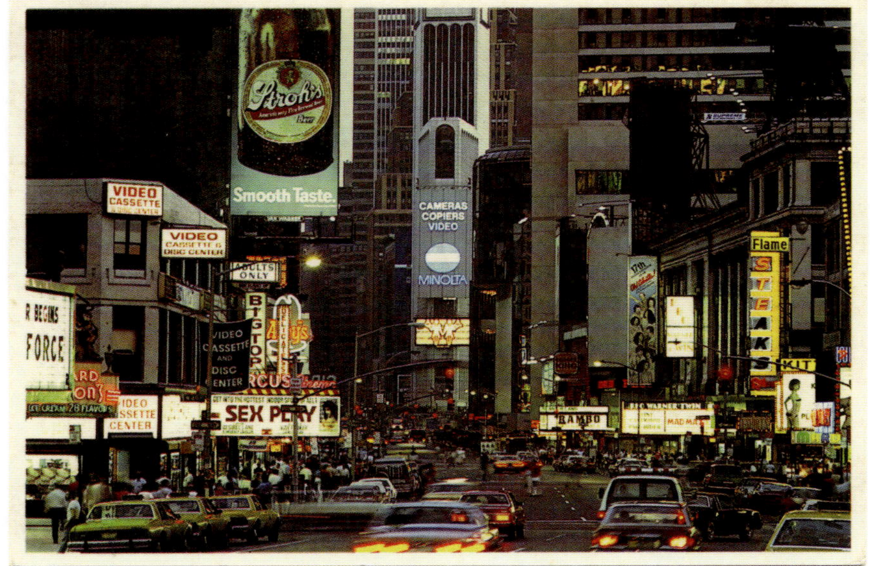

Stroh's
Smooth Taste.
VIDEO CASSETTE
VIDEO CASSETTE & DISC CENTER
CAMERAS COPIERS VIDEO
MINOLTA
Flame STEAKS KIT
FORCE
SEX PERY
RAMBO

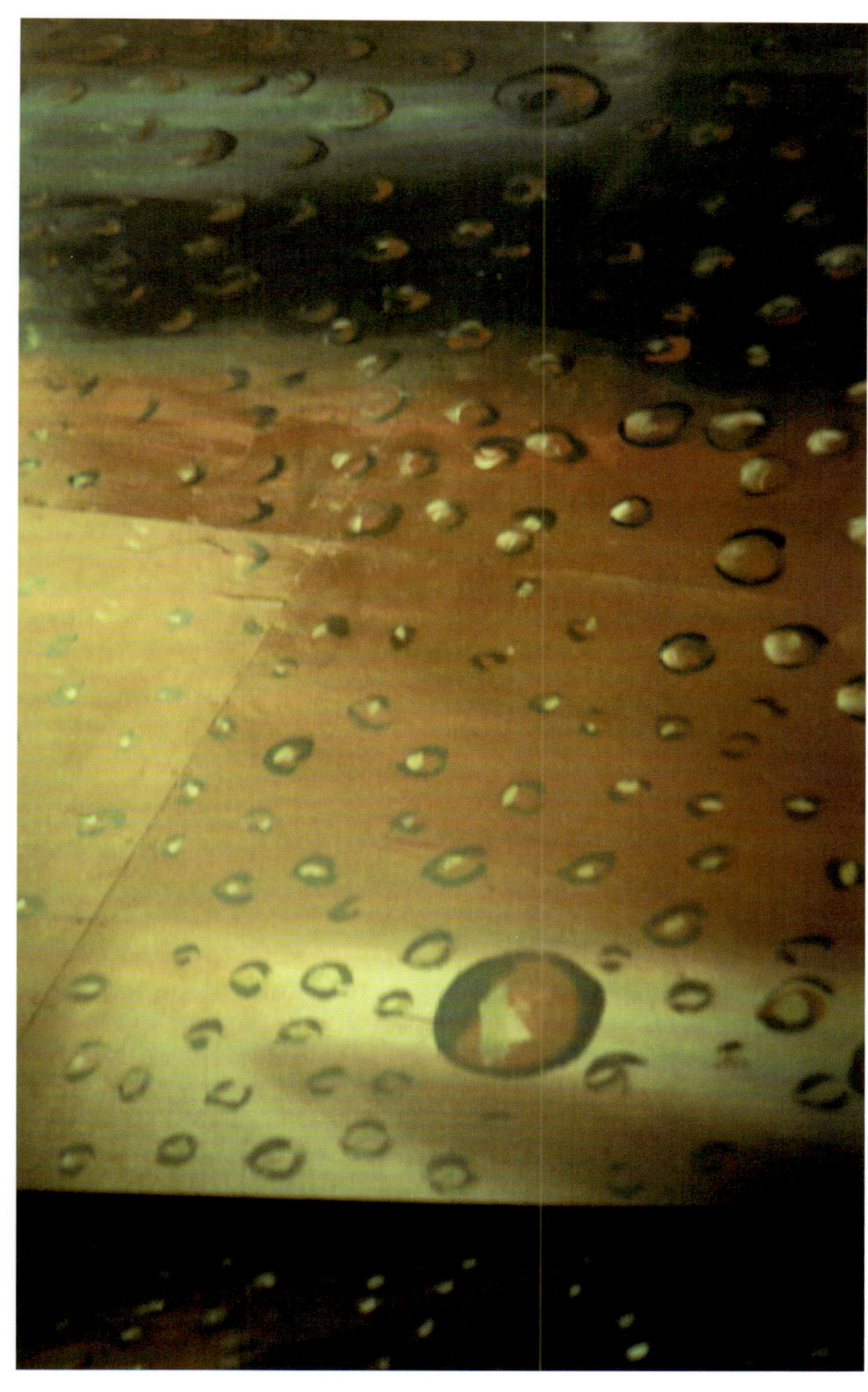

[108] *Stunt Artists*, 1985

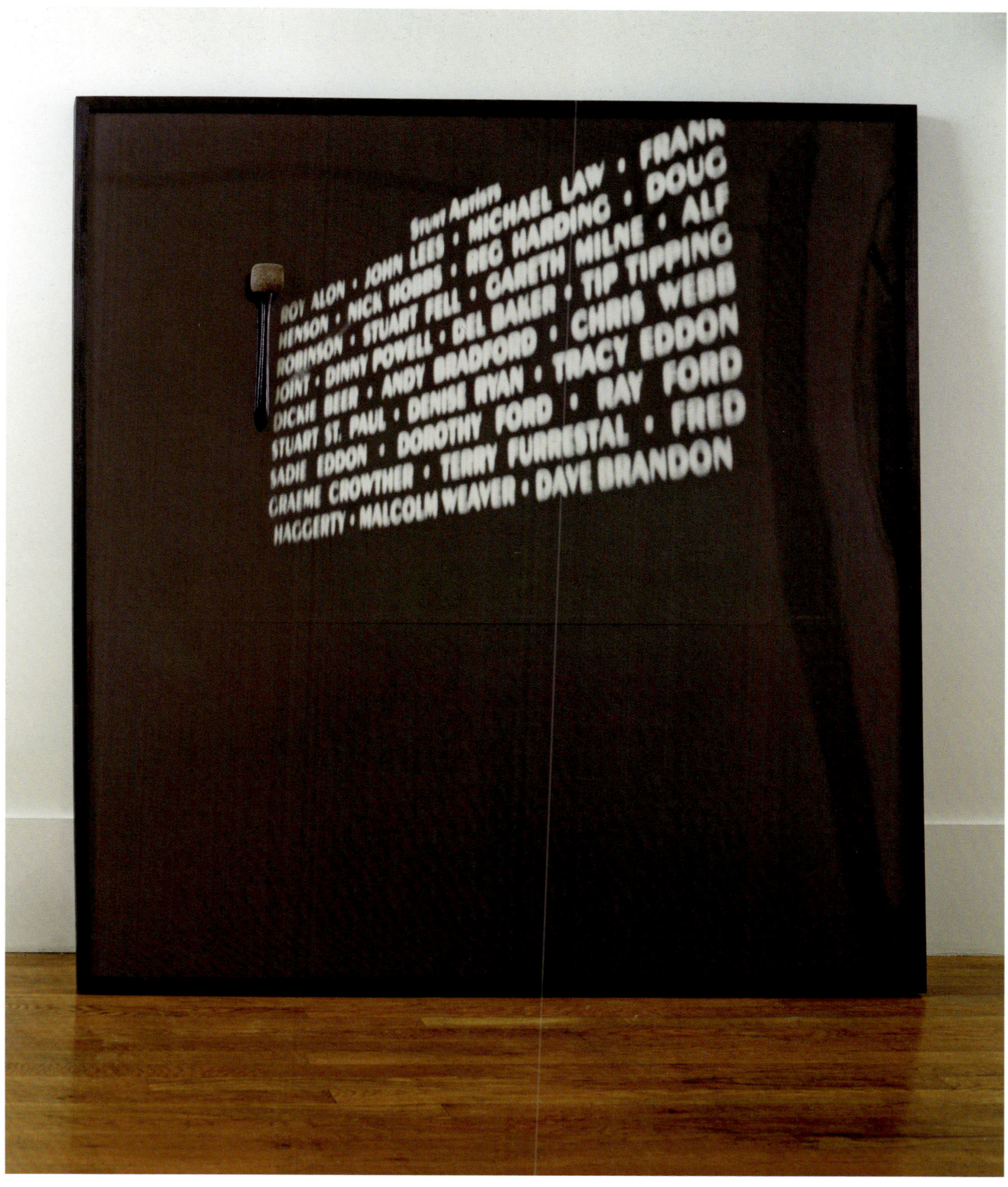
Stunt Artists
ROY ALON • JOHN LEES • MICHAEL LAW • FRANK
HENSON • NICK HOBBS • REG HARDING • DOUG
ROBINSON • STUART FELL • GARETH MILNE • ALF
JOINT • DINNY POWELL • DEL BAKER • TIP TIPPING
DICKIE BEER • ANDY BRADFORD • CHRIS WEBB
STUART ST. PAUL • DENISE RYAN • TRACY EDDON
SADIE EDDON • DOROTHY FORD • RAY FORD
GRAEME CROWTHER • TERRY FORRESTAL • FRED
HAGGERTY • MALCOLM WEAVER • DAVE BRANDON

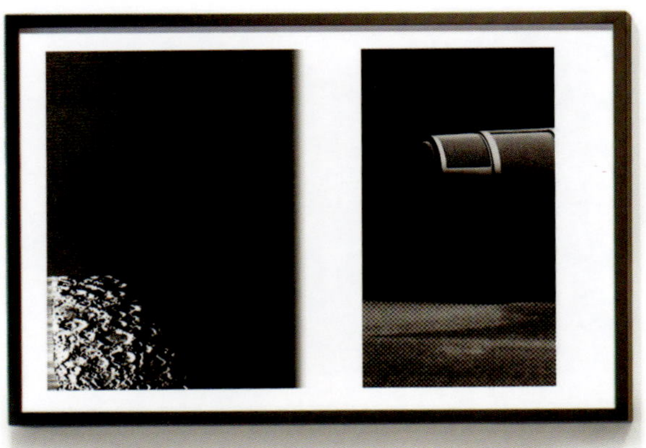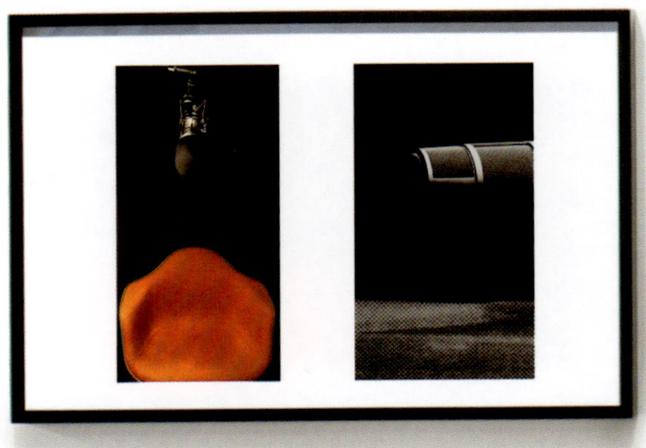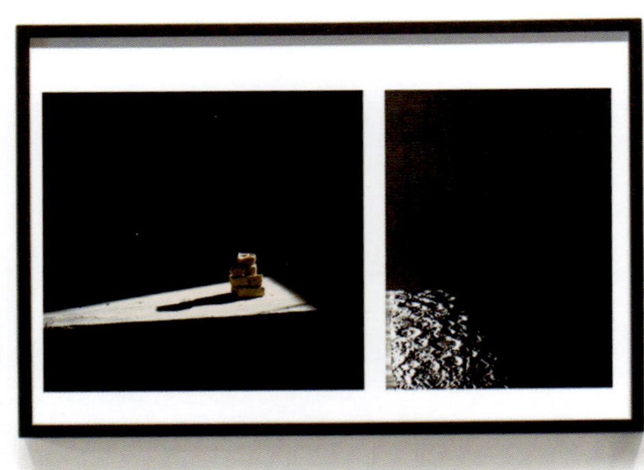

[109] Installation view (with diptychs from the series *Space Photography*): Inova, Milwaukee, 2009

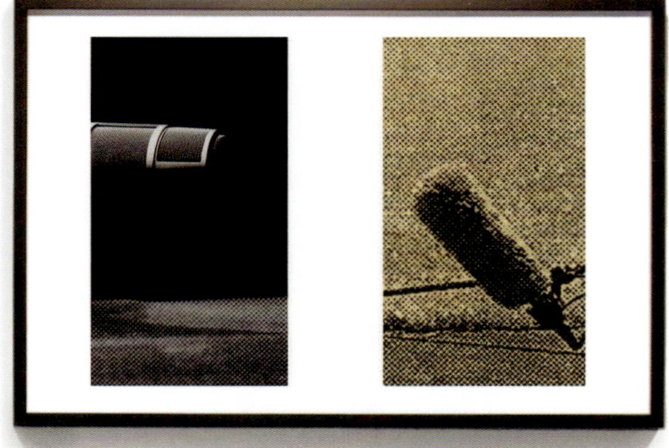

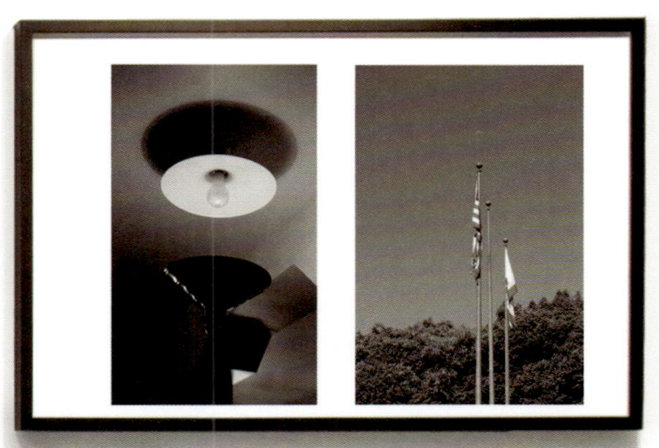

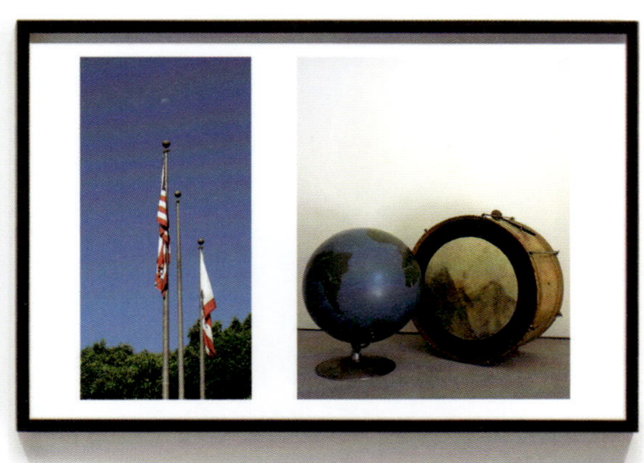

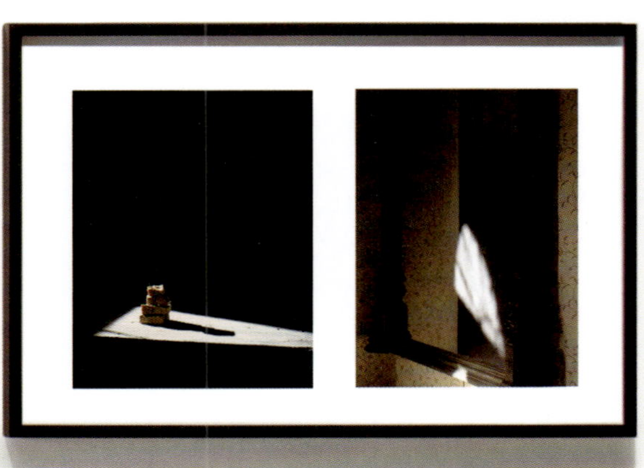

[110] *Diptych #14*, from the series *Space Photography*, 2009

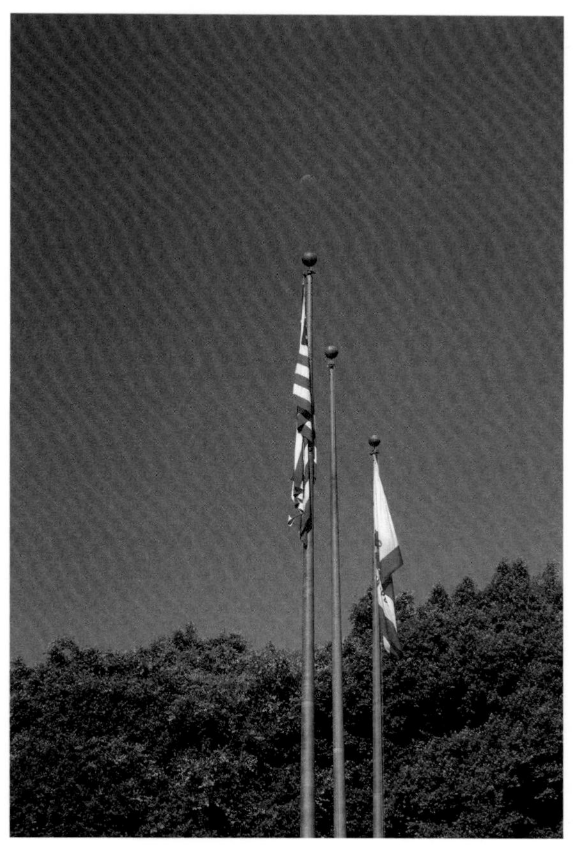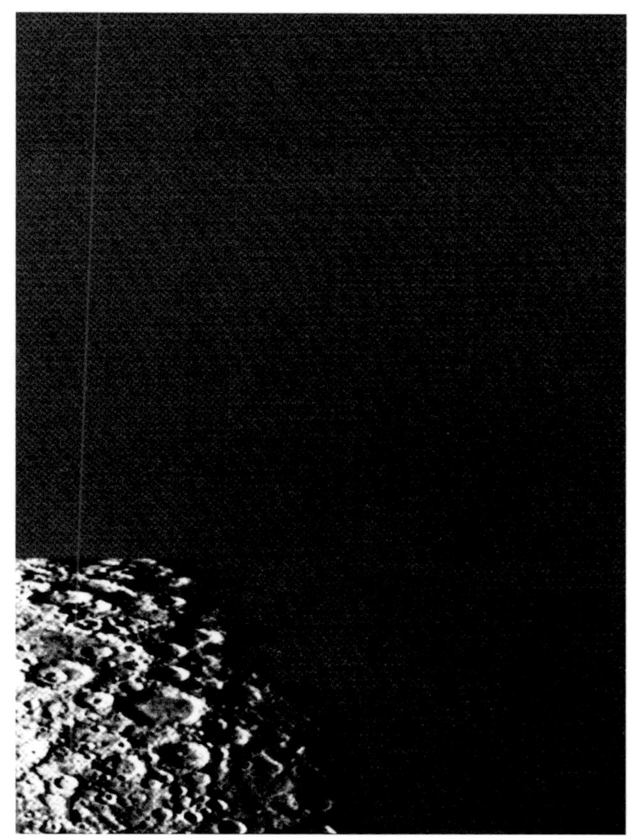

IMAGES

COVER
Composition with Speaker Cone (Blue), 1990
Type C print
31 x 20 inches

ENDPAPERS
details: *Map Folding Incident #1*, 2001
Paper map, wooden table, vitrine
90 x 36 x 36 inches
Photo: Charlie Deets

* denotes works in the exhibition

[1] detail: *Landscape*, from the series
Night Golf, 1983
B/W photograph
18 x 24 inches

[2] *Cartoon Curtain*, 1982*
Type C Print
32 x 30 inches

[3] Installation view: *Landmarks*,
The Kitchen, NY, 1982
with *Green Velvet Curtain**

[4] *The Formal Gardens Series, #16*, 1982
Type C print
14 x 11 inches

[5] *Central and Mountain*, 1985*
Bass drum with chalk pastel
and mallet
24 inches diameter x 15 inches deep
Photo: James Welling

[6] *Diptych #38* from the series
Space Photography, 2009
Inkjet print
26 x 40 inches

[7] *Green Towel Sequence #1*, 2004*
Type C print, box-mounted
35 x 25 x 3 inches

[8] *Cascade*, 1987*
Duratrans photograph
144 x 36 inches

[9] reference: Title still from
NASA film: *Planet Mars*
Photo: ©NASA

[10] reference: René Magritte, *Time
Transfixed*, 1938
Oil on canvas, 57 7/8 x 38 7/8 inches,
Joseph Winterbotham Collection,
1970.426, The Art Institute of
Chicago. 2011
© Herscovici, London / Artists Rights
Society (ARS), New York

[11] reference: postcard Times Square,
Photo: Alan Schein

[12] *Untitled*, 1992
Cibachrome
11 x 9 inches

[13] *Runaway Train Calendar*, 1988
b/w photographs, wood, hardware
10 x 8 x 6 inches
Photo: Andrew Moore

[14] *Times Square Cone*, 1989*
Wire rack, postcards of Times Square
38 x 22 inches diameter
Photo: Douglas M. Parker
Courtesy: Private Collection

[15] *Lever House*, from *The City at
Night*, 1998
Type C print mounted on aluminum
20 x 16 inches

[16] *Alley*, from the series *The City at
Night*, 1998
Type C print mounted on aluminum
20 x 16 inches

[17] *Appliance Store*, from the series
The City at Night, 1998
Type C print mounted on aluminum
20 x 16 inches

[18] *Conference Room*, from the series
The City at Night, 1998
Type C print mounted on aluminum
36 x 28 1/2 inches

[19] *Appliance Contact # 1*, 1999
Type C print
15 x 12 inches

[20] detail: *Appliance House*, 1999

[21] *Appliance House*, 1999*
Duratrans photographs in stainless
steel lightboxes
91 x 59 x 5 inches

[22] *Paper Cloud*, 2007
Type C print
40 x 21 inches
Photo: Oren Slor

[23] *Marshall Stack*, 1987*
3 handmade wood, vinyl speaker
cabinets, mounted & laminated color
photos, Marshall accessories
69 x 22 1/2 x 6 1/2 inches
Photo: Eeva Inkeri

[24] details: *Speaker I*, 1987
Speaker cabinets, speaker cone,
wood, enamel paint, photographs
mounted on wood, spotlight
74 x 40 x 11 inches

[25] Marcel Duchamp, *Bicycle Wheel*,
1913/51, (replica after original)
Bicycle wheel on painted wooden stool
© 2011 Artists Rights Society (ARS),
New York / ADAGP, Paris / Succession
Marcel Duchamp

[26] Jeff Koons, *New Hoover Convertibles,
New Shelton Wet/Dry 10 Gallon
Double-decker*, 1981-1986
Two vacuum cleaners, acrylic,
fluorescent lights
99 x 41 x 28 inches
© Jeff Koons

[27] *Coda Stack*, 1988
Speaker cabinets, Type C print, vinyl,
wood, B/W photograph, speaker cloth
72 x 36 x 24 inches

[28] *Single Speaker*, 1987
Wood and vinyl speaker cabinet,
graphite on gessoed wood
24 x 18 x 10 3/4 inches

[29] *Diptych #13*, from the series
Space Photography, 2009*
Inkjet print
26 x 40 inches

[30] Installation views: Metro Pictures,
New York, 1989 and 1988

[31] *Mouthpiece*, 1987
Type C print, speaker cloth, plexiglass,
etched brass plaque, plaster, wood
40 x 40 x 2 inches

[32] *Speaker II*, 1986
Speaker cabinet, fabric, wire mesh
51 x 19 x 10 inches
Photo: Maegan Hill-Carroll

[33] *Speaker I*, 1986
Speaker cabinets, speaker cone,
wood, enamel paint, photographs
mounted on wood, spotlight
74 x 40 x 11 inches
Photo: Brian Albert

[34] *Speaker Family Drawing*, 1986
Ballpoint pen on paper
17 x 18 inches
Photo: Brian Albert

[35] *Marshall Contact Sheet*, 1995*
Dye-sublimation print
12 x 8 1/2 inches

[36] *Conjunction*, 1987
Type C print
25 1/2 x 16 1/2 inches
Photo: Eeva Inkeri

[37] reference: segment of 35mm film
leader, "Rothko Element"
actual size: 3 3/4 x 1 3/8 inches

[38] *Conjunction Assemblage*, 1988*
Refrigerator door, speaker
facing, metal corners, handles,
Fender speaker cloth, framed
color photograph
75 1/2 x 30 x 5 1/2 inches
Photo: Eeva Inkeri

[39] *Earthquake*, 2004
Washers, dryers, speakers, screen,
audio and video of 16mm film
71 1/4 x 68 1/4 x 68 inches
Photo: Oren Slor

[40] *R.Shldr.*, 1990
speaker cabinet, Marshall speaker
fabric, shoulder pad, metal corner
19 x 14 x 6 inches

[41] *The Rounding of Corners*, 1991*
Cibachrome, shoulder pads,
corrugated cardboard frame
39 x 41 x 2 1/2 inches
Courtesy: Private Collection

[42] *The Porn Series, # 1*, 1982*
B/W photographs in blue frames
16 x 20 inches

[43] details: *The Porn Series, #2-7*, 1982*
B/W photographs in blue frames
16 x 20 inches

[44] reference: movie marquees
photographers unknown

[45] *Study for Untitled Tower*, 1999*
Type C print with colored pencil
on paper
24 x 18 inches
Courtesy: Virginia Cowles Schroth

[46] *Tower of Movie Marquees*, 2010
Steel, stainless steel, plexiglas,
electrical components and bulbs
15.5 x 9 x 5 feet

[47] *Composition with Speaker
Cone*, 1990*
Type C print
31 x 20 inches
Collection: Todd Thomas

[48] *Broken Bulbs*, 2010
Inkjet print
14.5 x 17 inches

[49] *and the*, 1987*
Movie marquee panel, plexiglas,
enamel paint, light fixture
19 x 20 x 6 1/2 inches
Courtesy: Dike Blair

[50] *A Salient Point*, 1987
Letter "O" from Texaco sign,
enamel paint, wood
48 x 60 x 24 inches

[51] *Listed Sign*, 1988
Movie marquee panel, wood and felt
letter board, enamel paint
20 1/2 x 27 1/2 inches
Photo: Eeva Inkeri

[52] reference: studio wall with photo of
Dike Blair's car running over my "O,"
and Richard Hamilton, *Diab DS-101
computer*, 1985-89

[53] *Alphabet and Junkyard*, 1989
Stainless steel, framed B/W
photograph
36 x 46 x 8 inches
Photo: Ellen Page Wilson

[54] Installation view: Michael Bennett
Gallery, NY, 1985 (with *Stunt Artists*
and *Central and Mountain*)
Photo: James Welling

[55] *+/- Landscape*, 1988
Type C prints in wood and vinyl frame
with metal corners, rubber feet
12 x 26 inches
Photo: Andrew Moore

[56] *Milk Crown*, 1987*
Cast porcelain
2 inches high x 7 inches diameter
Photo: Ellen Page Wilson
Courtesy: Private Collection

[57] *Skydivers*, 1989*
Lithograph
33 x 26 inches
Photo: Ellen Page Wilson

[58] Harold Edgerton,
Milk Drop Coronet, 1957
Dye transfer print, 14 x 11 inches
© 2010 Massachusetts Institute f
of Technology,
Courtesy:MIT Museum

[59] *Cast of Characters*, 1999*
Type C print mounted on aluminum
18 x 23 inches

[60] *Lexicon #2*, 1995*
Dye-sublimation print,
12 x 8 1/2 inches
Courtesy: Private Collection

[61] *Lexicon #3*, 1995*
Dye-sublimation print
12 x 8 1/2 inches
Courtesy: Private Collection

[62] *Aerial Phonograph*, 1991*
Cibachrome on record album, formica
base, turntable with motor
28 x 16 x 16 inches

[63] *Holding Pattern*, from the series
Road Movie, 1995
Type C print
19 x 19 inches

[64] *Steering Wheel*, from the series
Road Movie, 1995*
Type C print
19 x 19 inches

[65] *Glove*, from the series
Road Movie, 1995
Type C print, 19 x 19 inches

[66] *Held Open Space*, 1991*
Charcoal and crayon on paper
31 x 24 inches
Courtesy: Robin Weglinski

[67] *Orange Threshold*, from the series
Road Movie, 1995*
Type C print with painted
wooden frame
19 x 19 inches
Courtesy: Private Collection

[68] *Industrial Park*, 1999
Charcoal on paper
20 x 15 inches

[69] *U.N.titled Speaker*, 2002
Type C print, speaker fabric, concrete
25 x 20 x 31 inches

[70] *Mountain*, 2004
Inkjet prints mounted on
birch plywood
72 x 75 1/2 x 60 inches

[71] Interior of *Mountain*, 2004
Inkjet print
11 x 14 inches

[72] *Mountain Study #1*, 2003;
Ink on inkjet print
8 x 11 inches

[73] reference: Matterhorn
Henry White Warren,
The Matterhorn, from the book:
Among the Forces, 1898

[74] *Bag dance*, performance at the
Art Gallery of Nova Scotia, 1976

[75] *Movie Mountain*, 2004*
Type C print
14 x 11 1/2 inches

[76] *Side Show*, 1991*
Cibachrome
55 x 32 inches
Courtesy: Private Collection

[77] *Movie Chair*, 1984*
Wood & velvet chair, bronze,
enamel paint, lights pedestal
Dimensions variable
Courtesy: Michael Shorr
Photo: Charlie Deets

[78] *Diptych #8*, from the series
Space Photography, 2009*
Inkjet print
26 x 40 inches

[79] *Map Folding Incident #1*, 2001*
paper map, glue, wooden table
and vitrine
90 x 36 x 36 inches
Photo: Charlie Deets

[80] *Caruso Group*, 1985/2010*
2 pictures in easel frames: inkjet print
and b/w photograph
9 x 14 inches overall
Photo: James Welling
Collection: Peter Nagy

[81] *Smoke Screen #5*, 2007*
Inkjet prints on plywood and steel
96 x 48 inches
Photo: Brian Leatart
Courtesy: Private Collection

[82] reference: Pieter Bruegel the Elder,
The Tower of Babel, c. 1563
Oil on oak panel
44.8 x 61 inches

[83] reference: newspaper clipping
[see *Stack of Shims* image #89]
Photographer unknown

[84] reference: Ree Morton, *Untitled*, 1972
Branches, felt, flour, paint on paper,
tape and wood
Dimensions unknown
© Estate of Ree Morton
Courtesy: Alexander and Bonin, NY

[85] Jack Goldstein, *The Tornado, Three
Felled Trees, The Burning Forest*,
from *A Suite of Nine 7-inch records
with Sound Effects*, 1976
45 rpm vinyl records
© Courtesy: Estate of Jack Goldstein

[86] Installation view: Robbin Lockett
Gallery, Chicago, 1987

[87] *Globe Sightings: St. Mark's Place,
NYC*, 2000
Type C Print
38.625 x 32.5 inches

[88] *Overseas*, 1990*
box mounted C print
26 x 12 x 2 inches

[89] *Stack of Shims
(with wire photo)*, 1987*
Cedar shims, steel, framed color
photograph of newspaper clipping
65 x 18 x 7 inches

[90] *Sandwich Board*, 1983*
Type C print, wood, hinges, plexiglass,
enamel paint on tin
34 x 22 x 14 inches
Courtesy: Andrew Ong

[91] *Smoke and Snow*, 2010*
Inkjet print
22 x 27 1/2 inches

[92] *Forest Spirits, #12*, 1997
Iris print on rag paper
20 x 16 inches

[93] *Resting Place*, 1987
Kodak poster mounted on fiber
board, artificial ceramic logs, pencil
on painted plexi
57 x 38 x 18 inches

[94] detail: *Plywood Curtains*, 2008
Printed polyester fabric and
plywood panels
8 x 8 feet

[95] *Plywood Curtains with Shopping Cart,
Wilshire Blvd.*, 2009
Inkjet print
11 x 17 inches
Project produced by West of Rome
Public Art, 2010

[96] *Repeal*, 1990*
Cibachrome prints
19 x 39 inches

[97] detail: *Diptych #5* from the *series
Space Photography*, 2009*
Inkjet print
26 x 20 inches

[98] *Retroperspective*, 1988*
Pencil drawing
16 x 20 inches
Photo: Charlie Deets

[99] Installation view: Inova,
Milwaukee, 2010
Photo: Charlie Deets

[100] *Topology House*, 2002*
Inkjet prints on plywood
39 1/2 x 45 x 20 inches
Photo: Peter Meretsky

[101] *Globe Sightings: Stonehouse Road,
Bloomfield, NJ*, 2000*
Type C print
23 1/2 x 28 inches

[102] *9-Foot Pole*, 1989*
Aluminum pole, flagpole ornament,
wall-mounted wooden speaker,
speaker cloth
9 ft. x 12 inches wide x 20 inches deep
Photo: Douglas M. Parker
Courtesy: Margo Leavin

[103] Buzz Aldrin and the U.S. flag
on the Moon, 1969
Photo courtesy: NASA

[104] *Flagship Episode*, 1985
B/W photos, masonite, Type C print
clipped onto stained wooden board,
plexi, brackets
69 x 48 x 8 inches
Photo: Eeva Inkeri

[105] *Stroh's Sign Study #1*, 1984
Type C print
10 x 8 inches

[106] reference: postcard of Times Square
Photo: Alfred Mainzer

[107] detail: *Flagship Episode*, 1984
Type C print
30 x 13 inches

[108] *Stunt Artists*, 1985
Framed B/W photograph with mallet
55 x 50 inches

[109] Installation view: Inova, Milwaukee,
2010, (with diptychs from the series
Space Photography)
Photo: Charlie Deets

[110] *Diptych #14*, from the *series Space
Photography*, 2009*
Inkjet print
26 x 40 inches

[111] *Exit Triangle*, 2010
Inkjet print
37.5 x 70 inches

[112] detail: *Exit Triangle*, 2010

BIOGRAPHY

Born in Cleveland, Ohio, 1957

Nova Scotia College of Art & Design, BFA, 1979

Lived and worked in New York, 1979-2002

Lives and works in Joshua Tree and Los Angeles, 2002-Present

ONE and TWO PERSON EXHIBITIONS

2012 *Jennifer Bolande Landmarks*, Institute of Contemporary Art University of Pennsylvania, Philadelphia

2011 *Plywood Curtains*, West of Rome Public Art, Los Angeles

2010 *Mathematics and Myths of Yesterday and Today*, Thomas Solomon Gallery & Cottage Home, Los Angeles

Jennifer Bolande Landmarks, Institute of Visual Arts, (Inova), University of Wisconsin-Milwaukee

2008 Alexander and Bonin, New York

2004 Alexander and Bonin, New York

2003 Fotohof, Salzburg

2001 Alexander and Bonin, New York

1999 Alexander and Bonin, New York

PS1, Long Island City, New York

1997 Baron/Boisanté Gallery, New York

1995 John Gibson Gallery, New York

Kunstraum Munich, Munich

Kunsthalle Palazzo, Liestal

1992 Metro Pictures, New York

1991 Robbin Lockett Gallery, Chicago

1990 Galerie Urbi & Orbi, Paris

Galleri Nordanstad-Skarstedt, Stockholm

1989 Margo Leavin Gallery, Los Angeles

Metro Pictures, New York

1988 Metro Pictures, New York

Jennifer Bolande, Beaver College Art Gallery, Glenside

Jennifer Bolande and Tim Maul, Gallery 121, Antwerp

Jennifer Bolande and John Miller, Galerie Sophia Ungers, Cologne

1987 Robbin Lockett Gallery, Chicago

1986 Nature Morte, New York

1985 *Jennifer Bolande and Annette Lemieux*, Michael Bennett Gallery, New York

1983 *Jennifer Bolande and Victor Alzamora*, Artists Space, New York

1982 *Landmarks*, The Kitchen, New York

SELECTED GROUP EXHIBITIONS

2012 *This Will Have Been: Art, Love, and Politics in the 1980s*, Museum of Contemporary Art, Chicago; and the Walker Art Center, Minneapolis

2011 *Mixed Use, Manhattan: Photography and Related Practices 1970s to Present*, Museo Centro de Arte Reina Sofia, Madrid

2010 *Another Green World*, Carriage House, New York

Phot(o)bject, Presentation House Gallery, Vancouver

2007 *Stuff: Contemporary Art from the Collection of Burt Aaron*, Museum of Contemporary Art, Detroit

2006 *Sixteen Tons*, The Eli and Edyth Broad Art Center, University of California, Los Angeles

2005 *The Art of Design*, The Architecture and Design Collection, San Francisco Museum of Modern Art

The Forest: Politics, Poetics, Practice, Nasher Museum of Art, Duke University, Durham

2004 *Architecture & Arts: 1900/2000*, Palazzo Ducale, Genova

2003 *Living Inside the Grid*, New Museum of Contemporary Art, New York

Influence, Anxiety, and Gratitude, MIT List Visual Arts Center, Cambridge

The Photogenic: Photography Through Its Metaphors in Contemporary Art, Institute of Contemporary Art, University of Pennsylvania, Philadelphia

A Celebration of Contemporary Art, Museum of Fine Arts, Boston

Go Johnny Go, Kunsthalle Wien, Vienna

2001 *Big Nothing*, Staatliche Kunsthalle Baden-Baden

2000 *Private Investigations*, Presentation House Gallery, Vancouver

Insites: Interior Spaces in Contemporary Art, Whitney Museum at Champion, Stamford

Photasm, Hunter College/Times Square Gallery, New York

1999 *Trippy World*, Baron/Boisanté Gallery, New York

The Anagrammatical Body, Kunsthaus Muerz, Muerzzuschlag

1998 *The Cottingley Fairies and Other Apparitions*, Leslie Tonkonow Artworks & Projects, NY, Memphis Brooks Museum of Art, Memphis

ICON Bilder der Stadt, Galerie Fotohof, Salzburg

Night and Forgetfulness - in memory of Gilles Dusein, Musée d'art moderne et contemporain, Geneva

1997 *Deep Storage*, Haus der Kunst, Munich; Nationalgalerie, Berlin; Kunstmuseum, Dusseldorf; PS1, NY; Henry Art Gallery, Seattle

1996 *Just Past*, Museum of Contemporary Art, Los Angeles

Departure Lounge, Clocktower Gallery, New York

Making Pictures:Women and Photography, 1975-NOW, Nicole Klagsbrun, New York

1995 *Photocollages*, Le Consortium, Dijon

It's Only Rock and Roll, Contemporary Art Center Cincinnati; Lakeview Museum of Arts & Sciences; Peoria; Virginia Beach Center for the Arts; Tacoma Art Museum; Jacksonville Museum of Art; The Regional Center for the Arts, Walnut Creek, CA; The Phoenix Art Museum; North Carolina Museum of Art, Raleigh; Lowe Art Museum, University of Miami; Milwaukee Art Museum; Arkansas Art Center; Fresno Metropolitan Museum, CA; Austin Museum of Art

SELECTED GROUP EXHIBITIONS

1994   *Lessons in Life*, The Art Institute of Chicago

Synesthesia, Sound and Vision in Contemporary Art, The San Antonio Museum of Art, San Antonio

The Music Box Project, The Equitable Gallery, NYC; Long Beach Art Museum, CA; Spiral, Tokyo

1993   *Jennifer Bolande, Sophie Calle, Vik Muniz & Mike Scott,* Wooster Gardens, New York

1992   *Jennifer Bolande, Sylvia Gertsch, Marie-Therese Huber, Pipilotti Rist, Mio Shirai,* Shedhalle, Zurich, and Municipal Gallery of the City of Prague

1991   *Constructing Images: Synapse Between Photography and Sculpture,* Lieberman & Saul Gallery, New York, Tampa Museum of Art, Fla., Center for Creative Photography, Tucson

American Art Today: New Directions, The Art Museum at Florida International University, Miami

Anni Novanta, Galleria Comunale d'Arte Moderna, Bologna

1990   *The Readymade Boomerang,* Eighth Biennale of Sydney

The Cologne Show, Cologne

Sculpture, Margo Leavin, Los Angeles

Status of Sculpture, L'espace lyonnais d'art contemporain, Lyon; ICA, London; Lowen-Palais, Berlin

Viewpoints Towards the 90's: Three Artists from Metro Pictures, (Bolande, Kelley, Miller), Seibu Contemporary Art Gallery, Tokyo

1989   *A Climate of Site,* Galerie Barbara Farber, Amsterdam

Avant 1989, Villa Gillet-Frac Rhône-Alpes, Lyon

The Experience of Landscape: Three Decades of Sculpture, The Whitney Museum of American Art Downtown at Federal Reserve Plaza, New York

1988   *Graz 1988,* Stadtmuseum Graz

Made in Camera, Galerie Sten Eriksson, Stockholm

The Pop Project, The Clocktower, New York

Reprises de vues, Halles Sud, Geneva

Presi per Incantamento, Padiglione d'Arte Contemporanea, Milan

Works Concepts Processes Situations Information, Hans Mayer, Dusseldorf

1987   *Bolande, Dryer, Lemieux,* Lawrence Oliver Gallery, Philadelphia

Material Fictions, 49th Parallel, New York

Photo Mannerisms, Lawrence Oliver Gallery, Philadelphia

Playback, Galerie Hubert Winter, Vienna

1986   *Cinemaobject,* City Gallery, New York

Liberty and Justice, (Group Material) The Alternative Museum, New York

When Attitude Becomes Form, Bess Cutler Gallery, New York

1985   *Infotainment,* Texas Gallery, Houston; Rhona Hoffman Gallery, Chicago; Vanguard Gallery, Philadelphia; The Aspen Art Museum, Aspen; Galerie Montenay, Paris

Jennifer Bolande, Clegg & Guttman, David Robbins, Nature Morte, New York

1984   *Motives,* Hallwalls, Buffalo, New York

1982   *Public Vision,* White Columns, New York

Real Life Magazine Presents, White Columns, New York

Resource Material: Appropriation in Current Photography, Proctor Art Center, Bard College, Annandale-on-Hudson

SELECTED BOOKS and CATALOGUES

Space Photography, Jennifer Bolande, Zg Press, [2010]

Forest Spirits, Tim Maul and Ingrid Schaffner, Baron/Boisanté, [1997]

Road Movie, Jennifer Bolande, Baron/Boisanté, [1995]

Jennifer Bolande Philip Ursprung and Justin Hoffmann, Kunsthalle Palazzo, Basel/Liestal [1995]

Jennifer Bolande, Daniela Salvioni and Gertrude Sandquist, Nordanstad-Skarstedt, Stockholm [1992]

Jennifer Bolande, Jérôme Sans, Paris: Urbi et Orbi [1990]

This Will Have Been: Art, Love & Politics in the 1980s. Helen Molesworth, ed.; New Haven: Yale University Press, [2011]

Mixed Use, Manhattan; Photography and Related Practices, 1970s to the Present. Lynne Cooke and Douglas Crimp, eds. Museo Nacional Centro de Arte Reina Sofia, Madrid: MIT Press, [2010]

Sixteen Tons, Michael Darling, UCLA Department of Art, [2006]

The Forest, Politics, Poetics, and Practice, Kathleen Goncharov. Durham, North Carolina: The Nasher Museum of Art [2005]

Architecture & Arts: 1900/2004 A Century of Creative Projects in Building, Design, Cinema, Painting, Sculpture. ed. Germano Celant; Milan: Skira, [2004]

Each Wild Idea. Geoffrey Batchen; Cambridge: MIT Press, [2002]

Deep Storage. Ingird Schaffner and Matthias Winzen, London: Prestel, [1998]

The Readymade Boomerang: Certain Relations in 20th Century Art, René Block, The 8th Biennale of Sydney, [1990]

A Climate of Site; Robert Nickas; Amsterdam: Galerie Barbara Farber [1989]

Works Concepts Processes Situations Information, Robert Nickas, Dusseldorf: Galerie Hans Mayer, [1988]

Presi X Incantamento. Milan: Giancarlo Politi Editore and Padiglione d'Arte Contemporanea, [1988]

Made in Camera; Peter Anderson; Stockholm: VAVD Editions and Gallerie Sten Eriksson [1988]

Infotainment; Thomas Lawson, David Robbins and George W.S. Trow, New York: J. Berg Press [1985]

SELECTED ESSAYS and REVIEWS

2010   Bolande, Jennifer, "Jennifer Bolande Talks About Plywood
        Curtains," with an introduction by Sharon Lockhart, *1000
        Words, Artforum*, Issue XLIX, no. 3 (November 2010): 210

        Nisbet, James, "Jennifer Bolande," Thomas Solomon Gallery,
        Los Angeles, *Critics Picks, Artforum Online*, Oct. 2010

        Lawson, Thomas, "Jennifer Bolande," *East of Borneo*,
        www.EastofBorneo.org, November 2010

        Salvioni, Daniela and Lauf, Cornelia, "80s New York: Rearview
        Mirror" *Nero Magazine*, www.neromagazine.it

        Grabner, Michelle, "Jennifer Bolande" *Artforum, Issue XLIX, no.1*
        (Sept. 2010): 333-334

        Robbins, David and Bolande, Jennifer, "A Conversation:
        David Robbins and Jennifer Bolande" *Milwaukee Journal
        Sentinel,* (May 25, 2010)

2008   Maul, Tim, "Jennifer Bolande" *Art in America*, No. 5,
        (May 2008): 197

2005   Stone, Katie, "Jennifer Bolande," *Frieze,* issue 89
        (March 2005): 120-123

2004   Fels, Sophie, "Reviews: Jennifer Bolande," *Time Out, New York*
        (December 9-15, 2004): 82

        Lawson, Thomas, "Thomas Lawson on Media Moguls," *Artforum,*
        Issue XLIII, no.2 (October 2004): 93-94

2002   Nichols, Matthew Guy. "Jennifer Bolande." *Art on Paper*
        (March-April 2002): 88

        Schaffner, Ingrid , "The Unphotographable." *Art on Paper*
        (March-April 2002): 58-63

2001   Halle, Howard, "World Up." *Time Out, New York,* no. 320
        (November 15-22, 2001): 89

1999   Princenthal, Nancy, "Jennifer Bolande at Alexander and Bonin,"
        Art in America (January 2000): 113

        Schmerler, Sarah, "Jennifer Bolande." *Art on Paper* Vol.4 no. 3
        (January-February 2000): 80-81

        Siegel, Katy, "Jennifer Bolande: Appliance House." *Artforum,*
        Issue XXXVII, no.5 (January 2000): 88-89

        Arning, Bill. "Art Reviews: Jennifer Bolande," *Time Out New York*
        (October 7-14, 1999): 84

1998   Goldberg, Vicki. "Of Fairies, Free Spirits and Outright Frauds."
        New York Times (February 1, 1998): 48

1997   Griffin, Tim. "Projects, 3 new + 3 old." *Time Out New York*
        (January 16-23, 1997)

        Kimmelman, Michael. "Jennifer Bolande, Forest Spirits."
        New York Times (April 18, 1997)

        Griffin, Tim. "Jennifer Bolande, The Forest Spirits." *Time Out,
        New York* 84 (May 1-8, 1997)

1996   Aukeman, Anastasia. "Jennifer Bolande." *Art in America*
        (January 1996)

        Smith, Roberta. "Inside/Out." *New York Times*
        (September 20, 1996)

1995   Folland, Tom. "Jennifer Bolande." *Art Issues* no. 36
        (Jan/Feb 1995): 40

        Cotter, Holland. "Jennifer Bolande." *The New York Times*
        (March 17, 1995)

        Bolande, Jennifer. *Blind Spot,* no. 6 (1995) (photo essay)

1992   Cotter, Holland. "Jennifer Bolande." *New York Times*
        (June 5, 1992)

        Connelly, John. "Jennifer Bolande." *Flash Art,*
        (October-November 1992): 98

        de Bruyn, Eric. "Jennifer Bolande." *Forum International,* no. 14
        (September-October 1992): 104

        Batchen, Geoffrey. "On Post-Photography, Constructing Images:
        Synapse Between Photography and Sculpture." *Afterimage* 20,
        no. 3 (October 1992): 17

1990   Cyphers, Peggy. "New York Review: Jennifer Bolande." *Arts*
        (January 1990): 96

        Decter, Joshua. "Jennifer Bolande." *Flash Art*
        (January-February 1990): 129-30

1989   Marincola, Paula. "Something to Do with Jennifer Bolande."
        Artforum, Issue XXVII, no.5 (January 1989): 70-73 and Cover

        Magnani, Gregorio. "This Is Not Conceptual," *Flash Art*
        (March/April, 1989): 107

        Christov-Bakargiev, Carolyn. "Avant 1989, Villa Gillet-Frac
        Rhône-Alpes." *Flash Art* (March-April 1989): 124

        Messler, Norbert. "Jennifer Bolande, John Miller at
        Sophia Ungers." *Artscribe* (May 1989): 89

        Gargerie, Christian. "Graz 1988, Kunstverein." *Artscribe*
        (May 1989): 91-92

        Smith, Roberta. "Jennifer Bolande." *New York Times*
        (October 20, 1989): C28

1988   Graw, Isabelle "Still-Life." *Wolkenkratzer Art Journal* (Stuttgart)
        (January-February 1988): 54-56

        Jones, Ronald. "Jennifer Bolande: Robbin Lockett." *Artscribe*
        (March-April 1988): 89

        "Jennifer Bolande: A Salient Point (Detail): A Conversation
        Between Jack Bankowsky and Robert Nickas." *Flash Art*
        (May-June 1988): 78-79

        Jones, Ronald. "Hover Culture." *Artscribe* (London)
        (summer, 1988): 46-51

1987   Bankowsky, Jack. "Jennifer Bolande," *Flash Art* no. 135
        (summer 1987): 94

        Ottman, Klaus. "Jennifer Bolande, Moira Dryer, Annette
        Lemieux." *Flash Art* (April 1987)

1986   Indiana, Gary. "Talking Back." *The Village Voice*
        (February 11, 1986): 84

        Grundberg, Andy. "New Perspectives in Photography."
        New York Times (September 12, 1986)

1985   Halle, Howard. "The Anticipated Ruin." *Spectacle,* no. 3,
        (Los Angeles)

1983   Lawson, Thomas. "Victor Alzamora and Jennifer Bolande."
        Artforum, Issue XXI, no.7 (March 1983): 76

I would like to express my sincere gratitude to all who have contributed to
the realization of this book and exhibition. I am grateful to Inova curator,
Nicholas Frank, who took a leap of faith by initiating the process that led
to this book. Nicholas brought insight, consideration, perseverance and wit
to his roles as curator, essayist and editor. My deep appreciation to essayists—
Dennis Balk, Jack Bankowsky, Rosetta Brooks, Christina Valentine,
Nicholas Frank and Ingrid Schaffner for their astute readings of my work.
The ongoing dialogue with these individuals and their engagement
with my work, means a great deal to me. I am indebted to designer and
friend, Mark Voss, whose creative vision, perspective and commitment
was invaluable to this project from beginning to end. Special thanks to those
who, in different ways, helped in the realization of this book: Julie Ault,
Catherine Opie, Carole Ann Klonarides, Brian Butler, Russell Ferguson,
Vishal Jugdeo, Maegan Hill-Carroll, Daniel Hawkins, Donna Ratajczak,
Joel Wachs, and especially Lionel Bovier.

The exhibition was enriched by the considerable efforts of the Inova staff,
most especially director Bruce Knackert, who went above and beyond.
My thanks to Polly Morris, Mary McCoy, Neil Gasparka and also to the
Durfee Foundation for their contributions to the show. I am grateful to
Ingrid Schaffner, for bringing the exhibition to the ICA, and for organizing
its presentation there. Additional thanks to Claudia Gould, Robert Chaney,
Alex Klein, and to the staff of the ICA. My deep appreciation to the lenders
of works included in the exhibition for graciously sharing them with the
public for such an extended period of time.

Reflecting back on the span of time encompassed here has brought to mind
the many people and experiences that have shaped and supported my work
along the way. I'd like to take this opportunity to acknowledge just a few:
Gerald Ferguson, the Nova Scotia College of Art & Design, John Baird,
Helene Winer, Artists Space, Thomas Lawson, Susan Morgan, Howard Halle,
Matt Mullican, James Welling, Robert Hamon, Brina Gehry, John Miller,
Victor Alzamora, Moira Dryer, Amy Lowe, David Robbins, Nature Morte,
Alan Belcher, Peter Nagy, Robin Weglinski, Steven Parrino, Metro Pictures,
Cindy Sherman, Louise Lawler, Dike Blair, Margo Leavin Gallery, Tim Maul,
Paula Marincola, Daniel Levine, David Goldsmith, Todd Thomas, Mark Baron,
Elise Boisanté, Daniela Salvioni, Gertrud Sandquist, Justin Hoffmann,
Philip Ursprung, Dick Hebdige, Geoffrey Batchen, Cornelia Schulz,
Alexander and Bonin Gallery, Nancy Rubins, Chris Burden, Robert Hudson,
Mavis Jukes, Barbara Kruger, Emi Fontana, West of Rome Public Art,
Sharon Lockhart, Tim Christian, and Thomas Solomon.

Much love and gratitude to my family and to Cannon Hudson, my dear
partner in life, whose contributions to my life and work are immeasurable.

Finally, I offer my thanks to the artists whose works are represented in this
book. No less importantly, I owe a debt of gratitude to all the artists whose
works, while not here included, have inspired me over the years.

—JB

This book was published on the occasion of the survey exhibition
Jennifer Bolande Landmarks
Curated by Nicholas Frank

Institute of Visual Arts (Inova)
Peck School of the Arts
University of Wisconsin-Milwaukee
May 7-August 8, 2010

Institute of Contemporary Art (ICA)
University of Pennsylvania
Philadelphia, Pennsylvania
January 11-March 11, 2012

All exhibitions require the generosity of artists to achieve their full
realization, first and foremost in the creation of the artwork. But in
the case of Jennifer Bolande's *Landmarks*, the chance to work directly
with the artist to realize her first retrospective survey proved especially
rewarding. Her presence and careful guidance allowed insight into the
work that would not have been available otherwise, and her direct
involvement in the installation brought it to a level that would not have
been achieved without her particular readings of her own output over
time. I am deeply grateful for her singular generosity and commitment,
both to her own work and to this important occasion. Inova director
Bruce Knackert brings a rare dedication to his position, and without
his willingness to fulfill multiple roles, an exhibition of this scale and
magnitude would not be possible. My appreciation goes out to those
who voiced and lent their support and enthusiasm helped move the
idea from inception to realization, especially Ingrid Schaffner and
Thomas Solomon. A special thank-you to Polly Morris for her vision and
assistance, both early and late in the project. Thanks to those who over
the years presciently collected stellar examples of Bolande's work kindly
lent to the exhibition. Special thanks to the administration and staff
of the Peck School of the Arts for allowing Inova to achieve its full
potential with this important exhibition. Finally, our gratitude to the
Elizabeth Firestone Graham Foundation, the Andy Warhol Foundation for
the Visual Arts, the University of Wisconsin-Milwaukee, the UCLA Council
on Research, Suzanne Volkman, Michael Shorr and Anonymous for their
generous support of this book.

–Nicholas Frank

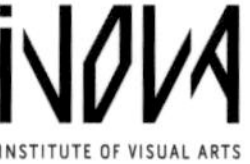

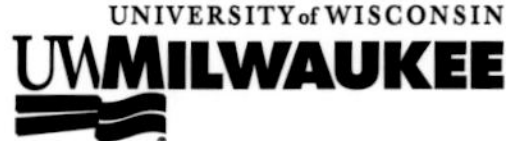

This book was made possible by the generous contributions of:
The Elizabeth Firestone Graham Foundation,
The Andy Warhol Foundation for the Visual Arts,
University of Wisconsin-Milwaukee, UCLA Council on Research,
Suzanne Volkman, Michael Shorr, and anonymous donors

Editor: Nicholas Frank
Design: Mark Voss
Cover Design: Cannon Hudson
Production: Maegan Hill-Carroll, J.R. Valenzuela, Daniel Hawkins
Printed by: Typecraft, Wood and Jones

Published by JRP|Ringier in association with
Institute of Visual Arts (Inova) University of Wisconsin-Milwaukee

Institute of Visual Arts (Inova)
Peck School of the Arts
University of Wisconsin-Milwaukee
PO Box 413
Milwaukee, Wisconsin 53201
(414) 229-5070
arts.uwm.edu/inova

DISTRIBUTED BY
JRP|Ringier
Letzigraben 134
CH-8047 Zurich
T +41 (0) 43 311 27 50
F +41 (0) 43 311 27 51
E info@jrp-ringier.com
www.jrp-ringier.com

ISBN 978-3-03764-260-3

JRP|Ringier publications are available internationally at selected book-
stores and from the following distribution partners:

Switzerland
AVA Verlagsauslieferung AG, Centralweg 16,
CH-8910 Affoltern a.A
verlagsservice@ava.ch, www.ava.ch

Germany and Austria
Vice Versa Vertrieb
Immanuelkirchstrasse 12
D-10405 Berlin
info@vice-versa-vertrieb.de, www.vice-versa-vertrieb.de

France
Les presses du réel, 35 rue Colson, F-21000 Dijon,
info@lespressesdureel.com, www.lespressesdureel.com

UK and other European countries
Cornerhouse Publications
70 Oxford Street
UK-Manchester M1 5NH
publications@cornerhouse.org, www.cornerhouse.org/books

USA, Canada, Asia, and Australia
ARTBOOK|D.A.P., 155 Sixth Avenue, 2nd Floor
USA-New York, NY 10013
dap@dapinc.com, www.artbook.com

For a list of our partner bookshops or for any general questions, please
contact JRP|Ringier directly at
info@jrp-ringier.com or visit our homepage www.jrp-ringier.com
for further information about our program.

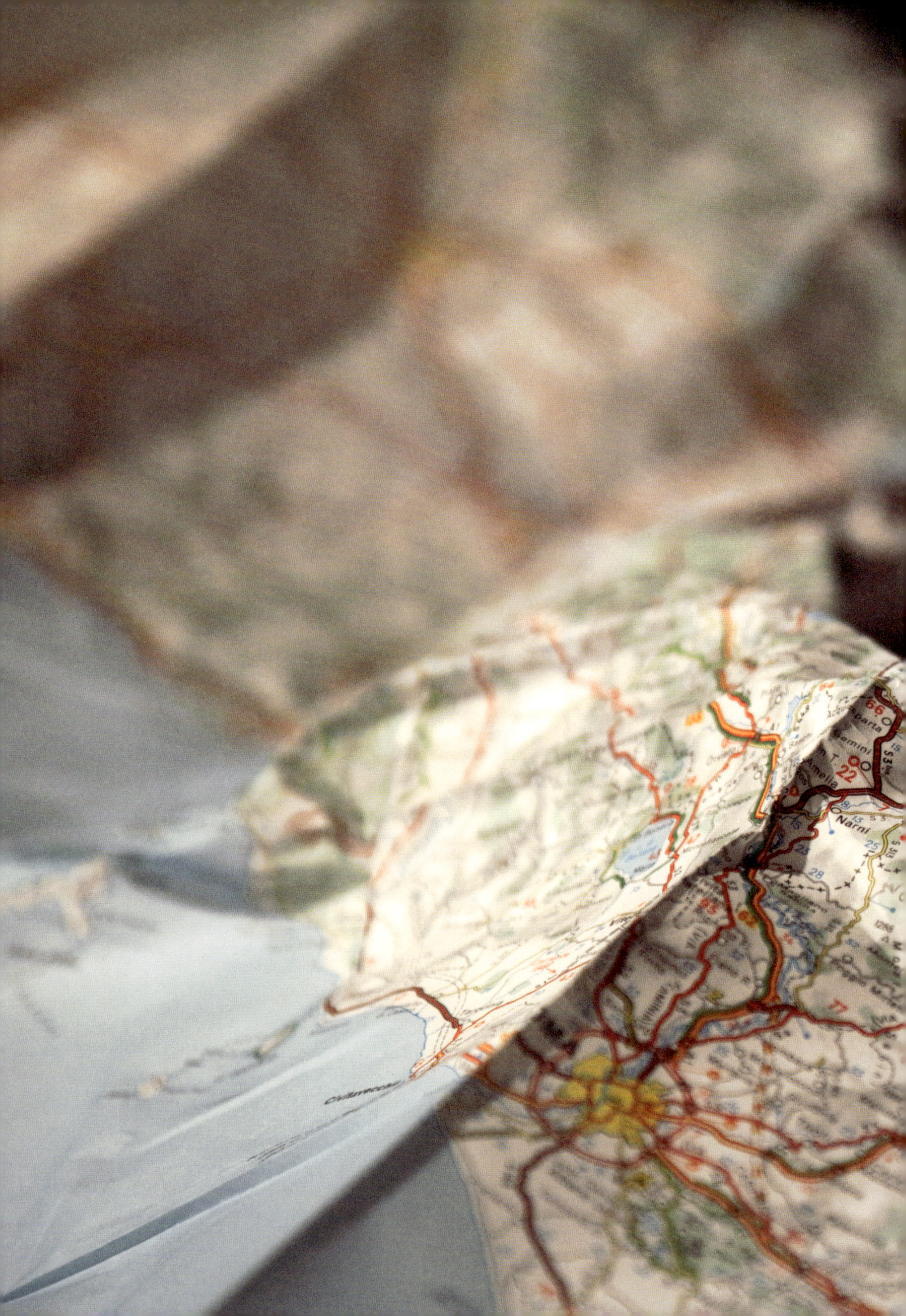

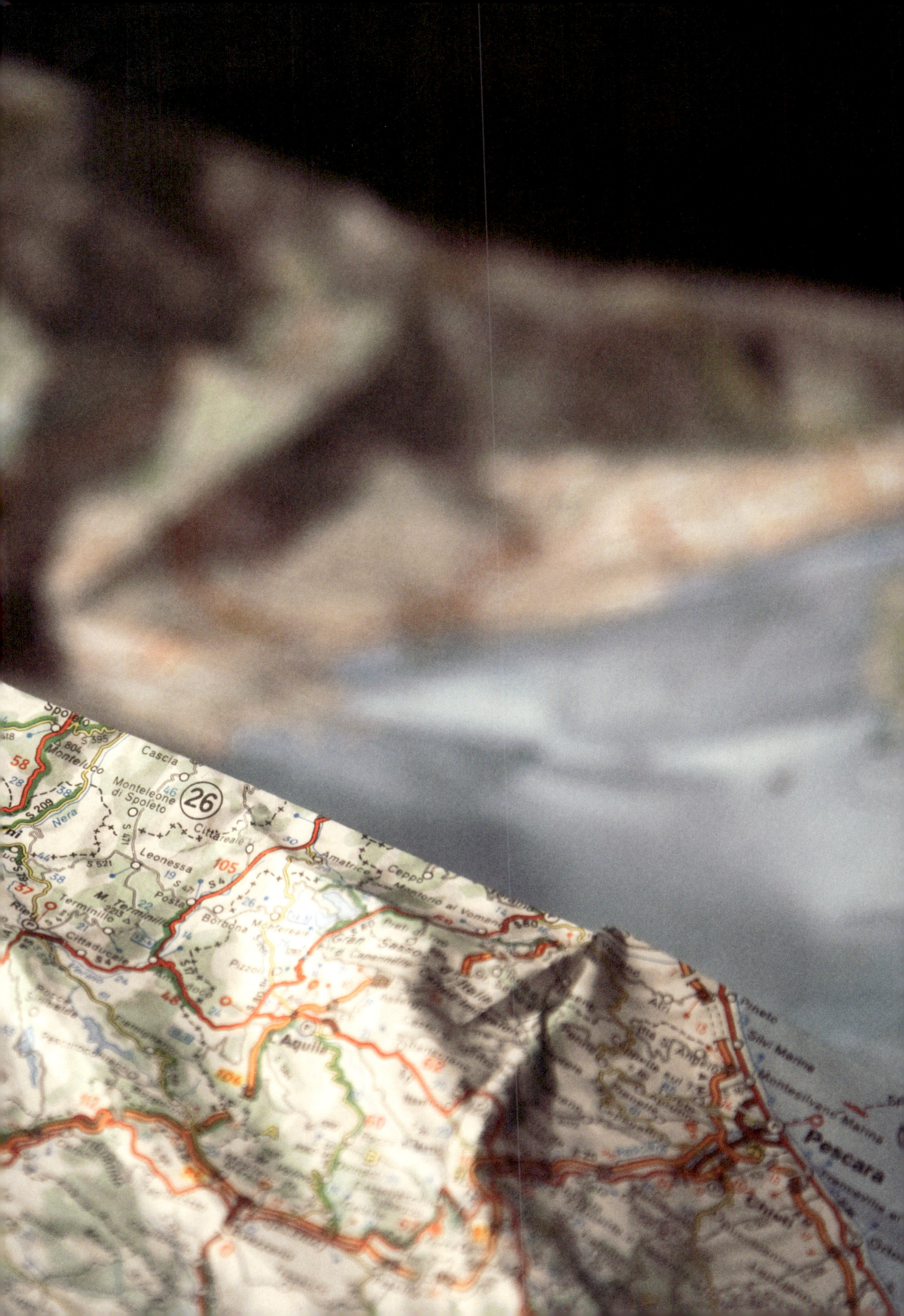
Spoleto
Cascia
58
Monteluco
Monteleone
di Spoleto
26
Nera
Cittareale
Leonessa
105
Amatrice
Ceppo
37
M. Terminillo
Posta
Borbona
Monterone al Vomano
Gran Sasso
Cittaducale
Pizzoli
Aquila
Pineto
Silvi Marina
Montesilvano Marina
Pescara